READING AS THERAPY

Reading as Therapy

WHAT CONTEMPORARY FICTION DOES
FOR MIDDLE-CLASS AMERICANS

TIMOTHY AUBRY

UNIVERSITY OF IOWA, IOWA CITY

University of Iowa Press, Iowa City 52242

Copyright © 2011 by the University of Iowa Press

www.uiowapress.org

Printed in the United States of America

Design by April Leidig-Higgins

The University of Iowa Press is a member of Green Press Initiative and is committed to preserving natural resources.

Printed on acid-free paper

Library of Congress Cataloging-in-Publication Data
Aubry, Timothy Richard, 1975–
Reading as therapy: what contemporary fiction does for middle-class Americans / by Timothy Aubry.
    p.   cm.
Includes bibliographical references and index.
ISBN-13: 978-1-58729-955-1 (pbk.)
ISBN-10: 1-58729-955-0 (pbk.)
ISBN-13: 978-1-58729-956-8 (e-book)
ISBN-10: 1-58729-956-9 (e-book)
1. Fiction — History and criticism — Theory, etc.
2. Reading — Psychological aspects.   3. Bibliotherapy.
4. Literature and society — United States.   5. Books and reading — United States.   I. Title.
PN3352.P7A84   2011
306.4'88 — dc22   2010030548

CONTENTS

ACKNOWLEDGMENTS

SEVERAL RESEARCH GRANTS made it possible for me to finish this book. I was supported in the 2007–2008 and the 2008–2009 academic years by PSC-CUNY, and in the spring of 2007 and the fall of 2008 by the Weissman School of Arts and Sciences Dean's Fund. I am especially grateful to the Whiting Foundation, whose generous grant allowed me to devote the 2007–2008 academic year solely to the task of working on this manuscript.

Certain sections of this book are revised versions of essays that appeared earlier. "Beware the Furrow of the Middlebrow: Searching for *Paradise* on *The Oprah Winfrey Show*," *Modern Fiction Studies* 52 (2006): 350–73, © Purdue Research Foundation, reprinted with permission of Johns Hopkins University Press; "Selfless Cravings: Addiction and Recovery in David Foster Wallace's *Infinite Jest*," *American Fiction of the 1990s*, Routledge (2008): 206–19; "The Pain of Reading *A Million Little Pieces*: The James Frey Controversy and the Dismal Truth," *a/b: Auto/Biography Studies* 22 (2007): 155–80; "Middlebrow Aesthetics and the Therapeutic: The Politics of Interiority in *The Pilot's Wife*," *Contemporary Literature* 49 (2008): 85–110, © Board of Regents of the University of Wisconsin System, reprinted with permission of the University of Wisconsin Press; and "Afghanistan Meets the Amazon: Reading *The Kite Runner* in America," *PMLA* 124 (2009): 24–43, reprinted with permission of Modern Language Association of America.

While I have been writing *Literature as Therapy*, many people helped me clarify my arguments, avoid pitfalls, and figure out what exactly I wanted to say. Several of my colleagues at Baruch College, including John Brenkman, Elaine Kauvar, Mary McGlynn, and Shelly Eversley, read and critiqued chapters, and I am indebted to their smart and illuminating feedback. The members of my reading group in the CUNY Faculty Fellowship Publications Program, Brij Singh, Sarah Covington, Sarah Chinn, Barbara

Montero, Nancy Berke, and Ting Man Tsao, helped me work through my ideas about *The Kite Runner* and Amazon. A number of friends, including Sandra Parvu, Michael Sayeau, and Evan Horowitz, reviewed parts of this manuscript and offered some indispensably honest and rigorous criticisms. I want to thank my editor, Joseph Parsons, for his encouragement and his thoughtful, hands-on approach and my two readers, Leah Price and Mark McGurl, for turning my attention to several pivotal questions, which I had neglected to address.

I began to wrestle with many of the arguments developed here as a student at Princeton University, where my advisers Michael Wood and Diana Fuss, as well as several other professors, including Jeff Nunokawa, Bill Gleason, and Claudia Johnson, did a wonderful job of challenging and inspiring me. I am grateful also to Sarah Fan, Deirdre Lockwood, Hollis Robbins, Jim Moyer, and Laura Baudot, who read and responded to chapters in my dissertation — which formed the intellectual basis for this project. Finally, I would like to thank my friends and family — my mother and sister in particular — for their love and support, and of course my wife, Tala, for keeping my life exciting when I wasn't stuck in the library.

READING AS THERAPY

HOW DOES FICTION help people? What forms of emotional support do books provide? Do they stave off loneliness? Do they offer useful examples of how to lead or how not to lead one's life? Why is the tingle of self-recognition that accompanies identification with a fictional character so satisfying?

To ask these questions is to recognize that many readers in the United States today treat novels less as a source of aesthetic satisfaction than as a practical dispenser of advice or a form of therapy. They choose books that will offer strategies for confronting, understanding, and managing their personal problems. They want to encounter characters who remind them of themselves, their family members, or their friends. In search of comfort and companionship, they also expect novels to validate their grievances, insecurities, and anxieties while confirming their sense of themselves as deep, complicated, emotionally responsive human beings.[1] For such readers, the subject of greatest interest, the one most capable of inspiring sympathetic identification, is the psychological interior.

Focusing on the functions that literature performs for readers in contexts outside the academy, this book examines what I will term contemporary therapeutic fiction. The pejorative category typically applied to the needs that I intend to foreground and the novels that aim to meet these needs is "middlebrow." Many intellectuals view the urge to identify with fictional characters as a naïve surrender of critical distance based on an embarrassing inability to recognize the distinction between literature and life. Moreover, the psychological emphasis of middlebrow fiction, scholars on the left have argued, fosters the self-indulgent impulses of its readers, promoting liberal individualism and the evacuation of the public sphere.[2] It is my aim to challenge or at least complicate this picture. Notwithstanding the attempts of critics to encapsulate the defining features or the essential ethos of the middlebrow, the texts that fall into this category, the messages that they purvey, and the needs that they attempt to satisfy turn out under close inspection to be heterogeneous and complex. And claims about the contemporary novel's prioritization of the private typically overlook its capacity to serve as a social currency.[3] Contemporary fiction offers emotional gratifications by dramatizing desires, anxieties, losses, and hopes, which readers experience as intensely personal, even while it provides the basis for intersubjective affective communities. The tendency of mainstream literary fiction to privilege the personal and the psychological, I argue, contributes to the development of a common therapeutic vocabulary, which is capable of inspiring unlikely forms of sympathy among strangers. Such elusive and decentralized social formations, typically predicated upon perceptions of shared emotions, are distinct from the public sphere in its traditional conception; but they have played and continue to play an important, generally underexamined role in shaping America's social and political history.

The works that I will discuss, Toni Morrison's *Paradise* (1997), Rebecca Wells's *Divine Secrets of the Ya-Ya Sisterhood* (1997), David Foster Wallace's *Infinite Jest* (1996), James Frey's *A Million Little Pieces* (2003), Anita Shreve's *The Pilot's Wife* (1998), and Khaled Hosseini's *The Kite Runner* (2003), though an eclectic mix, all aspire to be considered "literary" while appealing to a large audience of nonprofessional readers — two qualities that characterize the middlebrow genre. Many readers, no doubt, will argue that novels such as *Paradise* and *Infinite Jest* are too difficult to be placed in this category, while some might conclude that *The Pilot's Wife* and *The Kite Runner* have more in common with lowbrow genre fiction. And given my overall focus on the novel, some readers will quibble with my choice of *A Million Little Pieces*, since it is best remembered as a memoir whose author played too freely with the facts. I have decided to include it in this study, not only because scrutiny ultimately revealed it to be a work of fiction, but also because the controversy surrounding it exposed certain unacknowledged aesthetic truth criteria, that is, notions of what makes a text feel true, at work in the reception of both memoirs and novels, which are rooted in a therapeutic paradigm. My purpose in bringing together such a diverse set of works is not to equate their status or literary value, but to identify underemphasized continuities in their strategies for answering the needs of their massive readerships. I hope thereby to demonstrate the proliferation of features typically deemed middlebrow throughout the contemporary literary scene, which make it increasingly difficult to assert strict boundaries between high, middle, and low. The books I am considering exemplify subgenres that are rarely juxtaposed in critical conversations; disciplinary divisions tend to keep them isolated from each other thus obscuring important commonalities. Rather than reinforce the rigid categories that are typically imposed on these works, I intend to argue that their ambiguity within hierarchies of taste constitutes a crucial source of their appeal. Indeed, several of the works considered here inspire fantasies of escape from invidious cultural categories altogether through experiences that underscore emotional commonalities and allow readers to claim membership within an undifferentiated democracy of shared affect.

Postwar Middlebrow Culture

What defines the middlebrow, according to scholars, is an urge to offer a cultural education to middle-class consumers and a capacity to muddy the boundaries between high and low.[4] Starting in the 1930s, a host of initiatives, including radio and television talk shows, adult education courses, magazines, and innovative book publishing strategies, including the introduction of paperbacks on a massive scale and the Book-of-the-Month Club, aimed to expose millions of middle-class Americans, many of them newly middle class, not only to a broad range of artistic and literary works, but also to the idea that being cultured is a worthy aspiration.[5] The two most famous critics of American middlebrow culture, Dwight Macdonald and Leslie Fiedler, both respond with alarm to the new conditions of artistic production and consumption in the postwar period of the 1950s, namely: the growth of the corporate mass market and a greatly expanded reading public.[6] Macdonald contends that mass culture appeals to and fosters what is common, predictable, and formulaic in its consumers, thereby disseminating an insidious form of mass consciousness and creating the condition for widespread conformity. And middlebrow culture, or what Macdonald calls "Midcult," is even more dangerous since it is no less standardized, no less manipulative than mass culture, but is not recognizable as such. In their effort to satisfy the ambivalent desires of their middle-class consumers for edification and entertainment, middlebrow magazines, novels, and movies, according to Macdonald and Fiedler, combine elements of highbrow and lowbrow culture in ways that overlook distinctions between the two.

Most worrisome to Macdonald is the destruction of standards necessary to make aesthetic distinctions. The desire to reach, satisfy, and flatter the new middle-class reading publics of the 1950s, he argues, motivates medi-ocre, easily digestible work that exhibits only the superficial trappings but none of the genius or courage of high culture, while the glut of middlebrow works undermines consumers' intelligence and their potential for nuanced discrimination. Macdonald refuses to place blame upon either the artists or the consumers; both are victims and participants within a homogeniz-ing mass-market structure, and his characterization of the middlebrow as an "ooze" that "spread[s]" and "seep[s]," treats it as daunting primar-ily for its sourceless, contagious quality (54). Fiedler's position is similar to Macdonald's; he regards mass culture with greater sympathy, however, because it depicts the more disturbing sexual and violent impulses that the middlebrow studiously avoids. Highbrow and lowbrow works in fact both deserve praise for their "antibourgeois" energy, substantiated for Fiedler most persuasively by frequent efforts among middle-class readerships to censor them ("Middle" 542). To phrase it tautologically, the middlebrow resists extreme or transgressive gestures; its fundamental shortcoming for both Fiedler and Macdonald is that it disseminates, celebrates, and refuses to subvert middle-class values, chief among them a democratic fantasy of its own universal appeal ("Middle" 547). More frightening than the specific content of middlebrow aesthetic and moral values, then, is the effort to establish these values as axiomatic and to create one standardized culture for everyone.[7]

Several related historical developments generate the terror of confor-mity that Fiedler and Macdonald evince. Many phenomena now taken for granted, if not always welcomed, including the mass market, suburban sprawl, and the growth of corporate bureaucracies, were relatively new in the 1950s. Some observers feared that the individualistic entrepreneurial ethic had disappeared and been replaced by the mentality of the "organization man," the "other-directed" consumer.[8] This transformation was particularly disturbing given the perceived threat of Soviet communism. The American capitalist system suddenly appeared to be engendering precisely the homogenized, brainwashed population typically associated with the enemy. As Macdonald remarked, "The tendency of modern industrial society, whether in the USA or the USSR, is to transform the individual into the mass man" (8).

Many of the New York intellectuals, including Dwight Macdonald, Leslie Fiedler, Philip Rahv, and Lionel Trilling, had embraced Marxism in the 1930s, repudiated it in the wake of revelations about Stalin's brutal policies, and come to accept the United States' economic and political system as the best available option for protecting individual liberty and artistic expression — a collective shift documented by the *Partisan Review*'s 1952 symposium, "Our Country and Our Culture."[9] On the one hand, these scholars and writers were painfully equipped to identify the emergence of the tendencies that had provoked their original rejection of communism. On the other hand, they had no choice, in their view, but to opt for the better of two ideologies, and thus they could refer to no alternative system, no independent ground or political stance, as a basis for a radical critique of the United States or its self-promoting middle-class culture. Indeed, they were its beneficiaries, since the ranks of white-collar professionals provided an audience for their writings. Both Macdonald and Fiedler favor the United States for its democratic institutions and its potential to promote economic mobility and political equality, but they fear the effects these developments entail in the realm of culture. It becomes more difficult, however, to identify what exactly is wrong with a culture whose tendencies are logically concomitant with a system that one has decided to embrace. Unable to elaborate a wholesale rejection of American capitalism, Fiedler and Macdonald find the cause of the problem harder to locate or articulate; hence Macdonald's use of vague and viscous metaphors, and the tendency of both critics to treat the middlebrow threat as a stylistic or psychological ill without a specifiable origin.

Ironically, during the postwar period, many middle-class readers confronted challenges similar to the ones faced by the New York Intellectuals.

Within suburbia, as William Whyte argues, dissatisfaction and alienation were an indicator of status, a form of psychological capital, and a basis for further achievement. The upwardly and geographically mobile suburbanite could not afford to be comfortably attached to a particular place or position. Corporate and suburban environments required both integration and mobility, a readiness to fit in, but an ironic detachment that would subtly distinguish the striving individual from the rest of the crowd and prepare him or her to move suddenly and reintegrate within a new vocational or residential context whenever needed. Indeed, many middlebrow novelists, most notably John Cheever, Sloan Wilson, and Richard Yates, offered their readers an education in the proper mode of disaffection. They, like the New York Intellectuals who scorned them, were cultivating a particular attitude vis-à-vis mainstream American culture that would enable both assimilation and a capacity for critique.

Cheever's story "The Worm in the Apple," for example, seems to deride the blithe optimism and self-satisfaction that, according to Macdonald and Fiedler, characterize the American middle class: "The Crutchmans were so very, very happy and so temperate in all their habits and so pleased with everything that came their way that one was bound to suspect a worm in their rosy apple and that the extraordinary rosiness of the fruit was only meant to conceal the gravity and the depth of the infection" (*Housebreaker* 107). The impulse to question the happiness of the Crutchmans, with their unpromising surname, is one that Cheever's parodically chipper tone immediately invites. It is almost impossible to hear the statement "The Crutchmans were so very, very happy" as a straightforward report of the facts, and many, presumably, will substitute "*seemed* so very, very happy." Thus Cheever sets before his readers their own manner of hearing, their own automatic cynicism—which turns out to be just as easy a target for his satire as the Crutchmans' carefree complacency. Cheever's pervasive irony, in other words, does not apply only to the first part of the sentence, but also to the second: "one was bound to suspect a worm in their rosy apple." He is certainly questioning the Crutchmans' happiness, but he is also questioning the skeptical attitude that would question the Crutchmans' happiness. Those who register his mockery are invited to entertain the possibility that the Crutchmans are indeed happy—which is what the story's first line, after all, categorically asserts. This realization would be potentially uplifting, if readers were not also forced to confront their own cynicism. The game this sentence plays requires the assumption that most readers will doubt the happiness of the Crutchmans, only to have their jaded attitude mocked. Sadly, then, the reader is forced to accept: (1) It is absurd to assume that anyone who seems really happy must be unhappy. (2) There might actually be truly happy people in the world. (3) Nevertheless, I, the reader, am unhappy enough to doubt anyone else's appearance of happiness. (4) If Cheever's suspicions are correct, everyone who reads the story is unhappy enough to doubt anyone else's appearance of happiness. In short, if the Crutchmans are happy, they are the only ones. The lesson of this story, and many of Cheever's stories, is how to cultivate the correct attitude toward one's suburban existence. In subjecting his readers' cynicism to satire, Cheever is not preaching positive thinking; rather, he is teaching them how to be properly disaffected, how to modulate their own disaffection with a measure of salutary, self-protective irony — a mode that will enable them to integrate into corporate suburbia without entirely relinquishing their autonomy.

To be sure, Cheever's methods for managing the conflicting challenges of suburban life are more subtle than those offered by many of his contemporaries, but his gifts have only strengthened the case for him as a middlebrow writer who employs highbrow techniques, while avoiding a truly courageous, critical, or transgressive posture, thus supporting the comfortable vanity of his readers. Irving Howe describes him as a "cautious therapist making sure the patients don't fly into a rage and tear apart the modern furniture" (131). Ironically, Cheever and the New York Intellectuals are responding to the same situation; both are struggling with the sense of a more constricted intellectual life in the postwar United States, a narrowed set of critical positions, given the failure of Marxism in the Soviet Union and the perceived need, even among the erstwhile avant-garde, to support American capitalism.

But if this ideological pressure appeared to be producing a uniform middle-class monoculture disturbingly similar to the one enforced within the Soviet system, it was not, as Macdonald and Fiedler feared, eradicating hierarchies altogether, and Cheever's work is a good demonstration of this fact. Even within the apparently homogenous suburban landscape that he depicts, his characters are constantly trying to understand the invidious distinctions that structure their community. And for readers who find themselves in a predicament similar to his characters', Cheever's work offers a lesson in a particular style of suburban sophistication — one that asserts precisely by effacing its own claim to superiority. Macdonald and Fiedler identify an important feature of middlebrow culture, its egalitarian posture, but they underemphasize the struggles for status and cultural capital that this egalitarian posture conceals and, in a sense, energizes. Middlebrow culture, after all, is predicated as much upon the desire for upward mobility as it is upon the shared fantasy of a classless society, and the myriad degrees of perceived refinement that stratify both middlebrow books and middlebrow readers inspire a mode of cultural consumption all the more frantic and anxious because the hierarchy is neither obvious nor unambiguous. Paradoxically, the fear of aesthetic difficulty ascribed disdainfully by Fiedler and Macdonald to the middle-class consumer suggests a desire that serious literature be accessible precisely so that the consumer can, by reading and understanding it, distinguish her- or himself as cultured; hence the middlebrow mentality posits a populist fantasy while coveting the elite status that everyone purports to find objectionable.

In examining the middlebrow culture of the past fifteen years, I am focusing on a set of dramatically different historical conditions from those addressed by Macdonald and Fiedler. In the place of the binary division of capitalism and communism, which seemed to structure the modes of assimilation and critique available in the 1950s, American intellectuals, writers, and readers now increasingly lay claim to multiple subcultures based not only on gender, race, and sexuality, but also other affinities, including modes of consumption and styles of affect. Moreover the middlebrow has changed. A quick perusal of the novels sponsored by Oprah Winfrey, the foremost purveyor of middlebrow culture in contemporary America, will demonstrate that the middlebrow has relinquished the prudishness deplored by Fiedler. It no longer avoids the representation of unconventional sexual desires or disturbingly violent impulses. Middle-class taboos have relaxed, conceptions of normality have expanded, and the market has discovered ever more efficient means of commodifying and packaging modes of revolt; thus the boundary between middlebrow and avant-garde has become less obvious.

Equally important is the dramatic transformation of the publishing industry in recent decades. The spate of mergers and acquisitions has drastically reduced the number of independent presses, so that now a handful of massive corporations control all but a slender margin of the book market.[10] At the same time, Barnes & Noble, Borders, and Amazon have forced a large proportion of independent booksellers out of business.[11] Arguably many of the changes in the industry represent a response to an inhospitable market, with Americans reading fewer and fewer books each year, as other media increasingly monopolize their leisure time (Greco et al. 97–98). And the chain stores continue to enforce a draconian returns policy, sending back books to the publisher for a full refund if they do not sell within a narrow window of time (Hughes 13).

Desperate to maintain their companies' viability, business-oriented managers have come to dictate editorial decisions. As Andre Schiffrin, former editor and author of *The Business of Books*, remarks: "This [editorial] process has been skewed by the fact that decisions on what to publish are made not by the editors but by so-called publishing boards, where financial and marketing staff play a pivotal role. If a book does not look as if it will sell a certain number — and that number increases every year (it's about 20,000 in many of the larger houses today) — then the publishing board decides that the company cannot afford to take it on" (105–6). To help boards make these decisions, Amazon offers detailed information about the profiles and tastes of consumers. And BookScan, a technology developed in 2001, which records information about book sales within a massive database available to publishers for a fee, provides information about how many copies of a particular book have sold in any given week and where.[12] In considering new manuscripts, editorial boards more than ever before attempt to fit their selections into a pre-established market niche by categorizing them alongside previously acquired books with similar characteristics. Moreover, in order to maintain a sustainable profit margin, many publishing companies prioritize guaranteed blockbusters, thus engaging in fiercely contested bidding wars for best-selling authors, a practice that further reduces their resources and their ability to gamble on experimental, idiosyncratic, or innovative fiction (Lewis-Kraus 41). Thus almost all the books that end up on the shelves of Barnes & Noble or in the warehouses of Amazon are required to survive a market-oriented submission and editorial process designed to maximize profitability.[13] Even works that aspire to be serious literature are published only insofar as they are deemed likely to be remunerative. The consequence is that a large number of the contemporary works presented by the major publishing houses as serious literature, at the pinnacle of the cultural hierarchy, exhibit features that appeal to a large, nonexclusive readership.

What this means for the critic is an extensive, undelineated field of texts, many of ambiguous status, but staking some claim upon literary prestige — precisely, in short, what Macdonald and Fiedler feared. This is not, of course, a homogenous culture. A diversity of aesthetic strategies; ideological stances; degrees of difficulty; and categories, including literary, quality commercial, mid-list, and middlebrow, confront the contemporary reader. But the most successful works succeed at crossing these divisions, and what primarily interests me are border cases. Almost all of the texts I consider exhibit the trait that, according to Fiedler and Macdonald, both defines the middlebrow and undermines its easy identification: a sly capacity to maneuver between different cultural spaces so as to satisfy the multifarious and ambivalent desires of readers from a variety of social backgrounds. My intention is to identify a particular function often aligned with middlebrow protocols that in fact unifies various books across the complicated and unsettled field of contemporary literature, that is, the therapeutic. But this function, though generally rooted in a coherent set of philosophical and political assumptions, is itself capable, as I will shortly establish, of mobilizing multiple, contradictory desires, ideals, and agendas.

Middle-Class Readers

To argue that a novel performs the work of therapy raises an interpretive difficulty; such a task depends as much upon the sensibilities and expectations of readers as it does upon the novel's intrinsic textual properties. One of my central strategies for dealing with this problem will be to consider the ways in which texts imagine, address, and interpellate their readers. If novels in myriad ways construct the desires that they purport to satisfy, then they have also become extremely sensitive measuring devices capable of registering their readers' pre-existing needs. Whether or not authors in recent decades have become more consciously attuned to the requirements of the markets they seek to reach — a pertinent but difficult question — the publishing industry certainly has. Given the elaborate consumer-focused mechanisms that determine which books get printed and promoted, and how these books get edited and marketed, a careful examination of the texts that survive this process will necessarily yield important insights about the desires and anxieties of contemporary readers.

But of course literary works cannot always control or predict how they will be interpreted and used. As Alain de Botton demonstrated, a sufficiently determined reader can transform a work as intractably highbrow as Proust's *Remembrance of Things Past* into a self-help book. For Macdonald and Fiedler, after all, the middlebrow refers not only to a set of aesthetic qualities, but also to a set of interpretive tendencies; one of their greatest sources of anxiety is the manner in which certain readerships appropriate and misunderstand serious literature. As numerous reader-response critics have asserted, a work can acquire radically different meanings depending upon its audience.[14] Hence, I plan to consider not only how texts imagine and construct their readerships, but also how readers creatively appropriate and reimagine books in order to make them serve a variety of personal and practical functions. Both texts and readers are responsive to the same broader social imperatives; both have been shaped by the prevailing therapeutic paradigm. Necessarily, some of the arguments I make about what readers might do with a particular work are speculative, based on general sociological or historical information about prevailing anxieties or concerns, but I also consider ethnographic studies of contemporary readerships, as well as direct evidence of reader responses provided by Oprah Winfrey's book club and the customer reviews posted on Amazon.

In addressing middlebrow interpretive strategies, my aim is to be critical as well as recuperative. The insight developed within cultural studies and argued perhaps most cogently by Janice Radway in *Reading the Romance* (1984) that consumers are capable of appropriating and interpreting cultural commodities in diverse, creative, and at times subversive ways has obviously influenced my approach, as has Radway's argument that middlebrow responses to literature are often far more sensitive and intelligent than most critics have acknowledged.[15] At the same time, however, I would not deny the contention elaborated by scholars of political economy, typically in opposition to the approach of cultural studies, that corporate interests, mass-media mechanisms, and the demands of capitalism exert enormous influence over the ways in which the products generated within this system get interpreted and used.[16] A central claim of this book is that middle-brow readers operate within a particular conceptual horizon, namely, the therapeutic, dependent upon contextually specific cultural training. But I would also argue that this interpretive framework, though generally not subversive or radical vis-à-vis capitalism, is more flexible, more capable of accommodating critical, sophisticated modes of thought, and more open to communal aspirations than the left generally acknowledges. Therapeutic rhetoric, I argue, is capable of abetting a variety of positions within the political spectrum, of supporting both conservative and progressive institutions and initiatives, and thus it is important to pay attention to how it works in particular circumstances and for particular readers.

This book foregrounds that broad category of consumers no less vexed, no less resistant to definition than middlebrow, that is, middle class. Although the American middle class is a strategic or pragmatic concept, constantly expanded, diminished, and recast as it proves useful in various political contexts, and in another sense a fantastical ideal, a projection of illusory ambitions and imaginary self-conceptions, and in still another sense a fabricated scapegoat, embellished or defined tautologically for the sake of grandstanding invective, I will begin with some concrete, definitive characterizations.[17] My focus is the individual with a college education, employed or married to someone employed in a white-collar profession or career that requires at least a BA, whose economic status is relatively secure, whose overall family income is equal to at least twice the official poverty level in the United States, and who reads books outside traditional academic contexts. This profile characterizes the majority of regular readers in the United States, whether they choose literary, mid-list, or genre fiction; and middle-class preferences exert enormous influence on the publishing industry.[18] I would not claim, however, that the interpretive responses I explore are restricted to readers who meet all of the conditions for inclusion within the middle class. The middle class is a normative as well as a descriptive category, and it is clear, after all, that many Americans, of various economic backgrounds, approach books in the ways typically ascribed to middlebrow culture simply by virtue of having their interpretive tendencies shaped by American public schools, by publishers' marketing strategies, and by Oprah Winfrey's book club.

Women, most studies indicate, read fiction more than men do in the United States.[19] This fact, unsurprisingly, has been a cause for some alarm over the decades among male intellectuals. A fear of the female reader constitutes a crucial subtext of the critiques that Macdonald and Fiedler level against middlebrow culture. "Fit for a woman's magazine" is the accusation Macdonald reserves for his least favorite cultural products. The genre most often associated with female readers, the sentimental novel, whose roots Fiedler traces back to eighteenth-century England, has long been a subject of debate among scholars of American literature (*Love and Death* 43–80). The typical impulse, exemplified by Fiedler, Ann Douglas, and others, has been to deride this form as weak, escapist, puerile, and apolitical. Other scholars, such as Jane Tompkins and Philip Fisher, have worked to recuperate this genre, claiming, persuasively, that a contingent set of masculinist, modernist aesthetic assumptions have presented themselves as universal in order to marginalize the canon of American women writers, a canon which, they argue, adheres to a different set of protocols and standards. At the same time, some critics and historians have challenged associations between femininity and sentiment, identifying male authors who have contributed to the sentimental tradition and underscoring masculine forms of sympathy and affect.[20] The latter, in my view, is an important observation. If Amazon customer reviews are any indication, men are also quite capable of responding empathetically to literature; hence I do not believe that characterizations of middlebrow culture, whether positive or negative, can be understood as exclusive to women.

While academics have challenged sentimental responses to literature as unserious and ineffectual in practice, emotion, at least within popular culture, tends to claim an incontrovertible status whose force depends on its nondiscursive and anti-intellectual character. What right, one might ask, do scholars have to question the validity of readers' feelings? To accept this defense, in my view, is to deny that emotional responses to literature are themselves complicated forms of interpretation and knowledge, fully capable of holding their own when confronted with the rigors of critical debate.[21] Thus I have tried to take affect seriously in this book by placing it in a dialogue, as an equal partner, with other more rational forms of analysis. Most readers, after all, confront literature through a combination of emotive and rational responses, and I have sought to capture moments of compatibility as well as moments of tension between the two.[22] Overall, my approach eschews either an uncritical embrace or a categorical rejection of sentiment, focusing instead on its capacity to serve a variety of social and ideological functions depending on the context.[23]

An emphasis on middle-class, middlebrow readers may seem to imply an emphasis on white readers. Indeed, the manner in which whiteness both achieves and evades representation in contemporary fiction is a subject that I plan to explore. But the category of readers that interests me — those with a college education who have achieved some economic stability, who see themselves as at least moderately successful but desire even higher status, and who believe themselves to be leading respectable middle-class lives — encompasses a diversity of races in the Unites States. Although the middlebrow may once have been a primarily white domain, it is not any longer, and one of Oprah Winfrey's accomplishments has been to promote a diverse canon of books for a diverse audience of readers. Of central concern for me, then, is the capacity of middlebrow forms of identification to mediate encounters across racial and cultural boundaries.[24] In many instances, racial difference, it turns out, exerts a strange influence upon readers, serving not to preclude but to intensify their experience of identification even when they are confronting fictional characters from radically unfamiliar cultural backgrounds.

According to Janice Radway and Elizabeth Long, middle-class American readers tend to be pragmatic in their approach to literature. They want what Kenneth Burke termed "equipment for living"; they expect the same services that they expect from self-help books.[25] Studying the Book-of-the-Month Club (BOMC) and its efforts to satisfy its middle-class consumers throughout the twentieth century, Radway notes that middlebrow readers treat literature as a source of "cultural competence," status, inspiration, and guidance (*Feeling* 162). Members of the BOMC seek books that are entertaining but also edifying, books that help them escape but also understand and manage what they see as an increasingly bewildering and fragmented world. Long also notes contemporary readers' practical orientation. Nonprofessional readers, she observes, actively resist the protocols of dispassionate scrutiny that prevail inside the academy, embracing works that depict scenarios directly relevant to the challenges they face in their own lives (*Book Clubs*).

Undeniably, middle-class readers also seek cultural capital.[26] They are attracted to literature in part for its capacity to elevate their social status. The markers of this influence extend well beyond the more obvious displays of books on shelves and knowledge at cocktail parties. Though, as John Guillory has argued, canonical literature is no longer the central means of imparting forms of linguistic facility, it has throughout the postwar period, according to Joel Pfister, provided a form of psychological capital, teaching American readers how to imagine, articulate, and perform their interior affective experience so as to establish their position in society and distinguish themselves from their peers.[27] Cheever, for instance, models for his suburban readers a form of disaffection that both expresses and masks itself through a cheerfully impermeable irony. This pose is especially useful in a corporate landscape, where success depends upon a carefully modulated synthesis of assimilation and detachment. Other contexts, of course, will dictate different strategies; the competition for cultural capital in the contemporary United States is not predicated upon a single definition of success or status. Macdonald's anguished characterization of the middlebrow as a realm bereft of any shared aesthetic standards can be read as a reaction not to the disappearance but to the bewildering proliferation of cultural hierarchies structured around competing criteria and values. In researching the Book-of-the-Month Club, for instance, Radway is struck by the discovery, potentially fatal to the academic's hope of functioning as a public intellectual, that the middlebrow constitutes its own counterpractice in opposition to academic standards (*Feeling* 112). Although the two spheres are not entirely independent of each other, it is possible now to be cultured in a particular manner and to read books to this end without directly consulting or caring about academic tastes and protocols.

One sign of middlebrow readers' relative autonomy from the academy, ironically, is their persistent reverence for literature and for the category of the "literary." Scholars have challenged this special status by disputing the notion of the author as an individual genius, by treating novels and poems as if they were no different from other kinds of texts, and by analyzing them to uncover the ideological and economic forces responsible for their production. But readers outside the academy have not surrendered their piety. Audiences on *Oprah*, customers on Amazon, professional book reviewers, and authors themselves continue to treat great works of literature as quasi-sacred repositories of wisdom, containing truths about humanity relatively untainted by local prejudices or political biases. While the category of the literary and the features that distinguish it from other genres of textual production have recently regained their position in the academy as subjects worthy of interest, many scholars would probably agree that the efforts to demystify literature and to contest its purported autonomy have served a crucial function, generating remarkably productive interpretive frameworks, which have helped to relocate texts in the impure, pedestrian world where they are produced and read.[28] But some critical work has treated literary texts as if they were nothing more than historical documents, ignoring the special status that attends them and the unique functions that they perform for their readerships. The category of "literature," in my view, is not merely an illusory haze that discerning critics must see through in order to apprehend the real object of analysis; it is a constitutive feature of a text's social reality, of the conditions under which it achieves visibility and agency. Especially in considering middlebrow culture, the urge to contextualize literature involves understanding how it has been framed, packaged, marketed, and perceived so as to attain a status superior to other practices and forms of writing. One aim of my project, then, will be to investigate how contemporary texts have laid claim to the prestige attached to the concept of the literary and what special tasks this prestige has enabled them to accomplish.

The Therapeutic Turn

Middlebrow veneration, of course, rarely celebrates texts for their inaccessibility. And the greatness that American readers attribute to literature generally does not preclude, but in fact depends upon their ability to find personal relevance in the books that they read—a task they accomplish primarily by means of a character-centered interpretive orientation, focused on individual psychology. The paradigm that underwrites this approach, the therapeutic, typically inspires disdain among scholars approximately equal in degree to the enthusiasm that marks its most prominent adherents. The critical assessments offered by academics, though shrill, do identify legitimate dangers that the therapeutic poses to left and progressive ideals. But a thorough apprehension of its impact requires a rethinking of certain oppositional terms such as "private" and "public," "self" and "community," "individual" and "social," "affective" and "rational." Though I share many of the concerns and anxieties voiced by critics on the left, I also believe that the therapeutic paradigm is capable of accommodating modes of thought and action at odds with the conservative ideological role generally ascribed to it.[29]

Many historians, sociologists, literary critics, and philosophers, including Herbert Marcuse, Philip Rieff, Christopher Lasch, Fredric Jameson, T. J. Jackson Lears, Elaine May, Richard Sennett, Joel Pfister, Nancy Schnog, and Lauren Berlant, observe the therapeutic paradigm's emergence in the twentieth century. While their descriptions vary in terminology and emphasis, together they provide a fairly coherent picture. According to most of these accounts, the therapeutic has become the defining structure of thought and feeling in the United States, asserting individual happiness as the fundamental goal of life and prioritizing the private or the personal over the public or the social. Constituted by means of psychological terms and concepts, the subjective interior has become for Americans the site of greatest importance, interest, complexity, depth, and fulfillment in the world. And the place that is most conducive to exploring, expressing, and protecting this purportedly fragile but essential core, this true self, is the domestic or intimate sphere. Outside of its boundaries, in contact with strangers, the therapeutic subject experiences self-alienation. Yet societal pressures rarely receive blame for the psychological dysfunctions that the subject may suffer, and many have complained that the therapeutic worldview causes people to misrecognize problems with social, economic, or political origins as individual problems, mistranslating legitimate grievances that might be directed at institutional injustices into the language of mental illness or dysfunction and seeking solutions that address the psychological symptom rather than the social root cause. The therapeutic, according to some theorists, promotes the restoration of the established order in moments of crisis and fosters individual accommodation or adjustment to the status quo.[30] Thus critics have accused therapeutic rhetoric of both crediting individuals with too much agency, by insisting that they are solely responsible for their own mental well-being, and of undermining individual agency by forestalling concrete political action and treating subjects as the victims of pathologies beyond their control.[31] The term "self-help" and the books that fall into this category, often aligned with therapeutic strategies, mobilize both meanings: asserting a self that can supposedly help itself, while implicitly catering to a self that is in constant need of help, a self that is in many respects understood to be helpless.

Scholars have attributed the therapeutic turn to multiple causes. An early observer of the phenomenon, Philip Rieff, designates the breakdown of traditional sources of authority, namely Christianity and its rigorous communal demands, as the key development. Without a life-defining telos beyond the self, Americans treat individual well-being as the sole purpose of their existence. Thus psychological discourses replace religious ones as the basis for meaning, and the modern notion of interiority, which emerges at the turn of the nineteenth century, replaces God as the central object of mystery and contemplation.[32] This shift becomes more pronounced with the invention of modern psychotherapy in the late nineteenth century in Europe, propelled most forcefully by the practical and theoretical innovations of Sigmund Freud. Prior to his intervention, mental health practitioners attended almost exclusively to the insane or the extremely pathological and organized their work around the asylum. Licensed doctors specializing in neurology treated these patients and typically attributed their complaints to physiological disorders. Freud inspired a shift from the psychotic to the neurotic, placing emphasis on less extreme forms of mental illness, which doctors could treat through regular office visits, and he conceptualized the psychological sphere as distinct from the physiological.[33] Already popular in Europe, his ideas met an extremely receptive audience when he visited the United States in 1909, perhaps because an array of theories, methods, and strategies, including mesmerism, New Thought,

Christian Science, and the Emmanuel movement, many of them employing proto-therapeutic techniques designed to alleviate nervous conditions, had prepared Americans for a discipline that would focus upon the health and well-being of the mind.[34]

It was in the post–World War II era, however, that psychotherapy truly exploded, becoming the ubiquitous institution that it is today (Veroff et al.). As historian Ellen Herman observes, the war helped to remove the stigma attached to those who sought mental health services, since a large percentage of soldiers and veterans who considered themselves to be normal needed assistance (112).[35] In the years immediately after the war, the Veterans Administration (VA) paid for students to get PhDs in clinical psychology, created rigorous training programs, and redefined the role of the clinical psychologist so that it would include the practice of psychotherapy as well as research. During this same period, assisted by the VA and the newly created National Institute of Mental Health, numerous universities across the country established four-year graduate programs in clinical psychology. As a result, psychoanalysis, which had been one of the only options for people suffering from psychological disorders, found itself in competition with a variety of other methods, including client-centered, cognitive, and gestalt psychotherapy (Herman). In the years that followed, therapeutic notions of the self spread well beyond the boundaries of mental health practices and institutions and into the popular consciousness. As Lears maintains, "Now [therapeutic self-absorption] pervades our dominant culture, touching people who have never been 'analyzed' and who are only dimly aware of psychiatry" (304).

Large-scale social and economic changes helped to ready the ground for these cultural innovations. According to Pfister, the development of a vocational realm separate from the domestic space in the nineteenth century supported the production of private forms of subjectivity believed to thrive only in isolation from the public sphere and the dictates of sociability ("Glamorizing the Psychological"). Moreover, the growth of industrial capitalism throughout the twentieth century and the emergence of massive corporations and bureaucracies after World War II alongside cold war anxieties provoked a sense of uncertainty and individual powerlessness, which led people to prioritize the private and the psychological as the only sites of shelter, safety, and agency within an increasingly confusing social and political world. But of course the past sixty years have also witnessed extraordinary affluence in the United States, and some scholars have posited that the emphasis on the therapeutic is a consequence of the middle class's relative liberation from the necessities and austerities that material scarcity tends to entail.[36] Without such hardships, many Americans have the luxury to dwell obsessively upon their psychological health — a fixation that advertising campaigns have, by associating their products with the attainment of happiness, cleverly exploited.

The therapeutic became a dominant force during the cold war, one that underlined the importance of maintaining the private sphere in opposition to the state-centered mentality purportedly imposed by the former Soviet Union on its people.[37] Remarkably, however, therapeutic culture has become more pervasive since the cold war ended. In its need to justify its own existence, it has become increasingly adept at constituting and inventing the problems that it claims to solve — as evidenced by the popularization of new pathological identities including Attention Deficit Disorder, Obsessive Compulsive Disorder, Asperger Syndrome, codependency, and so forth.[38] Indeed the therapeutic has demonstrated a phenomenal capacity both to construct dysfunction and to translate all variety of challenges, dilemmas, and conflicts into its own terms — a capacity responsible for its persistent centrality within contemporary culture. In order to illuminate some of the strategies that therapeutic culture has employed to establish its continued relevance and usefulness, I want to turn now to an emblematic text that appears at the beginning of the period I am considering: John Bradshaw's 1990 best-selling self-help book, *Homecoming: Reclaiming and Championing Your Inner Child.*

A professional therapist who acknowledges his intellectual debt to a host of psychologists and self-help writers, Bradshaw traces psychological dysfunction back to childhood. In his view, the individual has certain needs at each stage of development that must be met in order for that person to progress to the next stage of maturity. If those needs are not met, the hurt, angry, unsatiated child will continue to live uncomfortably inside the mind of the adult, thus producing what he calls "spontaneous age regressions" (7). The only solution to this predicament is to learn, as an adult, to nurture one's own inner child in order to satisfy the needs that were not satisfied originally.

For Bradshaw, the inner child is not merely a figure for the youthful impulses that adults tend to ignore or repress; it is a hidden, well-nigh independent being living within the mind, which experiences its own continuous, subterranean development in response to the individual's manifest mental life. In short, Bradshaw anthropomorphizes the Freudian unconscious — a remarkable reversal of Freud's own effort to defamiliarize the operations of the mind, to make us feel like strangers to ourselves.[39] But Bradshaw's conceptualization, itself childlike in its simplicity, nevertheless strives to retain the notion, defended by Freud, of the subjective interior as complex, as bearing the intricate, subtle markings of the past in the present, as staging ongoing invisible dramas, as deeper, more obscure, and more interesting than everyday appearances might suggest. Bradshaw's image of the inner child preserves this valorizing picture of the human mind while rendering it less threatening, less alien, and more readily describable. The child not only offers a convenient figure for visualizing and understanding those aspects of the psyche that elude conscious apprehension; it also seeks to account for the individual's more irrational and destructive impulses while defusing the anxiety and self-loathing that attention to these impulses might provoke.

Bradshaw invites readers to nurture their inner child, and his advice at times seems to bear out an accusation frequently leveled against therapeutic culture: that it fosters the self-infantilizing, narcissistic tendencies of affluent American consumers. Many of the activities he suggests to help readers recover their sense of "I Amness" would likely be available only for those who have achieved a certain measure of wealth: "Get into a hot tub and spend time focusing on your bodily sensations"; "treat yourself to regular massages"; "in winter, wrap up by a warm fire and roast marshmallows"; "spend thirty minutes to an hour floating in a swimming pool on a warm summer day" (218). It is important to recognize, of course, that in instructing his readers to indulge in these activities, Bradshaw anticipates resistance. He recognizes that these luxuries must be constituted as deserved, as rewards for hardships suffered. Thus Bradshaw deploys psychological dysfunction as a means of justifying the self-love that he prescribes. The image of the inner child crystallizes the narrow circuit of victimization and entitlement that psychological discourse activates for members of the middle class. To imagine that one is harboring a fragile, confused, neglected child is to identify with a figure who appears legitimately wounded and who therefore deserves to be pampered. The popularity of self-help books such as *Homecoming* and the need for this strange vehicle of self-sympathy thus reveals not a complacently affluent middle class, but instead a population at least slightly uneasy about its privileges, one that requires periodic affirmations of its own victimhood and vulnerability in order to validate its various indulgences.

Bradshaw's book demonstrates that the central purpose of contemporary therapeutic rhetoric may not be only to resolve or cure, but also to construct and legitimize psychological dysfunction. One of Bradshaw's tactics, a common one in self-help books, is to offer surveys featuring questions vague and varied enough to allow practically any reader to identify a psychological problem. "Do you feel, or have you ever felt, *desperate* because a love relationship ended?" (83). "In social situations, do you try to be invisible so that no one will notice you?" (83). "Do you have trouble knowing what you want?" (106). "Are you a big worrier?" (106). "Do you fear anger in other people? In yourself?" (107). "Do you have trouble expressing your feelings?" (123). "Do you frequently feel uncomfortable in social situations?" (141). "Do you procrastinate a lot?" (141). For readers who fail to identify any strong indicators of psychological dysfunction, Bradshaw posits numbness as itself symptomatic: "In childhood you were most likely severely shamed and punished when you expressed anger. Your inner child learned to stop himself from feeling his anger. Over the years he became so numb that he didn't know he was angry any longer" (226).

While he asserts the ubiquity of psychological dysfunctions rooted in a mistreated inner child, Bradshaw also seeks to establish their severity, challenging any defenses and disclaimers that his readers might produce:

> If all this is shocking to you, that's great, because *shock is the beginning of grief.* After shock comes depression and then denial. Denial kicks

our ego defenses back in. It usually comes in the form of bargaining. We say, "Well it wasn't *that* bad. I had three squares [*sic*] and a roof over my head."

Please believe me: It *was* really bad. To be spiritually wounded, for your parents not to let you be who you are, is the worst thing that can happen to you. (78; emphasis in original)

Rivals for the distinction of "the worst thing that can happen to you" may come to mind, but Bradshaw proves his unyielding belief in this hyperbolic statement when he claims in two separate places that the results of a neglected inner child are either comparable to or more painful than incarceration in a concentration camp (48–49, 65). Central to his efforts to legitimize middle-class modes of suffering is the competition he invokes between material and psychological deprivations. *Not* having access to three square meals, for instance, is a concrete, socially recognized problem considered grave and worthy of compassion. By contrast, psychological problems are in many cases invisible — even to the sufferer. But this very invisibility allows Bradshaw to dispute any claims that psychological problems are the product of narcissistic delusion or exaggeration. Precisely because they are not available to consciousness and the distortions that it routinely practices, the inner child and its wounds are in fact *real*, and not merely a figment of the conscious imagination or the histrionic invention of middle-class self-pity.

Bradshaw tends to blame most of the individual's dysfunctions along with most of the world's problems on the traditional family. Reflecting the precarious and embattled status of the nuclear ideal in contemporary culture, this position might seem to contradict the therapeutic paradigm's general tendency to designate the private sphere as a site of safety and self-realization. But one could argue that the notion of the domestic sphere as an incubator of dysfunction actually empowers the therapeutic, allowing it to define within its own terms and conceptual scope the crises that it purportedly alleviates. Indeed, Bradshaw's premises enable him to frame a variety of historical phenomena within psychological terms: "I believe that the catastrophe of Nazism was rooted in the structure of the German family with its shaming and authoritarian parental rules. However, while these rules were taken to their extreme in Germany, they are not German rules. In fact, they are worldwide rules that have wounded children for generations and still exist today. Because the rules were considered normal, there was no awareness of how destructive they were" (254). Although uncharacteristic, this passage encapsulates the imagined explanatory ambition of contemporary therapeutic discourse. Bradshaw's account of Nazism as a product of widespread familial dysfunction appears to lend itself to the central criticism of the therapeutic paradigm: that it misunderstands social problems as private pathologies. In fact, the danger of his perspective is that it privileges the psychological dynamics of the domestic as the "root" or underlying reality, thus trivializing material, political, ethnic, and religious factors, relegating them to the status of symptom. But it would be a mistake to accuse the therapeutic, as some critics have, of eclipsing attention to social or structural realities in favor of the individual. As this passage on Nazi Germany demonstrates, therapeutic discourse attends to these realities precisely by means of psychological terms. Bradshaw treats the nuclear family as the expression of broader social norms. Thus the therapeutic paradigm represents not a retreat from, but rather an effort to theorize, social space — imagining it as molecular, consisting of divided but resonant spheres of dysfunction, all duplicating the same pathologies, all rooted in widely disseminated conventions, which are experienced and grasped most palpably in their private, psychological manifestations.

Focusing upon psychological needs that are, according to his theory, both universal and universally unmet enables Bradshaw to support certain ideological self-conceptions prevalent within the American middle class. The emphasis on the interior, evident in self-help books such as Bradshaw's, supports affluent readers in their belief that everyone suffers the same kinds of psychological hardships, and that they too are participating in painful struggles constitutive of the human condition. Such assertions are attractive in part because of pervasive feelings of weightlessness, sterility, shallowness, artificiality, boredom, banality, inauthenticity, and unreality, which have, according to numerous scholars, novelists, and critics, endangered the enjoyment of prosperity for Americans.[40] While mass-market commodities and technologies, such as television, designed, Daniel Boorstin argues, to produce "repeatable experience[s]," have diminished the capacity for intense sensation, spontaneity, and surprise (389), the growth of corporations, the loss of entrepreneurial possibilities, and the rise of jobs focused on the development and circulation of symbols and ideas rather than material products have undermined for white-collar workers their sense of importance, uniqueness, and individuality.[41] A world designed to make its inhabitants as comfortable and secure as possible has, in the eyes of many, radically reduced the opportunities for agency and heroism.

The notion, still celebrated in sneaker advertisements and fitness regimens, that life ought to be hard, stubbornly persists in the United States. The quintessentially American sensibility, the Protestant ethic, which advocates tireless labor, relentless dedication to the accumulation of wealth, and the deferral of gratification, emerged in response to the situation of economic scarcity in the eighteenth and nineteenth centuries. Some have concluded that it has been supplanted in the twentieth by a consumer mentality celebrating permissiveness and unrestrained indulgence. I would argue that it has survived, but in a distorted and displaced form.[42] It continues to insist, for members of the middle class, on the need for constant vigilance and work as requisites for the establishment of character and the achievement of secular well-being. And while it also continues to motivate the accumulation of wealth as one means to these ends, amid abundant material comforts, the Protestant ethic has come to redirect its energy into therapeutic endeavors, finding a new realm of struggle and perpetually delayed fulfillment in the psychological. For middle-class Americans, the interior now represents the staging ground for all the suffering, risk, trouble, and heroism that, owing to the residue of a worldview responsive to the demands of previous centuries, continue to be perceived as necessary aspects of a meaningful life.

If the claim that therapeutic strategies teach middle-class Americans how to be dissatisfied provokes the skeptical rejoinder that they have already mastered that particular skill, this is a sign of the therapeutic's hegemony. But, like any ideology, the therapeutic requires constant reaffirmation. What its discourses and practices do is validate and legitimize, or re-validate and re-legitimize, the forms of suffering and dissatisfaction that middle-class Americans, well versed in psychological introspection, are especially adept at experiencing, treating these interior hardships as a source of character. Recasting the imperatives of the Protestant ethic, the articulation of psychological difficulty enables individuals to imagine themselves as deep, courageous, complex, interesting, and authentic. Moreover, as Pfister has argued, a degree of dysfunction or maladjustment serves as psychological capital; it suggests a superior, more sensitive mind, and thus, carefully managed, increases one's social status.[43] The task of supporting the construction and performance of psychological trouble is one that both self-help books and novels perform. The latter, perhaps even more effectively than the former, are capable of transforming the vague, inchoate, private insecurities, anxieties, and disorders that many individuals experience into a compelling narrative — one that elicits sympathy and indirectly allows readers to feel sympathy for themselves.

Therapeutic Fiction

Modern fiction, I would contend, is especially well equipped to respond to the demands posed by the therapeutic paradigm. Indeed, one might maintain that a central function of the novel has been, for at least two centuries, to help middle-class readers narrate and manage their private problems. Franco Moretti has cogently argued that the particular narrative structures and formal properties of what he terms "serious fiction," including the habitual use of free indirect discourse, a prosaic fidelity to the details of everyday life, and an emphasis on meticulous factual description, are designed, in the nineteenth century, to represent middle-class experience in all of its fastidious regularity and paradoxically to make it exciting, worthy of interest and sympathy. He notes that the development of these techniques coincides with the emergence of the domestic sphere as a central and autonomous space, "when houses became more comfortable and luminous, and doors multiplied, and rooms differentiated their function, and one of them specialized precisely in everyday life: the 'living,' or 'drawing' room" (380).

Moretti's implicit suggestion is that a central basis for the appeal of serious fiction is its tendency to affirm middle-class lifestyles and values. The genre of fiction that he is characterizing, generally known as realism, has of course met with competition, both in the United States and Europe, from modernism, which aimed in many cases at a radical transformation of society, and from naturalism, which has typically sought to portray the conditions of the poor and the working class. But these countervailing trends were far more prevalent in the United States during the first half of the twentieth century than now. According to Thomas Schaub, fiction and criticism in the 1950s and 1960s rejected the naturalist, materialist attention to social realities, such as urban industrial conditions and class conflict, which characterized previous decades, and foregrounded instead the individual consciousness. The earlier emphasis, Schaub contends, was typically aligned with Marxist convictions, whereas the postwar orientation registered an emerging skepticism regarding the power of social institutions, political programs, or mass movements to solve various ills. Developments that I have already adumbrated, including revelations of Stalinist brutality, anti-radical patriotic commitments produced by the cold war, and the ascendance of global economic, political, and military systems capable of engendering apocalyptic scenarios — coupled with an official culture of consensus and positive thinking — all contribute to a climate of political pessimism on the left, making personal alienation, as opposed to radical activism, seem the only viable option for writers and intellectuals dissatisfied with the status quo during the 1950s.

In subsequent decades, American fiction seemed to be even more focused on the individual mind as psychological realism became the predominant literary mode, gradually supplanting naturalism, modernism, and postmodernism. It is important to note, of course, as Schaub does, that not everyone has understood this shift as a turn away from politics. An emphasis on consciousness for some writers entails revolutionary possibilities. While countercultural figures such as Norman Mailer or Ken Kesey may come to mind, the writers who most actively and successfully attempted to promote political change through psychological intervention were the feminist consciousness-raising novelists of the late 1960s and early 1970s. Influenced by Betty Friedan's efforts to make women's experiences more visible, these writers focused on characters' psychological problems, but they dramatized the insight, embraced by a variety of groups within the New Left, that the personal is political, explicitly showing how these problems stem from political and economic structures, including a patriarchal society, a discriminatory job market, and a belittling commodity culture.[44]

In many consciousness-raising novels, including Marilyn French's *The Women's Room* (1977) and Marge Piercy's *Small Changes* (1973), an awakening of the protagonist's consciousness leads her to participate in collective political action, and these narratives aim to produce similar forms of recognition and activism among readers.

Ironically, the various successes of the second-wave feminist movement, including the injection of millions of women into the job market, the enactment of equal opportunity laws, and the legalization of abortion, may have ultimately led to the ostensible depoliticization of women's fiction. Radical rejection of mainstream American society became less appealing and less tenable as many women found it necessary, if difficult, to reconcile themselves to an economic system they continued to see as antagonistic in some respects to their beliefs and interests, but which suddenly offered them unprecedented possibilities for success and social mobility. In the last few decades, novels that foreground women's experiences have become even more numerous, a trend most visible in the emergence of chick lit, the therapeutic heir to the consciousness-raising novel; but most of these books fail to offer an explicitly political understanding of the dilemmas that the characters confront, and they do not advocate deliberate political involvement. They seem, in other words, to accent the personal side of the personal-political equation. To take this equation seriously, however, is to recognize that even the most psychologically oriented, private dramas of contemporary women's fiction are not devoid of political meaning — an insight I take up in my chapter on Anita Shreve.

Reflecting the postwar embrace of the interior, several major critics formulate conceptions of literature's central function that emphasize its personal or psychological uses. Not long after Kenneth Burke published "Literature as Equipment for Living," Lionel Trilling described in *The Liberal Imagination* (1950) the "mithridatic" function of literature, an idea whose genealogy he traces to Freud and Aristotle: "At any rate, the Aristotelian theory does not deny another function for tragedy (and for comedy, too) which is suggested by Freud's theory of the traumatic neurosis — what might be called the mithridatic function, by which tragedy is used as the homeopathic administration of pain to inure ourselves to the greater pain which life will force upon us" (55–56).

In his essay "Literature as Therapy," Northrop Frye also attributes to Aristotle the idea that tragedy supports the achievement of psychic balance, arguing that it enables readers to inhabit a "counterenvironment" in which they can purge feelings of pity and terror that would otherwise be unbearable. But the most elaborate account of literature's therapeutic function is Norman Holland's, in *The Dynamics of Literary Response* (1968). Like Frye, Holland stresses the importance of the fictional status of literature in performing a salutary function. Divorced from the real world, works of fiction, Holland maintains, present us with situations that demand no action and require no sense of responsibility. The temporary state of extreme passivity engendered by the reading experience represents a reversion to infancy, which allows us to confront and satisfy repressed, primitive desires. Like dreams, literary works offer wish fulfillments rooted in our earliest childhood memories in a coded, managed form. It is through reading literature, in other words, that the individual can satiate the intense and irrational needs of the inner child.

A Freudian critic, Holland is both a product of the therapeutic paradigm and an astute observer of what draws readers to literature within the postwar period — though he does not view the interpretive responses that he describes as rooted in a particular historical context. Of particular interest is his claim that literature allows readers to experience intense emotions, which they ordinarily regulate and repress: "Rather than speak of regression, then, we can say our minds during the literary experience undergo a 'deepening.' It is as though a pianist had been confined to the upper three octaves because there was some danger if he played the low notes — perhaps an explosion would be triggered off, as, in everyday life, we feel it dangerous to respond to reality with much affect from the massive, primitive depths of our earliest selves. In the literary situation, though, we know no explosion will occur, for we know we are not going to act" (82). Holland here indirectly addresses a middle-class dilemma, the problem of banality, and suggests that literature provides the solution, allowing its readers to experience intense emotive dramas, which have come to be seen as a condition for complete and fully realized personhood. While literature's fictional status is essential, for Holland, in deactivating the reader's sense of responsibility, the experience he describes represents not an escape from, but a confrontation with, the deeper more basic reality of the inner self, a reality commensurate with the extraordinary scenarios depicted in great works of literature, and one so overwhelming that most people can confront it only in the guise of fiction. Thus Holland treats the apparent shallowness of everyday life as an illusory product of repression and imagines fiction as a means of access to the real pathos that American readers would otherwise fail to acknowledge. For those, in other words, who are bored by their actual lives but excited by fiction, Holland's account suggests, counterintuitively, that the former, boredom, is an illusion and the latter, excitement, the unrecognized reality.

The functions that Holland describes can obviously be performed by other media, including movies, television shows, and even video games, all of which share literature's fictional status. But the high-culture prestige of literature, most notably of serious fiction, allows Americans to approach the reading experience as a form of self-improvement. Even if fiction gratifies people's infantile desires, as Holland argues, it also enables them to imagine this gratification as psychologically salutary and intellectually elevating. Moreover, formal strategies particular to fiction, including free indirect discourse and first-person narration, integrate the represented interior thoughts of characters into the story far more seamlessly than equivalent devices in movies and television and thus appeal to those consumers, influenced by the therapeutic paradigm, who favor literature for its purportedly greater psychological depth.

A key element of the work fiction performs for readers is of course narrative. Within a secular, therapeutic worldview, the telos of life is individual happiness, but this is a state, as innumerable self-help books and therapists will insist, that ought not to be postponed or projected into some as yet unrealized future. The end of existence thus becomes the need to enjoy all the moments leading up to the end. But this displacement of meaning away from a broader communal purpose, a religious quest, or a distantly achievable state and onto every passing moment — each of which becomes a test, in quasi-Calvinist fashion, of whether the individual is leading a happy, fulfilling life — actually reduces life to a mere series of moments and thus potentially deprives these moments of the very significance that our fixation upon them is supposed to guarantee. Or to put it more simply, the therapeutic emphasis on immediate personal happiness runs the risk of making life feel boring and aimless — which of course becomes another problem that therapy then needs to solve. Faced with this situation, the task for the novel is to find a way to narrate experiences whose nonteleological character renders them impervious to narrative. This is what Lukács understood when he argued that the novel responds to a world deprived of any immanent purpose by attaching meaning to the passage of time itself and to the ongoing growth, flowering, and production of life that this entails (123–27). Building on Lukács's insight, Moretti claims that serious novels of the nineteenth century come to consist entirely of filler or description, and almost entirely lack turning points or plots. The narrative of the novel, then, is designed both to represent the modern experience of empty temporality, by re-enacting the forward movement of time through its own unfolding structure, and to reimagine this state, this movement, as meaningful in itself, precisely because meaning is nowhere else to be found. Indeed at times, as Lukács suggests, the novel makes the very loss of a governing telos into a source of lyrically sustaining pathos. More effectively and more poignantly than self-help or therapy, the enlivening prose of the novel attempts to elevate and exalt the prosaic character of middle-class existence.

Catherine Jurca, a scholar of American suburban fiction, finds middle-class anxieties about banality, or what Barbara Ehrenreich has dubbed "the problem of problemlessness" (19), to be largely meretricious. She describes such complaints as "empowering rhetorics of victimization, which somehow only seldom manage to be anything but rhetorical" (19). Though Jurca's identification of a histrionic register in certain evocations of middle-class suffering is persuasive, assessing the sincerity of these evocations seems an impossible endeavor. It is more critically productive, I would contend, to examine the aesthetic and rhetorical modes that middle-class laments and their legitimation require and the social and political consequences that they entail. The urge to feel part of a global humanity, unified by shared psychological suffering, though capable of promoting narcissism and eclipsing attention to tragic inequities, can also under certain conditions enable cross-cultural identification and compassion, which can in turn provide the basis for salutary acts of amelioration.[45]

Public and Private

A belief in the supreme importance of the public sphere and serious concerns regarding its erosion in contemporary American society tend to underwrite the distaste that the therapeutic provokes among critics especially on the left. To make sense of these concerns it is necessary to understand the ways in which theorists have conceptualized the private and the public. Numerous thinkers, including Hannah Arendt, Christopher Lasch, Jürgen Habermas, Richard Sennett, Anthony Giddens, and Michael Warner, to name just a few, have attempted to establish the defining characteristics of these two spheres. The debate is far too extensive to recapitulate here, but a few key assertions and distinctions are worth illuminating. Very generally, theorists maintain that the public is characterized by wide visibility, openness, and the coexistence and collaboration of strangers, while the private is characterized by hiddenness, exclusiveness, and intense familiarity among a limited number of individuals. In her description of how the two spheres operate in ancient Greece, Arendt identifies bodily functions with the private sphere, which she sees as primarily situated within the household and devoted to physical necessities and reproduction. By contrast, the public sphere is, in her view, a space of freedom and courage, removed from the immediate biological imperatives of survival, and consisting of dialogue designed to reflect upon and constitute the shared world of its citizens. Habermas offers a similar vision of the public sphere as composed of disinterested, rational debate aimed at reaching conclusions with universal validity; and both authors underline the unique capacity of the public to de-emphasize or bracket personal concerns and special interests particular to the individual in favor of the perpetuation and transformation of the common world.

Richard Sennett underlines the importance of the encounter with the stranger that public spaces enable. Like Arendt, he projects his idealized image of the public into a past historical era; in his case, the urban life of eighteenth-century France and England. According to Sennett's account, interactions between strangers in this context mobilized the spontaneous invention and expression of identity based upon the manipulation of shared codes of meaning. In city squares and coffeehouses, safeguarded by anonymity and liberated from the strict enforcement of class hierarchies, individuals could construct and redefine themselves by means of socially understood gestures, which were treated as self-sufficient signs capable of producing, like stage devices, their own immediate reality, rather than as symbols of a private interior. Only in the nineteenth century, Sennett contends, did language become burdened with the latter function. During that period a new ideological configuration emerged that insisted upon fidelity to a pre-existing interior essence, thus disabling the spontaneous expressiveness, the generative, transformational possibilities, and the capacity for constructive compromise that had distinguished an era concerned more with the requirements and theatrical possibilities of the public sphere than with the needs of the self.

It is tempting to situate the public within a clearly delineated space: a city square, a coffeehouse, or a salon. While theorists have paid particular attention to these locations, the public, as Arendt suggests, is impossible to designate or delimit a priori: it is any site where a group of people engage in a particular kind of discourse. It is defined as much by the style of discussion as it is by its physical (or virtual) context.[46] This unlocatability necessarily renders the division between the public and the private spheres ambiguous. Susan Gal has noted that the border is always shifting depending on the scale under consideration: "At a first look, the privacy of the house itself contrasts with the public character of the street around it. If we focus, however, on the inside of the house, then the living room becomes the public, that is, the public part of a domestic private space. Thus the public/private distinction is reapplied and now divides into public and private what was, from another perspective, entirely 'private' space. But even the relatively public living room can be recalibrated — using this same distinction — by momentary gestures or utterances, voicings that are iconic of privacy and thus create less institutionalized and more spontaneous spatial divisions during interaction" (82). The existence of these multiply "nested dichotom[ies]" undermines the purity of each sphere, demonstrating the inevitability of interpenetration, of elements purportedly specific to one domain asserting themselves within the other (83). For Habermas, the bourgeois public sphere in fact exists *within* the private sphere protected by the ownership of property and shielded from the mechanisms of power and the special interests that constitute the government—a position whose autonomy enables the public sphere to perform what Habermas sees as its defining function: opposing unfettered critical reason to the exercise of domination.

Given their uncertain, porous boundary, the private and the public spheres are always in danger of surrendering their distinctiveness. The slightly hyperbolic claims made by Sennett and Arendt about the strict delineation of the two spheres in previous historical periods are obviously designed to enable laments about the tragic collapse of the boundary in the twentieth century. While the influence of left paradigms has promoted an emphasis in the academy upon the absence of public and collective forms of consciousness in the United States, Sennett, Arendt, and Habermas are equally appalled by what they diagnose as the loss of the private. The public consists of the congregation of free, independent individuals, but, as both Arendt and Habermas note, the power to make a unique contribution to that sphere requires the ability to escape from it, to experience a life independent of its demands, to emerge into the visibility of the public from a place of privacy. Arendt eloquently summarizes the case as follows: "A life spent entirely in public, in the presence of others, becomes, as we would say, shallow. While it retains its visibility, it loses the quality of rising into sight from some darker ground which must remain hidden if it is not to lose its depth in a very real, non-subjective sense" (71). One culprit responsible, according to Arendt, for disrupting the boundary between the private and the public is industrial capitalism, which effectively removes the tasks aimed at satisfying life's basic biological necessities from the household and situates them within shared spaces, inserting necessity and unfreedom into what might have qualified, by virtue of its other properties, as a public sphere. This development in turn requires the household, liberated from the exigencies that once defined it, to offer possibilities of self-realization and fulfillment that have been removed from the public, thus instantiating what Arendt terms "the intimate sphere." At the same time, as Habermas and Giddens have noted, commodities and the mass media intrude into this sphere, curtailing its autonomous character. And in reciprocal fashion, familial, sexual, and psychological concerns increasingly relinquish their private character, intruding onto the public stage as a pervasive confessional culture insists upon the unabashed performance of the interior—a tendency that Sennett sees as especially damaging to American political discourse.

The danger of the therapeutic paradigm, according to Sennett, is not that it inspires a turn away from political and onto personal concerns, but rather that it has come to reconfigure the political in the United States, to reshape its characteristic modes of expression in alignment with an emphasis on "personality." Semiprivate, confessional styles of address now appear with greater influence than ever before upon the stage of electoral politics. The therapeutic, then, operates as a hybrid social formation, assuming functions that have been traditionally assigned to either the public or the private, while remaining distinct from each as a consequence of its hybrid character and the peculiar styles and strategies that this duality requires.[47] But how effective is the therapeutic in accomplishing the tasks that it has usurped? What issues is the therapeutic capable of coping with and what issues is it structurally guaranteed to misconstrue? Are its forms and protocols able to meet the personal and the political necessities that confront it, or is it doomed to produce failure and dissatisfaction as a consequence of its incongruities? How can the public or the private sphere perform its function if, owing in part to the therapeutic paradigm, the public sphere has ceased to be truly public and the private sphere has ceased to be truly private?

Habermas claims that individuals recognize their status as human beings through a focus on their interior subjectivity and thus become oriented toward a larger public of fellow humans, all unified by a shared sense of private autonomy. But he would likely argue that the subjective interior so frequently celebrated within therapeutic discourse is not in fact truly autonomous. Rather, under twentieth-century capitalism, individuals lead lives socialized to such an extent through commodities, mass media, and therapeutic discourse itself that their subjective experiences fail to qualify as private and therefore cannot contribute to an authentically public sphere dependent, in Habermas's definition, upon the autonomy of its subjects. "An inner life oriented toward a public audience tends to give way to reifications related to the inner life" (172). While it would be hard to question his image of the inner subjective realm as a site of social intrusion and market manipulation, arguably the individual autonomy that Habermas celebrates is so pure, so unalloyed as to become an impossible fantasy, establishing conditions for a legitimate public sphere that are unrealizable now or in the past eras that he imagines. Perhaps, then, it is necessary to consider the possibility and the political utility of impure public spheres based upon modes of semiautonomy and compromised privacy, in which the tension between public pressures and private barriers does not merely organize the encounter between the individual and the society, but in fact spreads and proliferates so as to constitute, in myriad entanglements, the very subjectivity of the participants.

Therapeutic discourse is capable of producing hybrid private and public affiliations perhaps most effectively by means of print and other media, among geographically dispersed audiences. One underexamined reward of the sympathetic identification promoted by the novel is the sense of solidarity that it produces not merely with fictional characters, but also with other actual and potential readers who respond in a similar fashion.[48] Michael Warner aptly observes that reading publics are characterized by an "intimate theater of strange relationality" (*Publics* 76). These are publics, he observes, composed of strangers, not only because their participants literally do not know each other, but also because the text's address functions as an open invitation to *anyone* capable of inhabiting the position of addressee, and thus cannot restrict in advance the empirical characteristics of its audience. And yet this collection of strangers is not entirely without a particular personality; it is defined by the style of address that beckons it into existence and by the reaction that only some experience in response to its call. Warner deliberately refers to this phenomenon as a "public"; he and other scholars, including Lauren Berlant, Nick Crossley, and Julie Ellison, are intent on establishing the role that a variety of traditionally unwelcome constituents, including style, emotion, bodily experience, and attitude, perform in shaping and consolidating public spheres.[49] Given that sympathy assumes a central role in the formation of these reading publics, they also might qualify as communities.

For the past few decades, activists and scholars have challenged the ontological privilege assigned by Marxism to class as a basis for identity and solidarity and have forwarded alternative modes of collective subjectivity premised upon other attributes and affinities.[50] But the conclusions we might reach about emotion — that most fugitive and ephemeral of states — as a basis for social organization will have to be tentative. What effects can a geographically and temporally disjointed empathetic response to a work of fiction achieve? What visible, lasting consequences, what forms of agency, what new self-conceptions can an imagined community of affect produce for its individual members or for society?[51] If these disparate identifications necessarily elude the more deliberate efforts to unify individuals around ideological goals, does this mean they lack real power, or simply that their power resists traditional measures?[52] And given the universality frequently attributed to emotional responses, how can we theorize the alliance between the transitory and the transhistorical, or between the local and the global embodied in shared modes of feeling?

Frequently serving to mediate these communities in the case of contemporary novels, autobiographies, and self-help books is a therapeutically inflected discourse focused on the individual subjective interior and capable of eliciting widespread empathy from readers. A tension between the content of the discourse, which is situated at the private or the personal scale, and its social function, which consists of supporting quasi-public affiliations among strangers, structures this particular formation. I would claim, however, that both the content and the function of the text are in these instances constituted by an internal hybridity, a complex knot of privacy and publicness that refuses theoretical unraveling. The apparently individual reference of therapeutic terms, the fixation on the particular character's internal struggles necessarily operates on more than one scale, signifying the widely experienced proclivities that the character instantiates, so that even the particular content of the work is freighted with a broader social resonance.[53] At the same time, the public-making function of a book is dependent upon a mode of participation experienced as intimate or personal, based on sympathies felt to be uniquely intense and specific to the reader and thus in a sense private.

While the therapeutic paradigm has become central within mainstream culture, many intellectuals tend to trivialize psychological states, including emotions, sensibilities, and attitudes, treating them as subservient to other events and developments. Journalists, for instance, speculate on how the mood of the country will affect the presidential election, or how the overall degree of optimism or pessimism might influence the economy. In order, however, to recognize the extraordinary sway of therapeutic discourse, it is necessary to acknowledge the psychological not only for what impact it might have on other spheres, but as important in its own right. This understanding requires, first of all, a sensitivity, increasingly underscored by scholars in the humanities and social sciences, to the social character of psychological states.[54] Emotional dispositions are often visible, transmittable, contagious, and subject to normative regulation. Thus it is possible to describe the ever changing psychological landscape of a nation as a phenomenon that is profoundly social both in its formation and in its reverberations, and as an important and real element of the shared world that its citizens inhabit. To be sure, the way this landscape both influences and responds to political and economic affairs merits serious consideration, but only insofar as this does not preclude a recognition of the significance of the psychological as a meaningful phenomenon in itself. I am attempting here to call attention to a mode of historical transformation that scholars have tended to characterize as symptomatic or effervescent, rather than as structural or foundational. But as Nancy Armstrong and Mary P. Ryan have maintained, the trivialization of this realm obviously depends upon a restrictive, masculinist conception of what counts as important, narratable history designed to efface the less conventionally conspicuous experiences, contributions, strategies, and forms of agency that have characterized those excluded until very recently from the public sphere in its traditional conception.[55]

The affective dimension of social life has become a central theme of my research in part because it is a reality that contemporary fiction is especially well equipped to register and to influence, and it thus represents the most immediate, if most elusive, measure of the difference that literary works are capable of making in American society. Each chapter in this book considers a particular set of desires, anxieties, frustrations, and needs that contemporary fiction helps, in therapeutic fashion, to clarify, alleviate, or manage. I have chosen to focus on books published since 1995, a period in which the therapeutic paradigm has been especially pronounced, with the popularization of new psychological pathologies, the growth of the anti-depression drug business, and the proliferation of twelve-step recovery groups. This scope, albeit narrow, has enabled me to examine a particular set of time-bound preoccupations with a thoroughness that a broader frame would not have allowed, while allowing me to consider how the therapeutic is operating *now*, and thus contribute to certain active and ongoing political and cultural debates. Moreover, in restricting my inquiry to the past fifteen years, I have attempted to demonstrate how a dominant social formation, the therapeutic, is capable of functioning in heterogeneous and at times contradictory ways — depending on the context in which it appears, the dispositions of its purveyors and consumers, and the needs it is required to serve.

The first two texts that I explore, Toni Morrison's *Paradise* and Rebecca Wells's *Divine Secrets of the Ya-Ya Sisterhood*, both respond in different ways to the atomization of American society. While Morrison describes an all-black post–Civil War utopian experiment and Wells depicts a small southern town that hearkens back to the subjects of early American regionalist fiction, both negotiate the complex tension between exclusivity and inclusivity involved in producing and sustaining communal intimacy — a tension that also shapes their strategies for addressing their respective audiences. Morrison keeps her readers at a distance from the world that she describes through a variety of alienating devices, even while she suggests that openness toward strangers is a condition for utopian politics. Examining the frustrated but determined efforts of the participants on Oprah's Book Club to make sense of *Paradise*, I consider ways in which Morrison's highbrow literary techniques both foster and endanger the egalitarian ideals that her novel celebrates. Like Morrison, Wells reminds her readers of their outsider status, offering them a fantasy of participation in the rituals of small-town life while periodically reminding them of their dependence upon mechanisms of mediation in order to experience a sense of communal belonging. In that chapter, I argue that therapeutic discourse, which *Divine Secrets* both deploys and critiques, serves as a compensatory response to the dispersal of traditional towns and communities in the past few decades.

The tension between highbrow techniques and democratic ideals at work in Toni Morrison's fiction is also present in David Foster Wallace's

Infinite Jest. His wry but reverential depiction of the anti-intellectual, earnest rituals practiced by Alcoholics Anonymous appears to repudiate the ironic, postmodern aesthetic strategies that his text addictively deploys. Wallace is intent on validating modes of empathy capable of eluding the narcissism, apathy, reflexive irony, and blasé hedonism that he sees as endemic to an overstimulated, late-capitalist consumer culture. Both he and James Frey, the two authors I consider in the middle section of the book, while radically different in their styles, respond to the idea that addiction is an alluring avenue of transgression, suffering, self-destruction, and self-redemption, which both typifies certain middle-class tendencies and seems to offer an escape from the perceived banality of middle-class lifestyles. And both writers attempt to create a reading experience that mimics the downward spiral of addiction and the arduous task of getting sober — Wallace through his dazzling but exhausting metafictional games, and Frey through his relentless and hyperbolic documentation of his physical pain. If Wallace's mimetic strategies involve some instances of exhausting verbosity, Frey's, ironically enough, involve blatant dishonesty. Examining the controversy surrounding Frey's memoir, *A Million Little Pieces*, and his two appearances on *Oprah*, I argue that his lies and exaggerations represent a self-defeating effort to create an aura of authenticity, thus revealing the precarious aesthetics of truth production that frequently shape middle-class self-representations.

The threat of terrorism operates in a manner analogous to the specter of drug addiction; and both have assumed center stage recently as the targets of wars declared by American presidents. My final two chapters on Anita Shreve's *The Pilot's Wife* and Khaled Hosseini's *The Kite Runner* explore the way in which depictions of the tragedies produced by violent global conflicts serve to valorize the everyday emotional struggles of middle-class Americans. Although Shreve's novel predates 9/11 by three years, her narrative, depicting a widow's gradual discovery of her late husband's affiliation with the Irish Republican Army, appeals to a contradictory set of attitudes regarding the insularity of the domestic sphere, a combination of explicit fear and unacknowledged desire in the face of external threats, which the Bush administration's War on Terror rhetoric subsequently exploited. The popularity of Khaled Hosseini's 2003 novel about Afghanistan, by contrast, can be read in part as a product of widespread exhaustion with the Bush administration's militant approach to international politics. Focusing on the visceral forms of cross-cultural identification with the narrator that are documented by the Amazon customer reviews of the novel, I explore the widespread belief in affective commonality as a potentially utopian engine for resolving the national, ethnic, and ideological divisions that 9/11 and Bush's response rendered painfully salient.

Initially motivating my interest in the therapeutic function of contemporary fiction was a desire to figure out what novels are doing for readers, especially in contexts outside of the university. Other scholars and critics have entertained the idea that fiction performs the work of therapy, but almost always with embarrassment or disdain, as indicative of a dangerously self-centered worldview's inescapable influence. At first tempted to argue that middlebrow literature is too complex, too diverse in its styles, structures, and themes to be reduced to a therapeutic tool, I have come to the conclusion that the therapeutic itself is equally complex, equally difficult to encapsulate. Indeed, as we will see, certain contradictions emerge among the therapeutic functions performed by the texts under consideration, demonstrating a flexibility that critiques such as those of Jameson, Sennett, or Lasch either fail to observe or else strategically ignore. Depending on the contexts, agendas, expectations, and needs that mobilize it, therapeutic discourse can support a variety of competing personal, social, and political agendas—at times promoting increased domestic insularity, at times providing the symbols necessary for communal, even global empathy. I am sympathetic to the worry that therapeutic values have diminished political and public engagement among Americans, but in my view a patient attention to particular instances of therapeutic work performed by contemporary fiction and a willingness to acknowledge the subtle differences among them can identify both risks and opportunities that a more categorical or dismissive theoretical framework might overlook.

CHAPTER ONE

Searching for *Paradise* on *The Oprah Winfrey Show*

JUST A FEW SENTENCES away from finishing Toni Morrison's *Paradise*, an arduous journey almost completed, the reader encounters an image of similarly exhausted travelers and a warning that the real work has only just begun: "When the ocean heaves sending rhythms of water ashore, Piedade looks to see what has come. Another ship, perhaps, but different, heading to port, crew and passengers, lost and saved, atremble, for they have been disconsolate for some time. Now they will rest before shouldering the endless work they were created to do down here in paradise" (318). Morrison awaits seekers of peace or rest with surprises, with reversals of conventional protocols. Labor will not be followed by leisure. Those in search of paradise will, after a long voyage in unfamiliar territory, eventually discover their reward: interminable toil. They should not, however, be dismayed by this realization, since, according to Morrison, such work is not a dreary alternative or an unfortunate but necessary prelude to paradise; such work is itself the essence of paradise — the generous domain of which is no longer up in the air, out of reach, but instead "down here," accessible to all.[1] Or, to understand Morrison's suggestion in a slightly different way, the experience of reading *Paradise* may be difficult, may demand substantial work from the reader, even after the book is done, but this work is in fact the point, a gift just as desirable as whatever ends the work might have been thought to achieve. With *Paradise*, then, Morrison hazards two propositions, both of which depend heavily on the inclinations of her massive middlebrow readership. The first is that her book, like the utopia its title promises, can be at once difficult and accessible, requiring a kind of hard labor that will not thwart but rather attract readers. The second is that *Paradise*'s power will not end on the last page, that the labor Morrison initiates will persist, indefinitely, after readers have put the book down.

Oprah Winfrey's March 1998 book club discussion of *Paradise* provides a good test of these propositions. The format of the episode is somewhat anomalous. Because the novel was thought to be so difficult compared to other books featured on the show, Winfrey decided not to host one of her usual informal dinner discussions. Instead she invited Morrison to lead a seminar for her and twenty of her viewers. Winfrey's suspicions that *Paradise* might frustrate some people turned out to be correct, but most of the participants, while puzzled, seemed determined to make sense of the text. The episode featured, as D. T. Max and John Young have noted, an unusually rigorous and extensive conversation about the language and meaning of the novel akin to what might take place in a college seminar, but it was nevertheless inflected by the therapeutic and personal priorities that usually prevail on Oprah's Book Club. Thus the show brought into dialogue the assumptions and inclinations of two very different interpretive communities. The audience's ambivalent reactions and the efforts of Morrison and Winfrey to make *Paradise* accessible reveal a great deal about how serious literature is used by contemporary middlebrow readers and what functions it is capable of performing for them. I have chosen to devote my first chapter to this staged negotiation in part because it brings the extreme poles of middlebrow culture — Morrison versus Oprah, serious fiction versus the rhetoric of self-affirmation, estrangement versus identification — together into one room. Thus the negotiation exemplifies the unlikely range of strategies, positions, and attitudes that this culture can accommodate.

Morrison, it turns out, harbors ambitious aims. Her novel depicts two ultimately failed utopian experiments: one rigidly policed, patriarchal, all-black town fanatically obsessed with preserving its racial purity and, nearby, a permissive and diverse commune-style household of women who have come to inhabit an abandoned convent. As she describes these two doomed efforts, Morrison seeks to promote a relationship between her text and her readers that can function as yet another model of utopian communal politics, a relationship whose difficult terms she refuses to dictate, insofar as they must be, according to her vision, the product of continual negotiation. Nevertheless, Morrison does attempt, in *Paradise* and on *The Oprah Winfrey Show*, to articulate certain conditions necessary both for good reading and for good politics. In particular, she insists on an openness to the unfamiliar and the heterogeneous seemingly at odds with the restrictive gatekeeping measures typically at work in conventional versions of paradise. Morrison's ideal, one might assume, would find a welcome embrace on *Oprah*, where the importance of tolerance and diversity is axiomatic. But *Paradise*'s narrative experiments pressure this reflexive stance, measuring its flexibility when confronted with forms of otherness that resist comprehension or identification. The questions I intend to explore, then, are the following: In what ways does Winfrey's book club discussion of *Paradise* promote, or fail to promote, the kind of work that serious literature, in Morrison's view, demands? Do Oprah Winfrey and her audience members adhere to, or do they in fact resist and revise, the protocols of interpretive response that Morrison prescribes? What forms of productive complicity and friction does Winfrey's show illuminate in the negotiation between serious literature's aspirations and middlebrow readers' inclinations — and in what ways does this negotiation either instantiate or endanger Morrison's utopian project?

Middlebrow Confusion

While an examination of Oprah's Book Club can yield useful insights about the dispositions, tastes, and desires of Americans, it would be misleading to claim that Winfrey is a straightforward representative of the average reader or that her book club episodes offer unmediated evidence of how ordinary people approach literature. To be sure, Winfrey and her production company, Harpo, encourage precisely this misconception through various strategies of self-presentation designed to make viewers forget that they are watching a carefully edited and choreographed production. In approaching her book club from a scholarly perspective, it is important to remember that Winfrey's staff chooses the novels by means of an elaborate process, it screens the participants for the book discussion, winnowing the thousands of contenders into a small group in order to support its image of the ideal reader, and it edits the content so as to emphasize certain interpretive approaches and to downplay others. Oprah's Book Club, then, is a packaged version of how American readers select, discuss, and use novels. But it is also important to keep in mind that Winfrey generates no profits from book sales and that her book club episodes often receive lower ratings than shows devoted to other subjects. Her motives in advertising and promoting certain works and certain styles of reader response are not, then, unequivocally cynical, self-interested, or economic. Moreover, her extraordinary power as a cultural authority depends upon her capacity both to recognize and to influence the desires of millions of Americans. Hence, whether as symptom or cause, her book club episodes do indirectly reflect certain reading habits pervasive within middlebrow culture. I intend to approach the conversations on her show as merely a trace of a more complicated, more elusive set of reading practices. Thus I plan to remain especially attuned to the moments in which participants hint at the experiences with the book that they may have had before the show or which they may anticipate having after — in other words, to all the interpretive work that does not lend itself to performative articulation or fit neatly into Winfrey's contrived format.

The standard practice on Oprah's Book Club, at least in its first incarnation from 1996 to 2001, is to treat fictional characters and the settings that they inhabit as if they were real, thus equating them with the nonfictional scenarios that Winfrey's show generally presents to its viewers. Frequently, an issue explored in the book with widespread resonance — such as spousal abuse, obesity, drug addiction, or mental illness — becomes the central topic, and participants are invited who have survived similar struggles in their own lives. Thus Winfrey treats novels as valuable insofar as they offer models for how to confront problems experienced by readers, and she expects her guests to emphasize their personal connection to the text.[2] That Winfrey ignores the fictional, discursive status of the books she considers, and that she abets the therapeutic tendency to translate political or structural grievances into personal terms are among the criticisms forwarded by scholars.[3] Others, however, praise her show for facilitating what they see as a critical public sphere for American women.[4]

While her approach frequently fails to address the specifically "literary" qualities of the texts that she introduces, Winfrey constantly invokes an intense reverence for novels. Her book club, of course, is only the latest installment in a history of middlebrow institutions designed to offer a cultural education to middle-class consumers — most of which combine the democratic belief that anyone can read and enjoy great works of literature with the motivational premise that reading these works confers prestige and distinction upon those who can appreciate their value. While a majority of the novels Winfrey chooses successfully navigate between the twin tasks of providing entertainment and disseminating cultural capital, the interpretive difficulties posed by *Paradise* risked jeopardizing this precarious balance, causing readers to question either the value of the book or their own intelligence, thus evincing a defensive state of uncertainty. During the discussion of *Paradise*, Winfrey's friend Gayle King remarks: "Ms. Morrison, are we supposed to get it on the first read? Because I've read it — I'm not even trying to be funny — because I've read it once, and I called Oprah and I said, 'Please, 'splain it to me.' So I'm thinking — so I'm now on my second read and I'm hoping I'll get it on the second read." A few minutes later, Winfrey echoes her friend's comment: "Because I — of course, I started with the epigram [*sic*]. I read it about three or four times. I went, 'Oh, I don't get it, let me move on.'"

Why is the expression "I don't get it" so characteristic of the insecure middlebrow reader? What differentiates the imagined act of comprehension encapsulated by "getting it" from the more culturally privileged forms of reception that rarely identify themselves in these terms? "Getting it" of course analogizes the act of interpretation with the act of consumption. It suggests only two possible relationships between the reader and the text: either you confront it as an alien entity beyond your grasp, or you take possession of it, view it as your own property. The expression admits no intermediary status, no state of partial comprehension. Moreover it imagines the transition from the first state to the second as instantaneous, likely involving what Winfrey frequently refers to as an "aha moment."[5] And once you "get" the book, once you "get" *Paradise*, your work presumably is finished, and you can relax. You have it in your possession, which means you are now among the elect and are thereby entitled to appreciate what has become your property, the book's meaning, without further struggle.

"I don't get it" is more ambiguous. It vacillates in its assignment of blame between the speaker and the text. Depending on the tone, it can easily betray a self-protective, sarcastically dismissive attitude toward whatever it is that one fails to get, which is why Gayle King feels compelled to remark, "I'm not even trying to be funny." Moreover, her comical slip into Black English, "please 'splain it to me," while self-mocking, can also be read as self-authenticating, a mark of pride in her own cultural identity, an identity that demands respect especially insofar as it keeps her at a distance from the realm of high culture. The implicit critique underlying her muted irreverence is that the book is elitist; its difficulty restricts its audience to a narrow set of excessively educated readers. Ironically, however, the irritation that motivates such skepticism is often based not only on the belief that literature ought to be widely accessible, but also on the unfulfilled hope that the reading experience will confirm one's own status as a cultured individual. Thus Winfrey remarks: "I was in a car, four women who were all — who have all read the book and are all — become defensive about their ability to read and their intelligence level. We're all saying, 'But, you know, I've read many books,' and, 'I went to this college' — and that's when I know everybody is being defensive, because people — this is a very challenging book" (*Oprah*, 6 March 1998). Their egalitarian fantasies displace onto the text the failing that they fear is their own, characterizing the text as categorically inaccessible, as if that quality were an intrinsic property and not dependent upon its readers' variable levels of training, even while their thwarted desire for the perceived status that would accompany their ability to understand the text serves, in its self-concealment, only to embolden their anti-elitist fervor. According to John Guillory, "in its institutions of middlebrow culture, our society expresses a certain ambivalence about high culture, an admiration tinged with resentment, a resentment troubled by guilt" ("Ordeal" 83–84).[6]

Given Morrison's agenda, which numerous critics have described as an attempt to imagine a more inclusive kind of paradise, it is safe to assume that Morrison is not interested in producing a text that divides those who get it from those who do not.[7] Rather, she aims to elicit forms of understanding and misunderstanding that are perpetually provisional — never enabling readers to rest on the side of either resigned incomprehension or complacent certainty. Her central project in the novel is to construct, with the help of the reader, new utopian models based on the negotiation between author and reader, and this joint venture of collectively envisioning and producing paradise will necessarily be a difficult, endless task. But not an impossible task; recall that the final passage of the book positions paradise "down here," a phrase that directly opposes the one Winfrey uses, punningly, at the beginning of the show to register her failure to understand the text: "over our heads." Morrison's "down here" contests the definitional inaccessibility of paradise implied by "over our heads," conceiving of it instead as a state that is widely available but dependent upon the constant labor of its participants, so that neither the excluded nor the included can surrender to the passivity that a more permanent status would enable. In her pursuit of accessibility, Morrison offers readers a text designed to make readers struggle and feel challenged, but also designed to make that struggle enjoyable. She remarks at one point during the show, "I wanted the weight of interpretation to be on the reader," underlining the burdensome hermeneutical labor that *Paradise* demands; but in another moment she comments: "That's because I want it to be a pleasant experience. I didn't want to write an essay. I wanted you to participate in the journey." In fact, a central purpose of Morrison's text is to impress on its readers the eternal, mutually constitutive relationship between struggle and pleasure, or between struggle and paradise, a relationship Winfrey herself suggests in a revelatory voice-over: "Wise author that she is, Morrison knows the rewards are twice as great when we readers get to unlock the secrets on our own."

But Morrison never allows her readers to unlock the secrets of *Paradise*. She refuses, for instance, to reveal the race and eventual fate of many of the main characters, as if her very purpose is to produce a work that can withstand the middlebrow urge to "get it." After Winfrey declares that she does not understand the epigraph, the two have the following exchange:

Ms. Morrison: I don't believe you Oprah.
Winfrey: It's true.
Ms. Morrison: I don't believe that you — that that happened to you. I think you think it didn't mean anything to you. I think you read it with some heightened expectation that it was in German and you

didn't speak German, but what I'm saying is that if I read it to you very slowly, one word at a time, you would know instantly what that meant.

Winfrey: Oh, I knew that it meant we were in for a major journey here. I knew that.

Ms. Morrison: Well, what's left to understand? There is nothing left to understand. That you got it is what I'm trying to tell you.

Winfrey: OK.

Ms. Morrison: You got it and you didn't believe you got it.

On the one hand, Morrison worries that Winfrey has preemptively elevated *Paradise* to such a great altitude in her mind that she has rendered it prohibitively difficult before even attempting to understand it. On the other hand, Morrison does want Winfrey to conceive of the text as difficult, and she seems pleased when the latter acknowledges it as such. Although even Morrison uses the phrase "you got it," what Winfrey has in fact correctly grasped, according to Morrison, is that she will not be able to "get" everything in the text, that *Paradise* will make her work by deliberately evading her comprehension. Morrison's aim here is to validate Winfrey's and her audience's confusion, to reassure them that it is precisely the point that they not "get it." But she also seeks to change the way in which they formulate or apprehend their own confusion — to replace "not getting it" with a different condition, less bent on dominating or possessing that which it cannot understand.[8]

The epigraph reads:

For many are the pleasant forms which exist in
  numerous sins
and incontinencies,
and disgraceful passions
and fleeting pleasures,
  which (men) embrace until they become
  sober
  and go up to their resting place.
And they will find me there,

and they will live,
and they will not die again.

Couched in a biblical style, the passage is not explicitly about the hard interpretive journey that Winfrey anticipates in reading the book but instead the journey to paradise. Morrison's affirmation of Winfrey's self-referential response, however, suggests a parallel between the two. To enter paradise it is necessary, the epigraph insists, not to avoid sin and failure, but to experience them dialectically as a means of achieving sobriety and redemption. The book posits the journey to paradise as predicated upon previous failures to achieve or reach a state of perfection. In fact, a genealogy of frustration, of failed efforts either to access or sustain utopia, underwrites the production of each community that Morrison depicts. Analogously, Morrison seeks to inspire a particular mode of reflection by systematically frustrating her readers' efforts, by requiring them to experience a series of interpretive disappointments. Thus Winfrey understands, or rather enacts, the epigraph's meaning—its implication that failure is an indispensable condition for utopian endeavors—precisely by failing to understand it, thus grasping that she needs to get past the desire to get the text.

Frustrating Identification

What exactly is so difficult about *Paradise*? Probably most baffling is Morrison's mode of exposition, especially in the text's early sections. The novel centers around the town of Ruby, which has a long history, a complex set of tacit laws, and a host of characters, all of whom are related to each other through an intricate mesh of alliances, bloodlines, sympathies, rivalries, and feuds. But Morrison defers delivering most of this information at first, almost always narrating, in free indirect discourse, from the limited perspective of individual characters, often visitors who know practically nothing about the town's dynamics. Thus she depicts a series of scenes, rich with opaque subtexts, but fails to provide the background information necessary to decipher them. Several of Winfrey's guests describe themselves as "lost" in reading the book, and most of them seem to appreciate Gayle King's plea for further elucidation. In fact, one might conclude, witnessing this scene of frustration, as Michael Perry does, that *Paradise* is simply an inappropriate text to introduce to Winfrey's middlebrow audience. I would argue, however, that Morrison's novel both deploys and transfigures many of the literary conventions that characterize the typical Oprah's Book Club selection, so as to interrogate the assumptions that support their operation. *Paradise*, in other words, is in fact aimed at a middlebrow audience, and its effects depend perversely upon a set of interpretive inclinations that it is intent on confounding.

The character of Mavis offers a useful example. A battered wife who escapes from her husband and eventually develops strength and courage in the Convent, a house inhabited by equally troubled, eccentric women, Mavis, at a glance, seems to epitomize almost formulaically the tropes that define what D. T. Max refers to as Oprah Winfrey's "therapeutic canon"(36). But if Morrison invites readers to activate their habitual expectations, she depicts Mavis's thoughts and actions as so painfully inexplicable and ir-responsible that they defy identification. Hurriedly buying groceries on a hot day, Mavis leaves her two infant children to suffocate inside a car with its windows shut. Then, harboring unfounded paranoid delusions about her remaining children's murderous intentions, she abandons them to the mercy of her abusive husband. Later Morrison describes Mavis's newfound confidence after her brawl with a fellow inhabitant at the Convent: "Pound-ing, pounding, even biting Gigi was exhilarating, just as cooking was. It was more proof that the old Mavis was dead. The one who couldn't defend herself from an eleven-year-old girl, let alone her husband. The one who couldn't figure out or manage a simple meal, who relied on delis and drive-throughs, now created crepe-like delicacies without shopping every day" (171). The moment incorporates the trappings of the quintessential inspira-tional narrative regularly featured on *Oprah*: the old insecure, incompetent Mavis is dead, replaced by a new, assertive independent woman. But her triumph includes some unpalatable ingredients, including her readiness to savor a vicious physical fight and her lingering hostility toward her daugh-ter, both of which cast Mavis's transformation as a disconcerting parody of the scenes of self-improvement that Winfrey generally celebrates.

Like Mavis, most of the characters in *Paradise* are elusive, fortified against identification. Their motives are rarely transparent; Morrison forces idiosyncratic deeds, offbeat metaphors, and cryptic quips to function as synecdoches for their histories, passions, and interior obsessions. Thus all of the characters seem gestural as opposed to round. And, of course, there are so many of them, no single one of whom assumes the leading role. For her refusal to create manifestly deep, multidimensional, stable characters, Morrison has won the admiration of poststructuralist critics who claim that she is subverting the essentialism presupposed by traditional, realist modes of characterization.[9] But what exactly does her text accomplish by disabling or hindering identification, especially when it represents such a valued interpretive response for so many of Winfrey's viewers?[10]

During the discussion of *Paradise*, the audience's reaction to the antagonistic relationship between Mavis and her daughter Sal exemplifies one particularly dangerous consequence of identification. If Mavis is, as Morrison acknowledges, an "incompetent" mother and the victim of abuse from her husband, Sal appears to be slyly vindictive and cold-hearted. Describing the reactions of her readers to these characters, Morrison remarks: "Somebody was asking me a couple of days ago or — or simply making an observation about this terrible child that Mavis had, her daughter who pinches her — and I kept saying, 'Why do you call her terrible?' I said, 'Think what it must feel like for an 11-year old girl to have a mother who permits her [*sic*] as a doormat and you watch this woman get knocked around by the father. She seems totally incompetent. You're terrified as a kid that that might be you'" (6 March 1998). At this point several of the guests express their agreement and it appears that Morrison will simply offer a trite lesson in the importance of not judging people too quickly, of understanding the circumstances that drive a character to behave in a certain way. But the discussion takes a more ominous turn: as Sal rises in the group's estimation, Mavis sinks. Although one audience member disagrees, she is quickly silenced, and the consensus, driven by Morrison and Winfrey, seems to be that Mavis, for her incompetence, is truly the one worthy of blame. Morrison convinces Oprah's audience of this interpretation by soliciting their identification with Sal. Her position, while defensible, nevertheless betrays a severe economy of empathy, a zero-sum game, undergirding the operations of identification obviously at work in the consumption of almost all narratives. Empathy for one character, in other words, must be paid for with antipathy toward another; identification with one character means alienation from another.

Having established Sal as worthy of compassion and Mavis of disapproval, Morrison abruptly and somewhat inexplicably redirects the conversation on to the topic of paradise:

> Ms. Morrison: Well, you know, it — I think in many cases, if not most, the damage — the psychological damage by watching that abuse is al — is worse than even taking it. They can't defend you, the children can't defend you, and you're not defending yourself, and they are in danger, because, A, "maybe I will grow up to be like that," which is nothing. It's kind of a renegoti — or rethinking that the whole idea of all paradises in literature and history and so on and in our minds and in all the holy books are special places that are fruitful, bountiful, safe, gorgeous and defined by those who can't get in.
>
> Unidentified Man #3: Yes, yes, exactly.
>
> Ms. Morrison: And you have to exclude and feel the status of being elect.
>
> Winfrey: Oh, got it. Key. That's key. That's key. (6 March 1998)

Morrison's point, presumably, is that Sal, in her state of misery and victimization, yearns for a happy functional family and thus exemplifies the position of exclusion that inevitably conditions visions of paradise. Ironically, however, the discussion that she has been leading has just enacted a process of invidious evaluation, deeming Sal, as the recipient of the audience's favor, the "elect," and deeming Mavis, as the recipient of their opprobrium, the "excluded," thus recapitulating the categories that Morrison wants to challenge. This exercise, however, should not be read as an effort to fix her readers' sympathies permanently, but rather as an effort to jar their initial adherences and push them into a state of fluidity. While Morrison does seek, by employing traditional middlebrow strategies, to elicit identification, she simultaneously strives to disturb its stable purchase, constantly undermining any settled sense of her characters by adding new inassimilable details, undermining whatever comfortable and frozen taxonomy readers might attempt to impose upon them. Morrison thereby requires readers to experience a novel kind of sympathy directed at individuals who remain manifestly unpredictable and unknowable. When accounting for her decision not to offer readers a "leading character," Morrison tells Winfrey, "Because I wanted to force the reader to become acquainted with the communities" (6 March 1998). A protagonist would offer readers prejudiced certainties, biasing their sympathy so as to create a permanent class of the "elect" and a permanent class of the "excluded." The emotional involvement that Morrison hopes to provoke, by contrast, resists this urge to order and divide her fictional world, and thus approximates the inclusivity and the readiness to embrace strangers that any productive rethinking of paradise, in her view, requires.

Identity Politics and the Afterlife

Morrison's most overt challenge to her readers' desire to know and understand her characters is her refusal to reveal the race of the Convent's inhabitants. The now famous first sentence of the novel, "They shoot the white girl first" (3), which describes the murderous attack of Ruby's men upon the Convent, produces a mystery that Morrison never solves. Who at the Convent is white and what race are the other characters? Whether this experiment serves to magnify or diminish the perceived significance of race becomes a subject of debate among Winfrey's guests. Morrison herself equivocates, claiming, "I mean, I said 'white,' which means that race is going to play a part in the narrative," then arguing, "it played another kind of role which was to signal race instantly and to reduce it to nothing," later remarking that "some readers were, you know, deeply preoccupied with finding out which was the single one, who was white," and finally summing up her agenda with the following pronouncement:

> Ms. Morrison: But the point is when you — you're right, but the point is you do have to know them [the women in the Convent] as individuals. That was why the racial information was withheld, because when you know their race, what do you know?
> Several Members of the Group: Nothing.
> Ms. Morrison: You don't know anything. (6 March 1998)

It is possible to interpret Morrison's comments as implying a trivialization of race in stark contrast to the obsession with race and racial purity that characterizes the town of Ruby. Morrison's alternative vision of utopia, one might argue, is a world in which people no longer care about, or even notice, each other's race — a world in which the apprehension and hence the reality of racial difference disappears, as it seems to within Morrison's depiction of the Convent. Such an ideal conforms to the racial politics most frequently articulated on *Oprah*: a post–civil rights stance, which holds that focusing on race hinders our capacity to understand each other as individuals.[11] This sentiment is in accord with an increasingly popular notion across the United States, in part responsible for attacks on affirmative action programs, that we are, or should aim to be, a post-race society.[12]

While such a position, according to Janice Peck, appeals to many of Winfrey's white viewers, Morrison obviously recognizes that the United States is nowhere near to achieving the post-race worldview that functions as an ideological fantasy on *Oprah*. In her study of white writers' figurations of blackness, *Playing in the Dark* (1993), Morrison contends, "for both black and white American writers, in a wholly racialized society, there is no escaping racially inflected language, and the work writers do to unhobble the imagination from the demands of that language is complicated, interesting, and definitive" (12–13). In that book she offers a compelling account of what blackness and black characters have been made to symbolize within white literary culture: "illicit sexuality, chaos, madness, impropriety, anarchy, strangeness, and helpless, hapless desire" (80–81).[13] Her suggestion that the imagination is hobbled by "racially inflected language" reveals a desire to escape racial categories, but also a recognition that no such escape is possible in the present moment. The first sentence of *Paradise* is nothing if not a reminder of the life-and-death importance that race continues to assume and the tragic consequences that it is capable of producing; and Morrison's entire oeuvre, after all, testifies to her rejection of any attempt to mend race relations or to end racism by forgetting America's history of slavery and racial inequality. Although one reader on *Oprah* declares that, "the beauty of that book for me was not knowing [the characters'] race," *Paradise* tends to sustain such states of serene color-blindness only for brief periods, typically interrupting them with jarring but indeterminate clues about the characters' race, coupled with reminders, often in the form of ambiguously tense confrontations, that race and racial difference, whether explicitly addressed or carefully evaded, continue to matter. Thus another reader admits, "we're busy guessing who was black and who was white," and another adds, "because [race] motivated the men to go out there."

The interpretive game that Morrison initiates, the search for clues that she invites, necessarily foregrounds the complex set of beliefs, practices, tastes, and characteristics that people associate with a given race. On the one hand, then, *Paradise* demonstrates how difficult it is, at least at this moment in history, to become truly color blind — that is, to subtract perceptions of race from the act of interpretation. Thus the text underscores the insufficiency of any solution to racial problems primarily dependent on the good intentions of individuals who claim that race is not a factor in their perceptions, judgments, and decisions. On the other hand, her relentless efforts to unsettle readers' confident ascription of racial categories to the Convent's inhabitants underline the inadequacy of any given, fixed understanding of racial categories for apprehending the behavior of individuals or the multiple ways in which they lay claim to (or disavow) their own racial identity. Race, as Homi Bhabha has argued, typically functions as a category of domestication — it produces the semblance, or fetish, of knowledge about the other. Challenging this function, Morrison's claim that knowledge of a character's race amounts to no knowledge at all entails the urge not to ignore racial difference, but rather to underline the epistemological difficulties that attend confrontations with this difference. Her textual experiments neither produce nor prescribe a disregard for the ways in which individuals' experiences are shaped by the discourse of race. Indeed, in contradistinction to the policing of racial purity epitomized by Ruby or the race-blind, liberal individualism often articulated on *Oprah* — both of which betray a desire for homogeneity — Morrison presents negotiations with racial difference as a valuable enterprise. But *Paradise* also seeks to expand the vocabulary of otherness, to recognize instances of heterogeneity, of opaque particularity, that elude racial categories and their tendency to colonize and reduce the incommensurable.[14]

The other major question that *Paradise* leaves unresolved, of course, is whether the Convent's inhabitants are alive or dead at the end of the novel. The men of Ruby never find the bodies of the women that they have shot, which inspires a diversity of theories among the townspeople about what has happened to them. Fuelling readers' uncertainty, Morrison concludes the book with scenes featuring the characters continuing to lead their lives after their supposed murder. Attempting to determine their status, one guest on *Oprah* notes the two references in the book to a chapter in the Corinthians, from which she quotes Paul's description of paradise: "Whether it was in the body or out of the body, I do not know." In paradise, according to Paul, people may or may not be liberated from their bodies — an equivocal condition that would coincide with the women's partial transcendence of any concrete racialized embodiment. Morrison responds enthusiastically to the guest's interpretation:

> Ms. Morrison: That's good. You open yourself up — to ask the
> question are they living or are they de — are they dead is to avoid
> the real question . . .
> Woman #17: Right.
> Ms. Morrison: . . . which is this other place.
> Winfrey: Which is the other place.
> Ms. Morrison: Yeah.
> Winfrey: OK.
> Ms. Morrison: You have to be open to this — yeah, it's not just black
> or white, living, dead, up down, in, out. It's being open to all these
> paths and connections and . . . (*unintelligible*) between.
> Winfrey: And that is paradise!
> Ms. Morrison: That is paradise.

Insofar as they are situated in "this other place," the characters are liberated from either/or labels: black or white, living or dead, bodily or spiritual. Earthly binary logic does not apply to their condition. Morrison affirms Winfrey's epiphanal identification of "this other place" as paradise — a term which may refer to a heavenly destiny but also, as the title of the novel, to the place of fiction. Only within a nonearthly world or within the world of the text can individuals escape the invidious categories that, in rendering their bodies legible, serve as a condition for personhood.

When she first raises the question of the racial status of the Convent's inhabitants, Winfrey remarks, "Did it drive you crazy not knowing whether some of the key characters — what race they were? Well, we talked about that in our study group. It drove a lot of people crazy that we even wanted to know what color they were, but then a lot of people wanted to know what color they were" (6 March 1998). The curious assumption that Winfrey and at least some of her readers make is that there are definite, correct answers to their questions about the race and final status of the women at the Convent. These readers, in other words, approach the characters as if they were empirically real and thus in possession of physical, psychological, racial features as unequivocal as those of any living, nonfictional individual. Objective information about these characters, in the view of these readers, exists, but Morrison has stubbornly refused to reveal it. In response to the guests' frustrations, she insists: "I mean, that you enter the landscape of a novel. You enter it fully. You suspend disbelief, and you walk in there like an innocent but who trusts, and you trust the narrator, you trust the book. It's risky, it might disappoint you, but that's the way you go in it. And things that you cannot sort of fathom become instantly recognizable and knowable under those circumstances. You walk in. 'Does this — is this really technically possible for'— that's hardly the point. You suspend disbelief of everything that might not be possible in the material world" (ibid).

Her suggestion is that insofar as her characters are fictional they are not susceptible to modes of categorical empirical scrutiny, and thus there may be no answer to questions about their race. Inhabiting a different ontological space, one that is sustained entirely by the text, the characters are not bound by the constraints of the material world. Their race, if it never receives unequivocal treatment in the novel, simply does not exist as a determinate phenomenon that can yield answers to the readers' insistent questions. Although this is a fairly simple fact about how novels operate, it enables Morrison to analogize the fictional landscape, and the otherworldly liberties, ambiguities, paradoxes, and thrills that it nourishes with "this other place," that is, heaven. The novel, Morrison seems to be implying, is as close as mere mortals can get to paradise.

Readers might be forgiven for conflating the characters with real people, given that Morrison's meticulous realism often invites this response. Significantly, *Paradise* baffles comprehension not only by withholding, but also by volunteering information about the world that it describes, often in copious doses but in fragmented form. The difficulty of the early sections consists of trying to process the onslaught of hints, allusions, and details, many of which Morrison offers prematurely without adequate explanation. Clarification gradually arrives and the material eventually assumes a coherent shape so that attentive readers could by the end of the novel inscribe accurate floor plans of the Convent, a map of Ruby, an intricate family tree cataloging all of the relations between its citizens, and a chronology of the town's happenings, major and minor, over the course of several decades. This surplus of information in conjunction with its elliptical, haphazard, and desultory delivery conveys the illusion of a world that is not merely staged for the reader's benefit, but that exists independently in all of its Byzantine, chaotic reality, whether or not anyone is paying attention to it. And this of course is precisely the mimetic fantasy that Winfrey's readers reflexively entertain — one that supports their belief that the race and fate of the characters exist as objective facts awaiting detection.[15] Yet the world's recalcitrant facticity is also what makes it so challenging for readers to negotiate; it refuses to unfold itself in an intelligible or reassuring manner.

Winfrey and later Morrison explain the rationale for the text's bewildering exposition in almost identical terms. Morrison tells the audience: "I wanted — you have to look at each one of these people and figure out who each one was and then see their relationship to each other and how that changed in each of these paradises. And I wanted the weight of interpretation to be on the reader, the way you do when you walk into a town. When you walk into a neighborhood, you don't know anybody. Do you really just want to know the one person who seems to know everything about the neighborhood?" (6 March 1998). Her remarks are helpful but paradoxical. The fictional landscape, as Morrison suggests, is an unfamiliar one constituted by its own peculiar logic. In order to convince readers to enter this landscape, she compares the alienating effect of her novel to an experience that is likely familiar: entering a strange neighborhood — a situation potentially disconcerting but also exciting, which might be called a familiar experience of the unfamiliar. Thus, Morrison attempts to familiarize her fiction by invoking a common scenario that defamiliarizes our everyday perceptions. But her advice, which justifies her fiction by arguing that its methods of information delivery actually mimic the way that individuals experience and process new surroundings, clashes slightly with her advice that readers should "suspend disbelief of everything that might not be possible in the material world" (ibid.). In some moments, she suggests that the world of *Paradise* works nothing like the world that readers are required to navigate in their ordinary lives, and in other moments, she suggests that it works exactly like the world that they know, replicating its modes of disorientation and obscurity to a disturbing degree.

When Morrison insists that readers "suspend disbelief of everything that might not be possible in the material world," she is, I would argue, seeking not only to encourage a sensitivity to the fictional status of the novel's projected landscape and the liberties that this status enables, but also to inspire a utopian form of thought that is not weighed down by a reflexive attachment to the world as it currently is and the laws believed to constitute and limit its possibilities. But the attempt to provoke radical utopian thinking risks alienating those readers to whom Morrison's ideal of inclusivity requires her to appeal. She does not seek, after all, to posit a paradise that is entirely "above our heads," out of reach, so radically removed from the familiar world as to be unimaginable and inaccessible. Morrison's project requires the readers' participation. As she declares on the show: "Novels are for talking about and quarreling about and engaging in some powerful way. However that happens, at a reading group, a study group, a classroom or just some friends getting together, it's a delightful, desirable thing to do. And I think it helps. Reading is solitary, but that's not its only life. It should have a talking life, a discourse that follows" (6 March 1998). Morrison seeks to work with her readers, to envision paradise by negotiating with their established interpretive assumptions, by presenting a fictional world, however bewildering, that resembles the world that they have encountered in their everyday lives. Her strange synthesis of realism and utopianism thus provokes a dialectic in which her readers confront unanticipated difficulties resulting not from a forced surrender of familiar interpretive procedures, but from an intensified engagement with those procedures designed to inspire a transcendence of the positivistic assumptions to which they are typically wedded. To put it another way, *Paradise* requires readers to work not against, but *through* their habitual ways of thinking about fiction.[16]

If fiction, owing to its special capacity to defy the rules that appear to shape the material world, provides an analogue to paradise, this insight yields the reciprocal conclusion that paradise is always itself a fiction, defined by its otherworldly character. But this does not entail that it is necessarily useless, insubstantial, or even radically divorced from reality. Morrison's novel works to inspire her readers to inhabit paradise, but as a fiction, to allow this fiction to recast and transform their everyday experience. Morrison asks readers, in short, to *live* this fiction, and thereby to elude the invidious logic that divides people into the categories of black or white, living or dead, included or excluded.[17] But even in its efforts to transcend the more painful realities, Morrison's fiction, of course, strives to remain answerable to the world that it yearns to escape and to those readers whose willingness to envision paradise depends upon a negotiation with the world that they know and the modes of thought that they have already comfortably assimilated.[18]

Difficult Love

The text's strategy of inundating the reader with information but withholding explanation of its meaning produces a state of saturation and desire, of knowing too much and, at the same time, of never knowing enough — a state that reproduces the staggering, uneven trajectory of love. Playing on metaphorical associations between darkness and racial otherness, Morrison describes the love affair between Deacon, the patriarch of Ruby, and Consolata, a resident at the Convent: "He drove, it seemed, for the pleasure of the machine: the roar contained, hooded in steel; the sly way it simultaneously parted the near darkness and vaulted into darkness afar — beyond what could be anticipated. They drove for what Consolata believed were hours, no words passing between them. The danger and its necessity focused them, made them calm. She did not know or care where headed or what might happen when they arrived. Speeding toward the unforeseeable, sitting next to him who was darker than the darkness they split, Consolata let the feathers unfold and come unstuck from the walls of a stone-cold womb" (228–29). Consolata's relationship with Deacon includes all of the vertiginous gaps of knowledge and startling leaps of intuition that are peculiar to early intimacy. In their late-night drive, darkness does not thwart their progress, but rather invites it. As they "[part] the near darkness" they seem almost to leap ahead of themselves, to leap ahead of the present moment, apprehending traces of a future not yet arrived, knowing things about each other they should not yet know. But their uncanny vision remains partial and their movement forward simply leads them further into darkness. In fact, unremitting darkness sustains their understanding of each other by demanding continuous interpretive activity, thus constituting understanding as an ongoing, endless process, rather than as an instantaneous act of appropriation. Morrison here is trying to teach readers ways of unknowing that are neither defeatist nor covetous in relation to the subjects that elude their mastery.

Viewing the task of interpreting *Paradise* and, by extension, the task of approaching otherness to be akin to falling in love has the potential to recast the difficulty of the text. The serious labor that is required, the frustrated desire for complete comprehension, and the sense of perpetual uncertainty can be understood, like love, to be sources of pleasure. But the other less appealing consequence of this equation is that love, while pleasurable, must also be understood as extremely difficult, a point made in *Paradise* by the unsympathetic, dogmatically conservative Reverend Senior Pulliam: "Love is divine only and difficult always. If you think it is easy you are a fool. If you think it is natural you are blind. It is a learned application without reason or motive except that it is God" (141). Although Pulliam functions as anything but a mouthpiece for Morrison's views, his insights in this instance defy immediate dismissal, and it is significant that Morrison presents his sermon before she identifies the speaker, forcing the reader to assess its validity without the prejudice that his persona is likely to inspire.[19] Here she borrows from an unlikely source an element of rigor for her utopian vision, whose emphasis on nonauthoritarian inclusivity might otherwise imply unrestrained permissiveness. The Convent runs the risk of becoming too lax, allowing its members to do and think whatever they want, until Consolata, the oldest woman there, decides to impose certain demands and rules on the community, insisting that they do the work necessary to establish a truly fulfilling utopian space: "I call myself Consolata Sosa. If you want to be here you do what I say. Eat how I say. Sleep when I say. And I will teach you what you are hungry for" (262).

In her apparent assumption of power, Consolata seems disturbingly dictatorial, but her methods do not usher in a regime of repression similar to Ruby's. On the contrary, the rituals and regulations that she installs incite spontaneous modes of artistic creation from the Convent's residents: self-portraits painted on the floor, lyrical confessions, narrated dreams. Analogously, the central motto of Ruby, inscribed on its monumental oven, "Beware the Furrow of His Brow," initially designed to elicit from the townspeople strict obedience to a higher authority, becomes an object of subversive reinterpretation. The younger generation debates its meaning and eventually rewrites it altogether, so that it reads "Be the Furrow of His Brow" (143), and finally, "We Are the Furrow of His Brow" (298). Influenced by the various countercultural and radical political movements of the 1960s and 1970s, this gesture does not reject the importance of authority. While *Paradise* dramatizes the dangers of hierarchical power structures, it also portrays, in the Convent, the risks of unconstrained liberty. The alternative model Morrison presents, in the rewriting of Ruby's motto, is a form of authority, of regulation that demands discipline, but that emerges from within rather than from above the community and thereby requires not only obedience but also the creative labor of constant renegotiation and revision.

The rhetoric of *Paradise* often assumes a piously didactic tone like the inscription on the oven, but Morrison's purpose is not to impose an unambiguous moral or message on the reader, not to silence doubt or division, since it is, in her view, only through an inclusive dialogue that paradise can be reimagined. As Morrison remarks on *Oprah*, "I wouldn't want to end up having written a book in which there was a formula and a perfect conclusion and that was the meaning and the only meaning." Winfrey's book club, Morrison seems to hope, can provide readers a forum in which to debate the meanings of her text—notwithstanding the danger that her authorial presence might quell a democratic dialogue. *Oprah* is a promising site for this kind of discussion; like many middlebrow institutions, as Sherryl Wilson has argued, it relies upon the authority of experts, while simultaneously challenging any monopoly these experts might claim upon knowledge, asserting the countervalidity of ordinary people's immediate experience (117–18). And Morrison's hopes do not seem all that far-fetched; the show features robust, if somewhat truncated, debates about theology, race, and aesthetics, which only occasionally reach a consensus. One reader, apparently not intimidated by Morrison's purported genius, stridently questions her novel's artistic value: "I was lost because I came into — I really wanted to read the book and love it and learn some life lessons; and when I got into it, it was so confusing I questioned the value of a book that is that hard to understand" (6 March 1998).

The woman's remark merits consideration. She, like many of Winfrey's audience members, approaches literature with passion and a readiness to challenge herself intellectually. *Paradise*'s difficulty, however, effectively blocks her critical engagement. Her response echoes the observations made by Gayle King and Winfrey that *Paradise* might be simply "over our heads," impossibly inaccessible. Their attitude, which, as I have argued, vacillates between awe and dismissal, also includes as a target Princeton University, a "center for higher learning." Their comments imply a critique of the elitism and exclusiveness that characterize the entire world of so-called high culture along with the academic institutions, such as Princeton, that support, celebrate, and embody this world. The widely acknowledged insularity of high culture and academia remains a justifiably vexed issue, but it is especially pertinent in the case of Morrison, who explicitly thematizes inclusivity in her text. On the show, she remarks that all paradises validate themselves, problematically, by excluding certain individuals — a practice her own institution, Princeton University, unapologetically enshrines as the sine qua non of its high status. Indeed, at the opening of the show Winfrey underscores the connection between paradise and Princeton, posing a question many, including F. Scott Fitzgerald, must have pondered before her: "Could we find paradise inside Princeton?"

Morrison's answer to this question ought to be an unequivocal *no*, given that she wants to redefine paradise as a state of openness. But her text runs the risk of denying readers access; its difficulty constitutes a daunting admissions process. One of the most disturbing aspects of Morrison's textual challenges is the way they replicate the fictional town of Ruby's paranoid, self-protective methods for dealing with intruders. The community essentially stonewalls Misner, the new liberal-minded minister who has been assigned to work in the town. On hearing the clichéd expression, "no harm in asking," Patricia, an acquaintance of Misner's, responds in the following way: "Yes there is. Harm. Pat sipped carefully from a spoon. Ask Richard Misner. Ask him what I just did to him. Or what everyone else does. When he asks questions, they just close him out to anything but the obvious, the superficial" (216). This closing out is precisely what Morrison does to the reader, at least in the early segments of the book. It is an interesting tactic given her obvious dissatisfaction with Ruby's exclusionary practices, suggested even in Patricia's sudden disgust with the town's treatment of Misner, and given Morrison's own definition of paradise as a state of openness. Why, then, does she place the reader into the position of excluded outsider? Is paradise, as she suggests, available to conceptualization only from a place of exclusion?

Motivating Pat's aloof treatment of Reverend Misner is a secret desire for his affection. He is an eligible bachelor, and she is in fact wooing him in her own coy manner. Thus, Morrison implies, the gesture of ostensible exclusion might also be read as a covert come-on, and the obstacles to comprehension that *Paradise* deploys might actually be understood as an effort to allure readers. Arguably, Morrison's project is to sever the link between textual difficulty and exclusiveness, which has conditioned the reception of twentieth-century literature at least since the advent of modernism, and to realign difficulty with the task of furthering inclusiveness. All of the challenges *Paradise* offers function as lessons in how to approach otherness, how to approach one's relationship with people, practices, and concepts that are profoundly unfamiliar, that resist easy categorization. A paradise with open boundaries, a paradise whose definition and whose practical embodiment remains perpetually receptive to novel interventions would depend on precisely the rigorous modes of dialogue and interpretation that Morrison requires from her readers. Her utopian politics challenge the emphasis on intimacy, familiarity, and resemblance that often seems to energize the forms of identification fostered on Oprah's Book Club, in order to promote a utopian model that can accommodate the encounter with strangeness, obscurity, and difficulty.[20] Yet the potential consequence of Morrison's demands — made in the hopes of promoting a more inclusive society — has been ironically to exclude large segments of enthusiastic readers.

The episode devoted to *Paradise* was one of the lowest rated book club discussions in the history of the program. Undeniably, then, millions of readers were turned off by Morrison's novel. But this fact does not entail that *Paradise*'s rhetorical strategies are inherently disengaged from the needs and expectations that characterize Winfrey's middlebrow audience. While the category of readers who have managed to enjoy Morrison's book is much narrower than the massive readership that regularly participates in Winfrey's book club, the former category may be defined not by a greater degree of sophistication or cultural mastery than that which character-izes the typical middlebrow reader, but rather by a simple willingness to struggle. What Morrison's novel demands is an ideal middlebrow reader — one who confronts the text by means of familiar interpretive strategies, but is open to the experience of frustration and willing to treat this experience as a critical, constitutive condition for understanding *Paradise*, a process that is never completed. And, like the reader's interpretation of the novel, paradise, in Morrison's conception, refuses the peace that would attend the sense of its finalized achievement.[21]

Both Morrison and Winfrey work hard to prevent the audience from giving up on the novel. Their comparison between reading the text and en-tering a strange neighborhood is effective but also potentially self-defeating. Elucidating the reader's encounter with unfamiliarity through analogy to a familiar circumstance is a way of domesticating the text's strangeness, ren-dering it recognizable. But part of *Paradise*'s power, frustratingly enough, lies in its capacity to leave readers in the dark, bewildered and disoriented, without any conventional map or model for how to proceed, without know-ing why or how they have gotten lost, thus forcing them to improvise new strategies of interpretive navigation. Explaining the difficulty by relating it to a common experience, while reassuring, runs the risk of disabling this effect. The woman who complains about the text's inaccessibility responds to Winfrey's guidance in a telling fashion:

Woman #7: You should have told us that. It would have been easier for me. I w —

Winfrey: But I'm telling you now.

Woman #7: Ok I'll go home and . . .

Winfrey: I'm telling you now, that you have to open yourself. It's like a life experience. It's getting to know people, getting to know people in a town. It's not everything laid out.

Woman #7: No, that makes sense. (6 March 1998)

The woman wishes she could have been spared any readerly discomfort, any experience of difficulty irreconcilable with a clear agenda. Her comment "I'll go home" declares a desire to return to familiar surroundings. She will reread the book only on the condition that she can circumscribe its strangeness within the safety of her own home.

The reader's wish to return home complements an analogy invoked several times on the show between reading the book and going on a journey. Winfrey, for instance, repeats one reader's warning about *Paradise*: "And someone said—had said that, 'It's challenging, it's like taking a trip, but you'd better have your bags packed. You better not have your bags empty'" (6 March 1998). While many an English major at Princeton University has learned the importance of "unpacking" as a mode of interpretation, Winfrey's audience seems dedicated to the reverse process. What exactly does it mean to approach a text with your bags packed? On the one hand, this metaphor could imply a refusal to discard or question any of your carefully sealed conventional assumptions, associations, and prejudices. On the other hand, it evinces a willingness to leave home behind, to travel somewhere new, even if a condition for this journey is that you carry with you certain familiar items, devices that will help you navigate and domesticate the unfamiliar territory. Both the plan to go home in order to reread the text and the urge to pack your bags constitute the reading process as an interchange between returning to and departing from the familiar safety of what is known—a paradoxical mode of reflection also at work in the middlebrow experience of identification and in any productive reimagination of paradise.[22]

What the strangely matched pair of Morrison and Winfrey—attempting to embody and enact the reconciliation of serious literature and middlebrow culture—are suggesting is that, as you struggle through this difficult work of fiction, you can bring all of your baggage with you. In fact, it will come in handy. Your urge to identify with fictional characters, though dangerous in its favoritism, covert narcissism, and concomitant cruelties, will nevertheless enable you to transgress your own boundaries, apprehend unfamiliar modes of subjectivity, and thus begin the dialogue necessary to constitute a more inclusive community. The desire to "get" literature, while assuming that the task of understanding involves a single, manageable act of acquisition, also evinces a healthy sense of confusion and a willingness to be challenged — a willingness crucial for persevering in the ongoing process of understanding that Morrison hopes to initiate. Your tendency to treat the fictional world as if it were real, while potentially limiting your willingness to believe in the miraculous, may allow you to imagine promising forms of proximity between the world you already know and the utopian world that remains as yet a fiction. Finally, the automatic gears of your racial consciousness may grind loudly to a halt as you read *Paradise*, but the dissonant noises they will make are necessary to register the potential for a less routine, more unknowing approach to heterogeneity.

Winfrey's discussion encourages several of her guests to rethink their frustrations and to reconsider *Paradise*. As anyone who has found relief in sharing anxieties and concerns with fellow readers after trying to make sense of a difficult text will recognize, forums, including classes, book clubs, and online discussion boards, often provide a necessary and salutary scaffolding that enables readers to continue grappling with the disorientation and self-doubt that such a text may provoke. While Morrison's invitation at the end of her novel to continue the work necessary to sustain paradise appeals to an imagined community of readers, the initial resistance of Winfrey's guests to *Paradise* demonstrates the circumscribed capacity of any individual book to inspire the kind of work that Morrison envisions, at least in the absence of concrete communal structures of mutual support and guidance. Read in a certain context, like a book club, *Paradise* becomes less exclusionary, not because its difficulties disappear, but because, as an explicit subject of discussion, the purposes that these difficulties may serve become more evident. If *Paradise* does appeal only to a restricted audience, then obviously the inequality between modes of access to these supportive contexts deserves as much blame as the text itself. Moreover, I have focused primarily on the ways in which *Paradise* addresses or excludes college-educated middlebrow readers, but of course this is already a privileged population whose belief in its own taste as an arbiter of a book's universal appeal depends upon an effacement of the specific, class-rooted educational advantages that have produced this taste. Even if *Paradise* had met with praise and devotion among all of Winfrey's regular book club participants, in other words, this would not have proven it to be unequivocally inclusive. Given the cultural stratifications and multiple literacies that continue to exist in the United States, the measure of a book's democratizing function cannot be the impossible ideal of total accessibility; rather *Paradise* furthers its political ideals by working with the audiences that it can reach, narrowing its appeal precisely in order to challenge the unacknowledged privileges and exclusions that middlebrow reading strategies can abet.

One obvious threat to Morrison's egalitarian ideals, in Oprah's Book Club itself, is the authorial role she assumes on the show, which places her in a position of superiority relative to the audience, so that she becomes the genius dispensing wisdom for the benefit of the ignorant masses. Her function in this seminar is undeniably pedagogical, but it is important to note that she does not get the final word. By contesting the value of Morrison's book, the audience demonstrates an irreverent skepticism indispensable for producing a paradise based not on answers from above, but on a dialogue from within, "down here." The readers' bold articulation of their dissatisfaction and their claims about the book's inaccessibility actually comprise just the kind of inclusive, democratic dialogue to which Morrison hopes *Paradise* can contribute, thus continuing the difficult, endless work she imagines on the final page. Moreover, this is work that promises to persist beyond the boundaries of the book club discussion. Almost all of the participants on the show express a desire to reread, an act that may represent a return home, but their return, in this case, has the potential to transfigure home into a disturbingly, auspiciously unrecognizable place.

If Morrison's readers evince, in some moments, an urge to retreat from the disorienting strangeness that her novel represents in order to return home, in the next chapter I consider a genre designed to respond to the converse impulse: the anxiety that home itself has become a place of estrangement. Contemporary regionalist fiction, as we will see, appeals to the desire for communal ties outside the isolating boundaries of the domestic sphere, thus envisioning a state of belonging, a kind of home denied to individuals by the privatized social landscape of contemporary America.

CHAPTER TWO

Therapy and Displacement in
Divine Secrets of the Ya-Ya Sisterhood

BEWILDERED BY CROWDS, factories, and cities of unprecedented scale, Americans in the late nineteenth century turned to novels about small towns, local customs, and preindustrial crafts. The genre they embraced, now known as regionalism, depicted the idiosyncrasies of tight-knit rural communities in New England, the South, and the newly settled Midwest and, while subtly acknowledging the threat of sweeping change, catered to nostalgia for a traditional, communal mode of life perceived to be vanishing with the onset of modernity.[1] Though frequently ignored by critics, regionalism persisted as an important category of fiction in the twentieth century, and its popularity is arguably greater now than ever before. Among the titles featured on Oprah's Book Club, for instance, a surprisingly large number depict quirky, rural communities, charming because they are apparently nothing like the rest of the United States.[2]

Contemporary regionalist novels frequently market themselves on the basis of their paradoxically exotic settings — places so quaintly American in their use of mythic national imagery as to be practically un-American, or at least alien to the experience of most readers who currently reside in the United States. A question worth exploring, then, is why do regionalist novels emphasize the difference between the locales they describe and the country inhabited by the rest of Americans, a country which presumably includes their readers? What is the appeal of this foregrounded domestic foreignness? What forms of dissatisfaction with the contemporary

United States do these novels presuppose, and what compensations do they provide? If regionalist novels inspire a fantasy of inclusion within old-fashioned, tight-knit communities, why do they simultaneously remind readers that they are voyeuristic outsiders? How do the complex combinations of identification, yearning, and estrangement that such novels promote serve both to intensify and to complicate the fantasies that they produce?

In *Paradise*, Morrison proposes that democratic utopian communities must be capable of embracing the stranger. In the novel that I consider in this chapter, Rebecca Wells's *Divine Secrets of the Ya-Ya Sisterhood*, therapeutic discourse emerges, remarkably enough, as the primary vehicle for promoting this embrace. Wells's novel describes the vibrant, small-town culture of Thornton, Louisiana, while depicting beyond its borders a fragmented social landscape. The protagonist, Sidda, has left Thornton, the town of her childhood, behind and currently resides in New York City. A successful theater director, Sidda makes disparaging remarks about her mother, Vivi, who continues to reside in Thornton, in an interview with the *New York Times*. The ensuing article, which suggests that Sidda's mother was abusive, enrages Vivi, and the novel focuses on their painstaking reconciliation. Sidda's defining characteristic is her addiction to therapy, and the novel suggests that therapeutic practices have come to serve as a compensation for the loss of local intimacies fostered by small-town communities. Indeed, the central conflict of *Divine Secrets*, the conflict between Sidda and Vivi, exemplifies a confrontation between therapeutic and regionalist worldviews. While the novel evinces nostalgia for Vivi's lifestyle and celebrates her anti-modern wisdom, its narrative structure and its modes of address to the reader adhere to therapeutic protocols. Thus the book attempts to bridge the two paradigms whose incongruity it dramatizes, lamenting the loss of old-fashioned communities while providing the basis for ad hoc therapeutic affiliations capable of accommodating a disjointed, decentered world of strangers.

A Sense of Place

To understand why regionalist or local-color novels have achieved such popularity in recent years, it is worth examining some recent trends in the United States' social geography. While regionalism in the nineteenth century responded to the emergence of disorientingly large metropolitan centers, at the turn of the twenty-first century it responds to an inverse process: the migratory dispersal of Americans away from traditional cities and towns. According to Joel Garreau, increasing numbers of Americans today find themselves living in sprawling corporate technoburbs, what he calls edge cities. Most of these residents live nowhere near a traditional downtown, work in isolated office parks, and frequent massive corporate-sponsored shopping malls.[3] While Garreau is an advocate of these new formations, he acknowledges the concerns voiced by some critics that edge cities feel artificial or sterile, lack historical resonance, and discourage communal activities. Owing to their newly fabricated character, their un-bounded, uncentered organization, their corporate-driven homogeneity, and their frequent eschewal of a municipal, political identification, these places fail even to register as singular, distinctive places, and this may par-tially account for why Americans are attracted to novels with richly de-scribed and unique settings. Edge cities, of course, are a logical extension of the suburbs; both cater to Americans' desires for physical autonomy and geographic mobility. Many of the complaints now aimed at edge cities were once aimed at the suburbs; but the latter nevertheless offered a compelling setting for fiction, as evidenced by the work of John Cheever, John Updike, and Richard Yates, among others, whereas the former seem to have in-spired an urge to return, at least in the realm of fantasy, to old-fashioned, small-town communities where fewer and fewer Americans actually live.[4]

A related trend in the past three decades, carefully documented by Rob-ert Putnam in *Bowling Alone* (2000), is the steady decrease of communal orientation and civic engagement in the United States. According to his findings, participation in social activities ranging from the institutional to the informal has diminished precipitously in recent years. People visit town meetings, join professional organizations, play cards, vote, and so-cialize less frequently than they did thirty years ago. Among the causes he catalogs are increased work-related time pressures, suburbanization and sprawl, residential mobility, the emergence of a globalized economy, and television. He also notes that the World War II generation, motivated by intense patriotism, became exceptionally engaged in civic and communal affairs, while subsequent generations have not discovered an equally energizing cause. Putnam's central argument is that communal engagement produces all variety of individual and societal benefits, including less crime, a more vibrant and participatory democracy, and lower rates of depression, to name just a few. Though some Americans clearly cherish their relative isolation, the widespread interest in novels about small-town life suggests that many share Putnam's view; they desire the local, tight-knit communities that historical developments have rendered all but unattainable.

Near the opening of *Divine Secrets*, Sidda leaves Manhattan in order to spend some time poring over her mother's scrapbook in a friend's isolated family house, which is located a few hours' drive from Seattle, through "vast corporate 'managed forests'" (23). The governing perspective of the novel thus places readers at a distance from Thornton, initially requiring them to imagine Sidda's hometown while situated within precisely those contexts most destructive and most alien to American small-town life—the city and the technoburb. This distancing effect serves to underscore Thornton's exotic singularity. Manhattan barely registers; the nameless area in Washington where Sidda stays impresses her primarily with its relentless drizzle, and therefore Thornton, by contrast, emerges as the only well-evoked and particular *place* in the entire novel.

Sidda alerts readers to Thornton's small-town status when discussing her decision to postpone her wedding: "I know how word spreads in Thornton" (11). And it is a place with a powerful physical presence. Phrases such as "the oaken smell of good bourbon; a combination of lily of the valley, cedar, vanilla, and somewhere, the lingering of old rose" (42) and "the pungent aroma of the *cochon de lait*, or the sight of that pig roasting over the slow fire, or the huge vats of boiling water for the corn. . . . The presence of the bayou, the feel of liquid Louisiana land" (126) frequently delivered in a list, removed from any verbs, any signs of action or movement, characterize southern Louisiana, and particularly Thornton, as an overwhelmingly sensual, palpably particular, stubbornly timeless state of being. Her constant reminders of Louisiana's intense humidity suggest that its unique and heavy presence can be immediately felt. It has its own defining atmosphere. Moreover, Wells's periodic use of French establishes Thornton's foreignness. When Sidda invites her fiancé, Connor, to visit her family in Louisiana, she jokes, "Shots and passport up to date?" (330). After they have arrived at their hotel, Connor notices a rare flower bush in the courtyard and remarks, "I can't believe I'm in America" (351).

If Connor finds Thornton to be foreign, then Sidda's mother, Vivi, and her friends Caro, Teensy, and Necie, the self-named Ya-Yas, notable for their brash, flamboyant tendencies, present themselves as even more exotic than their immediate surroundings. Vivi's scrapbook, which bears the same title as the novel, records their outlandish pranks and misadventures. Though many of these episodes took place while they were still young, the adult Ya-Yas are unruly drinkers, incorrigible flirts, and unapologetic hedonists. Sidda's lifestyle is nothing like her mother's and the contrast between these two characters suggests that a particular historical and social context — the mid-century rural southern town — enables the charming deviance, the impassioned waywardness of the Ya-Yas. Because they have lived together in the same place among the same people for their entire lives, they have developed an unspoken choreography, an idiosyncratic language, just as Thornton has evolved a durable sense of identity, a local texture that is conspicuously missing from the cities, suburbs, and technoburbs designed to accommodate a more transient population.

Though the Ya-Yas are a compelling group, it is important to note that their allure depends upon a problematic appropriation of racial otherness. Vivi and her friends, though white and middle class, conceive of themselves as members of a primitive tribe with their own language and rituals. At the age of eleven, the four of them sanctify their bond with a blood pact in the middle of the night. Vivi supplies the group's mythical genealogy, which begins: "Long before the white man showed up, the Mighty Tribe of Ya-Yas, a band of women strong and true and beautiful, roamed the great state of Louisiana" (70). The group, ironically, has spent the afternoon helping Vivi's mother to whiten with turpentine a black Virgin Mary statue that Vivi's father has brought back from Cuba, but, after their self-exoticizing forest ritual, they use makeup to "color her skin brown again" (74), thus symbolically confirming their own unwhitening. The applied blackface is an artificial layer, but its purpose is to reproduce the statue's original condition, just as their forest ritual is designed to assert their tribal origin. In both cases, performances of blackness pretend to enact the recovery of a prior, more primordial status.

The Ya-Yas' claim to a nonwhite tribal ancestry and their veneration for a black Mother Mary represent the children's inchoate enactment of the central influence that black female housekeepers and nannies have exerted upon them as surrogate mothers. In various subtle and overt ways, the Ya-Yas, who retain their name and their tribal identification as adults, play at being black—a cultural appropriation predicated upon complex feelings of superiority, envy, and insecurity.[5] In the very first scene of the novel, a Billie Holiday quote scrawled on the blackboard, "SMOKE, DRINK, NEVER THINK" (ix), seems to license the Ya-Yas' rowdy, drunken card game, played while their children are left unsupervised. Their game uncannily replays a moment, narrated later in the novel, when Vivi, as a child, visits the "colored car" during a journey home from Atlanta and is shocked to discover Ginger, her black nanny, smoking, drinking, and playing cards with her fellow black passengers (108). Moreover, in what has become a familiar trope in contemporary American culture, the text occasionally requires black people to channel and perform intense modes of affect to which the white characters then paradoxically assert a superior claim precisely by refusing to display these feelings outwardly, by identifying them with an incommunicably subtle private core.[6] "Often the music flowed from black people whose songs touched a sadness inside Vivi that she herself had no words for" (165). At times, Wells evokes the destructive racial hierarchies that complicate and in moments undermine the modes of cultural transmission and intimacy between black workers and the white families that they support. And she frequently seems to recognize the racism that underwrites the Ya-Yas' embrace of tendencies that they implicitly associate with blackness, including primitivism, criminality, spontaneity, sensuality, irrationality, soulfulness, and so on. But in many moments, Wells seems to corroborate and applaud, through her breathless prose, the efforts of the Ya-Yas to unwhiten themselves, to evade what they see as the staid banality of middle-class whiteness, without disowning any of its privileges. The implicit assumption is that white America is excessively sterile and rational. To escape it, the characters lay claim not only to the exotic allure of a small southern town but also to the vital tribalism that they identify with African Americans.

Therapy and Intimacy

Viewing a photograph of the Ya-Yas as teenagers, Sidda remarks: "They are lazy together. This is comfort. This is joy. Just look at these four. Not one wears a watch. This porch time is not planned. Not penciled into a DayRunner" (79). Sidda lacks not only Vivi's casual, carefree attitude toward time, but any kind of informal community of female friends. "Sidda's professional life had crowded out most of her girlfriends" (120), and the only close relationships she does maintain are with people she has met and worked with in her career as a theater director. A key difference between Sidda and Vivi of course is that the former, unlike the latter, supports herself financially, and one might read the nostalgia that the book invites for Vivi's lifestyle as merely a retrograde desire to return to traditional gender roles.[7] But Wells is also exploring how the modern, urban context that Sidda inhabits has shaped her in contradistinction to Vivi, and proposing that Sidda's departure from Thornton, though instrumental in furthering her career aspirations, has also required a sacrifice of certain habits and virtues whose value the book is attempting to measure.

It is significant that Wells underlines Sidda's professionalism, given that the emergence of professionalism, as sociologist Magali Sarfatti Larson has argued, typically coincides with the disintegration of traditional tight-knit communities. Professionalism is an institutional framework designed to depersonalize particular skills and trades, to wrest them away from communally recognized family traditions and to produce a functional and task-specific form of trust between strangers. The protocols of professionalism legislate disinterested judgments based upon purportedly universal forms of knowledge abstracted from personal or emotional investments. A review of a play Sidda has directed compliments her work for maintaining a "touching equipoise between personal involvement and professional detachment" (3). But, if Sidda has achieved a productive balance between the two in her directing, the novel suggests that she has allowed her professionalism to saturate her social life to an unhealthy degree. She envies the Ya-Yas' capacity "not to have to constantly 'work' on things, the way we do now" (43) — suggesting the inescapability for Sidda of unspontaneous, labored forms of social intimacy that require an exhausting measure of negotiation and analysis.

The concept of "working" on a friendship conflates professional strategies and personal desires and thereby testifies to the presence of the therapeutic paradigm. Sidda admits that the money she has spent on therapy by the age of forty would be enough to "buy a small country somewhere" (39). But therapy for Sidda, as her mother recognizes, has become more than merely a financially onerous weekly ritual; it has become a reflexively operative worldview, a way of being. Sidda decides to postpone her wedding because she "[doesn't] know how to love," a claim that provokes her mother's rejoinder: "You have had too much therapy. Or not enough" (25). Vivi's ironic remark maintains that therapy has done more than simply fail to meet its stated aims; it has made Sidda into a less healthy individual, thereby guaranteeing her continued need for even more therapy. While talking with Teensy about their relations with their own mothers, Vivi remarks, "What my thoroughly analyzed daughter doesn't understand is that you don't have to spend thousands of dollars in therapy to consider things like this" (255), suggesting that the therapeutic profession has, for Sidda and the entire generation that she represents, secured a financially lucrative monopoly upon introspection, foreclosing other informal, noninstitutional strategies for achieving self-knowledge.

One of Vivi's central complaints about her daughter's dependence upon therapy is that it encourages her confessional impulses. The latter's imprudent response to the *New York Times* reporter is a perfect example. In that instance, Sidda mistakenly treats the reporter as she would a friend, confusing the private and the public, the personal and the professional. By contrast, Vivi categorically opposes the therapeutic paradigm's tendency to encourage the discursive confessional, the "talking cure." In response to Teensy's suggestion that she resolve her conflict with Sidda by telling her about her own past emotional struggles, Vivi replies, "No, no, no. Not my style. This is *my* luggage. These are *my* trunks" (255). Vivi is so opposed to talking about her problems that, even after she suffers a nervous breakdown and spends some time in a mental hospital, she refuses, except on one occasion, to discuss the episode with her Ya-Ya sisters. The novel's title suggests a group of friends whose bonds are based upon their secrets, but the paradoxical implication of Vivi's reticence is that kept rather than revealed secrets sustain close relationships. Even as a child Vivi grasps this notion: "Every time I think I know my friends, they surprise me. They are full of secrets I will never know" (74). Here Wells asserts that the untold secret and the absolute maintenance of personal privacy provide the basis for psychological depth. Vivi's friends seem complex and interesting to her because they do not tell her everything; densely suggestive silences intensify their intimacy.

It is also important to note that the Ya-Yas do not *need* to tell each other all of their secrets, because they have grown up together in the same town; and thus they have lived their various secrets in each other's presence. The novel frequently underscores the quotidian forms of nonverbal communication that shape the Ya-Yas' relations. In one scene, for instance, Vivi helps Caro with her oxygen tank "without offering"; and "without acknowledgement," Caro accepts her help (15). They have developed complementary habits, automatic rituals, and reflexive forms of empathy, which render verbal communication unnecessary. At the same time, their capacity for reserve is required by the tight-knit community that surrounds them. If Thornton, in other words, facilitates the development of unlabored intimacy, it also encourages a perpetually performative stance, designed to preserve individual and familial privacy in response to unavoidable communal visibility. The Ya-Yas, whose pranks and escapades repeatedly appear in the town newspaper, lead relentlessly public and publicized lives. They are always putting on a show, at times for the sake of entertainment and at other times as a means of self-preservation. After Vivi survives a harrowing semester in a repressive Catholic academy, where she practically starves herself to death, she returns to Thornton anxious to hide the psychic aftereffects of her experience and becomes "a high priestess of self-presentation" (233).

Vivi's careful regulation of her personality does not appear to interfere with her friendships. In several instances, *Divine Secrets* contends, contrary to the assumptions of our contemporary confessional culture, that intimacy and performative self-presentation need not be understood as mutually exclusive. Upon learning that Sidda has postponed her marriage because she fears that she does not know how to love, Vivi writes her a letter, in which she contends:

> *God* knows how to love, Kiddo. The rest of us are only good *actors.*
> *Forget love. Try good manners.* (25)

Vivi worries that her daughter's unguarded indulgence in therapeutic self-analysis has interfered with her ability to treat her fiancé in accordance with socially determined standards of propriety. The novel, near the end, returns to Vivi's advice as Sidda achieves an epiphany: "*I have been missing the point. The point is not* knowing *another person, or* learning *to love another person. The point is simply this: how tender can we bear to be? What good manners can we show as we welcome ourselves and others into our hearts?*" (346). Sidda's analogy for becoming close to another person is the act of hospitably inviting a guest into one's home. It is an apt metaphor; playing host involves allowing another person into one's interior, inviting that person to cross the boundary between the public and the private, but not without maintaining, even within that interior, a measure of decorum, a public persona. The question "How tender can we bear to be?" suggests a motive: intimacy is painful and thus its enactments require a self-protective interior lamination. But this mannered glaze also serves another purpose; it preserves an image of the infinitely deep, unknowable self. Paradoxically, the intimate gesture of opening one's interior to the other seems to require the decorous veiling and concomitant construction of even deeper, unrevealed interiors.

Vivi's unorthodox equation between intimacy and good manners yields several interpretations, but what is most important to note is the way the small-town community enables this equation. Thornton demands a performative, publicly oriented demeanor, but it simultaneously promotes silent modes of solidarity that in fact depend upon the maintenance of socially determined civility. The prevailing form of intimacy encouraged by therapeutic practices, by contrast, involves the disclosure, rather than the preservation, of secrets, and may be understood as a compensation for the loss of such small-town communities. In the absence of locally rooted relationships, therapeutic discourse serves as a surrogate for common history, condensing the sustained temporality of habitual contact into the punctual discursive confessional. Strangers seeking to become friends in cities, suburbs, or technoburbs, with no shared past to build upon, are, in other words, obliged to *tell each other everything*.[8]

According to Christopher Lasch, the therapeutic paradigm in fact effaces history, producing a perpetual immersion in the present (13). And Wells seems to register, as Trysh Travis has argued in her astute reading, the profoundly dehistoricizing influence of Sidda's therapeutic preoccupations ("The Divine Secrets"). History, of course, signifies at least two different related phenomena: a chronological succession and accumulation of experiences and a series of significant events that reverberate across the nation or the world. Sidda detaches herself from history in the first sense by departing from Thornton, a town which preserves a communally enshrined memory of her past. But Sidda also seems isolated from history in the second sense. While the narrative situates Vivi's life in relationship to major historical events, it focuses in its depiction of Sidda on her private psychological ruminations and domestic problems. She seems unwittingly to repeat the struggles her mother faced when she was younger, but in a distinctively therapeutic register. Sidda is terrified that her fiancé, Connor, will die or abandon her — a fear that uncannily recapitulates her mother's loss of her one true love, Jack, who died in World War II. Sidda's recovery of history transforms her mother's confrontation with disastrous global events into a purely psychological struggle. Whereas a world war intrudes so as to destroy Vivi's hopes, the danger Sidda faces in her reiteration of her mother's narrative is nothing other than her own anxieties. Her fear of abandonment leads her to postpone her wedding and thus threatens to provoke the very abandonment that she fears. In circular fashion, her private psychological fixations constitute the very problem that in turn motivates and exacerbates her fixations. Just after reading a series of letters written by her mother as a girl about the premier of *Gone with the Wind*, Sidda reflects: "*What is my civil war about? Is it the fear of being held in the warmth of familiar love versus the fear of running through the fog, searching for love? Each holds its own terrors, extracts its own pound of flesh*" (114). War, for Sidda, is nothing more than a metaphor for her own ambivalence; therapeutic dilemmas have replaced historical ones.

The narrative decisions of *Divine Secrets* seem to encourage a preference for Vivi's mode of being over Sidda's. Vivi's life is in a significant way *eventful*; it poignantly registers many of the national transformations and upheavals of the past seventy-five years, and it thereby includes all kinds of uncertainties, risks, and tragedies, whereas Sidda's life seems relatively banal. Though Sidda attributes a timelessness to the Ya-Yas' experiences, the novel presents these instances as states of blissful evasion, all the more powerful because history always lurks in the background ready to disrupt a serenity whose permanence is manifestly an illusion. By contrast, reading Sidda's episodes, one yearns for enlivening intrusions; the repeatedly invoked drizzle that ceaselessly falls during her retreat to her friend's house signals a decrease of narrative energy whenever the text shifts from Vivi's colorful and dramatic childhood to Sidda's self-involved meditations. One could argue that this difference is simply the product of time scales: the narrative covers a few weeks of Sidda's life versus several decades of Vivi's; but this choice could also be seen as a reflection of the two characters' respective worldviews, signaling the significant role communal and national history play in Vivi's consciousness compared with the fairly minor role they play in Sidda's.

The community, the larger society, and history itself all seem to press palpably upon the Ya-Yas, and their lives exemplify an embodied, almost tactile worldliness in stark contrast to the cloistered introspection that characterizes Sidda. Thus Wells challenges the typical perception that small-town life entails provinciality. In one episode she dramatizes the power of Vivi's intensely local perspective to encourage global empathy. During an oppressively hot summer night near the very beginning of World War II, the teenage Ya-Yas surreptitiously scale Thornton's water tank in order to take a dip in the town's water supply. "From the top of the water tower, Vivi felt a relief spread through her. What a sweet small-town thrill this was, like the delight of watching a parade from the top of a tall building" (157–58). Vivi's physical standpoint allows her to see a good portion of the town, but she also begins to visualize the parts of the town she cannot see, the insides of houses, the insomniacs lingering by their open iceboxes, the candles burning inside the local Catholic church. Then, "winging higher still, Vivi left her town, went up so high she could no longer see the trees or the boulevard or the faces in ecstasy or worry. . . . She lifted above her town until she could see Bunkie and Natchitoches and how the Cane River was more like a lake, and how the Garnet River fed into the Mississippi" (158). By the end of her reverie, she imagines that "she could see the whole little Earth, blue and white, spinning around in terrifying magnificent space. No people, only hearts, hearts beating, countless hearts; and the sound of breathing" (159). This epiphanic glimpse of humanity's magnitude, however, is accompanied by terror, by the sense of her own "impermanence," and she unwillingly retreats from her lofty perspective, succumbing to the fear that her boyfriend, Jack, will die in the war. But her personal anxieties quickly lead back into an unbounded transport of empathy, as she and her Ya-Ya sisters submerge themselves in the tank, crying so that their tears join the communal water, and Wells remarks: "They cried because Jack's enlistment had cracked open their tight universe to the suffering world" (160).

Tom Lutz notes that American regionalism typically displays not merely an urge to capture a particular region's local color, but a capacity both to inhabit and to stand outside of that region as evidence of a larger cosmopolitan vision capable of comprehending a diversity of specific cultures. Likewise, Bruce Robbins and Pheng Cheah maintain that local, regionalist attachments necessarily underwrite all productive forms of cosmopolitanism.[9] *Divine Secrets* confirms the notion that the two perspectives, regionalist and cosmopolitan, can operate symbiotically. Vivi's local orientation appears to lead, as if in accordance with a deterministic physical law, toward an expansive identification with all of earth's humanity, then contracts again to focus on her own personal relations, before expanding once again into a palpable compassion for the suffering that ties all people together — the entire movement of expansion and contraction resembling, significantly, a beating heart.

Thornton, as a distinctive place, is available for Vivi's visualization. From the top of the water tower, she can see a considerable portion of it, and she can visualize the rest, which is why she identifies her exhilarating panoptic experiences as a "small-town thrill." Thus, her immediate surroundings offer a concrete, mentally mappable embodiment of a community, transforming society from an abstraction into a tangible image. What she can see allows her to picture what she cannot see, which in turn allows her to imagine what she cannot know. Her capacity to comprehend humanity as a community of beating hearts requires not merely the explicit synecdoche of the heart standing for the individual, but also a parallel synecdoche of the local, palpably immediate, cognitively manageable town of Thornton standing in for the otherwise ungraspable world. And as she imagines all of the various bodies of water in the area connecting to each other, she enters the town's water supply, cries into it, and thus enacts symbolically her sense that her individual suffering is merging with the suffering of her town and of humanity in general. Her global empathy requires that she be immersed, physically and emotionally connected to one particular place, which can, through its metaphorical and physical confluence with all that surrounds it, mediate between her and the larger world. At the same time, her capacious vision serves to ennoble her own personal anxieties, endowing them with world-historical significance.

Of course, Wells's celebration of Vivi's regionalism is equivocal. If Thornton serves as a platform for Vivi's global vision, it also runs the risk of insulating her: she accesses the rest of the world by means of a "crack" in her "tight universe." She gains her new perspective not from within the town, but only when she finds herself above it, placing herself in a position to see it as a discrete, finite object, rather than as the horizon of her existence. If Vivi feels capable of apprehending the entire world's suffering in this moment, throughout much of the narrative her attention is more narrowly focused on her community and her immediate circle of friends. Their club, the Ya-Yas, is fairly exclusive, and as such it represents a danger that, according to Robert Putnam, attends all small, tight-knit communities: an inability to assimilate outsiders.[10] Vivi empathizes with people, in other words, only to the extent that she can imagine them as a part of her local community.

To put it another way, the automatic, silent trust predicated upon shared history and a common culture functions well among the Ya-Yas, but obviously cannot serve as the solidifying agent for an open public sphere within the heterogeneous population of a modern city, suburb, or technoburb. As a means of promoting trust, understanding, or empathy among strangers deprived of a shared history or culture, therapeutic discourse becomes necessary. It constitutes resemblances and affinities between people by decontextualizing, disembodying, and deracinating them — by obscuring the local attachments that connect individuals to the distinctive, culturally specific places they inhabit and focusing instead on their interior characteristics. Vivi's water tower vision of the world as a community of beating hearts, stripped of all external or contextual features, ironically enough, obeys the same logic, demonstrating that Vivi's local orientation must be supplemented by a therapeutic perspective in order to provide a grounding for her cosmopolitan epiphany.

The book's paradoxical suggestion is that therapeutic discourse is best suited to operate among strangers. In fact even Vivi seeks out strangers in certain moments to fulfill her private therapeutic needs, confessing her problems as a form of catharsis. She occasionally visits Catholic priests, and she regularly sees a massage therapist. Her sessions with the latter closely approximate the typical therapeutic office visit, and during one conversation Vivi not only cries, but feels a need to discuss her internal psychic rifts. " 'I'm thinking,' Vivi said, 'about an afternoon in my life when all the cracks were clear. Like a pile of broken crockery' " (242). She then adds, trying to recover her characteristic taciturnity, "It is not in my personality to talk like this," followed by "My God, I'm starting to sound like Blanche DuBois: '*I have always depended on the kindness of strangers.*'" Her massage therapist's response is telling: "Maybe I'm not a stranger." The two are involved in a professional relationship, and yet Torie asks Vivi to view her as a friend. Her tentative refusal of Vivi's characterization instantiates the central paradoxical task of the therapeutic: the professionalization of intimacy — a process that enables the private confessional to function among strangers.

Of course, therapeutic discourse works to produce intimacy between strangers even outside of strictly professional contexts. This is the peculiar, generally unacknowledged, but most politically promising feature of the therapeutic paradigm.[11] Though critics argue that therapy abets the pervasive atomization of contemporary social life in the United States, one might understand therapy as a response to atomization, an effort to mediate new kinds of interactions and group identifications in the face of these developments. While its ostensible content is generally the personal, the domestic, and the familial, therapeutic discourse facilitates relations between people outside of the private sphere, fostering intimacy among strangers. In fact, estrangement becomes, paradoxically, the very basis for intimacy in the therapeutic encounter; Vivi can reveal her psychic rifts only to someone whom she does not know; the sense of anonymity shields and depersonalizes her embarrassing confession. Furthermore, the universalizing vocabulary of therapeutic discourse and its division of the psyche into categorizable constituents enable people from divergent contexts to recognize and identify with each other in the absence of shared history or culture. At the very least, then, therapeutic discourse enables subjects to engage with other people by means of a general sense of relatedness or commensurateness — a mode of anti-privatizing empathy capable in certain circumstances of providing the foundation for decentered, psychologically inflected communities of strangers, or what some might term a public.

In lamenting the disintegration of the public sphere, Richard Sennett celebrates urban contexts for enabling creative, performative interactions between strangers oriented toward the reshaping of a larger shared world; he claims that these public forms cannot thrive within smaller, more localized communities where, he contends, each individual is primarily concerned with realizing, preserving, and expressing his or her interior essence. But Wells's novel seems to invert Sennett's scheme. The theatrical, mannered, public modes, which Sennett locates within the city, Wells identifies with small-town communities, such as Thornton, where constant visibility necessitates the maintenance of decorum and where characters reject self-absorption in favor of stoical flamboyance. Sidda, who lives in Manhattan, is the one who dwells most obsessively upon her private psychological tendencies. Rather than operating within tight-knit, provincial communities as Sennett suggests, therapeutic discourse seems to serve as the necessary equipment for urban dwellers, who are surrounded by strangers and who assert connections with each other through the articulation of generically understood psychological problems, which promote pragmatic fantasies of immediate intersubjective resonance. The public virtues thus seem divided between the two orientations, regionalist and therapeutic, neither of which can, on its own, provide the basis for a robust public sphere. The former promotes sociability and civic investment but also exclusivity and insularity; the latter allows strangers to identify with each other across various social divisions, but it can also lead to narcissism and to factitious forms of intimacy, as Sidda discovers from her interactions with the *New York Times* reporter. Thus Wells seems to favor a synthesis of the two, a synthesis that she also seeks to establish in her relationship with her readers.

Intimate Readerships

Standing above the town of Thornton, Vivi imagines a community of unseen strangers unified by the resonance of their beating hearts. Her expansive, publicly directed gaze in this instance might serve as a metaphor for the manner in which the novel *Divine Secrets* or its author, Rebecca Wells, addresses an audience of unseen readers. In the "Note to the Reader" that prefaces HarperCollins's second edition of *Little Altars Everywhere*, released after *Divine Secrets* achieved enormous popularity, Wells remarks upon the peculiar intimacy that connects her as an author to her readers — most of whom she will never meet in person. "I've been thinking lately about the intimacy that exists between us, writer and reader. And the more I reflect, the more grateful I am for this gift, because the process of a book's coming to life is not fully complete until your imagination meets mine on the page. The words evoke pictures and something altogether new is created, something different from the limits of my own skills and imagination" (vii). Her observation yields an insight similar to one voiced by Michael Warner in his analysis of reading publics. According to Warner, print media works through a paradoxical combination of personal and impersonal rhetorical postures and modes of response (*Publics* 76). When you read a good book, you may feel singled out, as if it were addressed exclusively to you, but at the same time you know that you are unknown to the author. A text constitutes its audience by satisfying certain desires, thus appearing to know its readers in advance, but at the same time it addresses itself to an unrestricted general public and as such makes a paradoxically intimate appeal to strangers. Wells asserts that the act of reading creates "something new," beyond the limits of her own "skills and imagination." The productive intimacy between her and her readers, in other words, depends upon the reader's unanticipated responses, based upon experiences, dispositions, and interpretive tendencies that are, in the ideal reading situation, unavailable to the author's knowledge. To be drawn into intimacy with Wells, then, you must feel yourself personally addressed, but *as a stranger.*

The initial appeal of Rebecca Wells's first novel, *Little Altars Everywhere*, according to Travis, depended upon its publication by a small independent Seattle press, Broken Moon, and the sense that this was not a generic product designed for a mass audience. After HarperCollins acquired *Divine Secrets*, her second novel, Wells's popularity grew gradually, in part as a result of her own energetic and dramatic readings at independent bookstores. These in conjunction with word-of-mouth recommendations and the spontaneous emergence of Ya-Ya fan clubs across the country eventually transformed her into a best-selling author. Hoping to capitalize on readers' enthusiasm, HarperCollins created a Web site for Rebecca Wells designed to facilitate discussions, disseminate information, and encourage the formation of more Ya-Ya groups. While this strategy aimed to control what had been a disorganized, largely consumer-driven phenomenon, HarperCollins eschewed a proactive, high-budget publicity campaign for fear of undermining precisely what was drawing readers to Rebecca Wells. It was, after all, her noncorporate, offbeat persona that paradoxically made her books so widely marketable. As Travis remarks: "Clearly the publication and promotional history of Wells's books illustrates that an unknown author can in fact penetrate — and then capitalize on — today's corporate literary marketplace. In an age fully — achingly — conscious of the degree to which celebrity, synergy, and rationalization shape cultural production, this phenomenon is heartening; so heartening that, ironically, it becomes the sign by which the product is marketed" ("The Divine Secrets" 142). Allowing readers to feel that, unsolicited by any manipulative market mechanisms, they had discovered an authentic voice ostensibly addressed to their own private desires and had thus joined a fellowship of similarly inclined, similarly lonely readers, HarperCollins was able to extend the sense of intimacy and grassroots solidarity that Wells inspired across a large cross section of the middlebrow book market.

Wells's narrative strategies of course contribute to this effect. While the intimate reading public that *Divine Secrets* fosters is radically different from the small-town community that it describes, the book obviously appeals to readers' fantasies of belonging to the Ya-Yas' exclusive club. But

Wells both energizes and frustrates these fantasies through her inconsistent narrative devices. In some moments the novel describes an archive of the Ya-Yas' experience, allowing both Sidda and the reader to experience the past through its present traces, including letters, newspaper clippings, and photographs. At other times, the past emerges in the form of a character's memory of it, including Vivi's recall of her boyfriend's death in World War II or Sidda's meditations about her mother's effort to help a desperate cosmetic saleswoman. In a few instances, one character narrates her memories of the past to another character, as Caro does when she describes Vivi's nervous breakdown to Sidda. In all of these cases, the novel offers some foregrounded mediation between the readers and the experiences depicted. But in several other scenes Wells chooses to dispense with these devices, simply describing various experiences as if they were happening in the present, often providing a careful evocation of the characters' thoughts and feelings, thus producing, through the lack of any retrospective distancing device, in conspicuous contrast with other flashbacks in the book, the sense for readers that they are simply there, participating in the Ya-Yas' experience. The relative underemphasis on intermediation, in other words, allows readers, in these moments, to imagine that they are living the history, rather than simply witnessing its recovery through a discursive recapitulation.

Whether or not this strategy is deliberate, and whether readers are even explicitly conscious of these narrative shifts, they are likely to feel as they read the book at times drawn into and at times kept out of the Ya-Ya club, at times immersed in a fantastical identification with the group, at times aware of the gap between their desire and its fulfillment. Simultaneously included and excluded, readers are privy to the mode of southern hospitality that Sidda celebrates when she wonders "*what good manners can we show as we welcome ourselves and others into our hearts?*" (346) — a mode that lets people in, but only as guests. Wells offers readers the fantasy of belonging to an exquisitely inaccessible small-town community, but at times underscores the status of this community as mere fantasy and the position of the reader as voyeur. Thus this teasing narrative game is likely only to intensify the reader's experience of the fantasy while exacerbating the yearnings that the novel is incapable of fully satisfying.

Although the provocation of desire for an unrealizable, imaginary community may seem cruel, it has served a productive function, engendering communities of readers allied precisely by this unappeased desire. *Divine Secrets* has been not only a choice of numerous book clubs; it has also inspired social clubs modeled upon the group depicted in the novel. These clubs exemplify an interesting hybrid social formation; they bring together strangers, facilitate dialogue about all variety of subjects, and thereby operate as a quasi-public gathering, but one that is capable of accommodating intimate disclosures of the kind that traditional, masculine conceptions of the public have strived to exclude. Travis issued a questionnaire to the members of a Ya-Ya club, and one respondent offered an especially illuminating observation: "We speak about how we wish things were like they are in Rebecca's Thornton, LA. People are born, grow up and die knowing the same people there. I am the only one in the group who is actually from Colorado. We feel so much is lost by moving around, always seeking the greener grass, that it gives no time to develop lifelong friendships that once were. So we just tell each other everything from the past and then fake it!" ("The Divine Secrets" 154). Deprived by the contemporary social landscape of the opportunity to live their histories together and thereby cultivate the regionalist form of intimacy that they expressly desire, the respondent and her friends, according to their own reports, first encountered each other as strangers. Thus they were required to employ the discursive confessional characteristic of therapeutic practices as a substitute for, or mimetic condensation of, shared history.

If the book *Divine Secrets* describes no adequate alternative to the traditional small town, it offers itself as the closest approximation. Motivating the novel's plot is Sidda's discovery after her interview with the *New York Times* critic that her confessional impulses are risky, that they foster and thrive upon the dangerous illusion of familiarity and trust between strangers. The Ya-Ya clubs that have formed around Wells's novel may seem to depend upon a similar illusion, but if their members lack a unifying context, at the very least they have an imagined context offered by the book itself. Their gestures and disclosures do not operate within an absolute vacuum. What binds these readers together is not their membership within a small-town community, but their shared longing for one and their willingness to make the fiction of one serve as a platform. Their desire provides the strange basis for the compensatory, therapeutic measures designed to appease this desire. *Divine Secrets*, in other words, unites therapeutic practices and regionalist fantasies.

Obscure Wisdom

The fragmented world that most American readers inhabit may make them eager to receive another offering rooted in the book's small-town setting: the promise of wisdom. Considering Caro's argument about Vivi, "however she fucked you up — and I'm sure she did — every mother fucks every kid up — she did it with style," Sidda reflects, "therapy *has* done *some* good. Five years ago I would have gone catatonic if someone spoke such blunt crazy wisdom to me" (171). Although this passage suggests that it is precisely her time in therapy that enables her to remain calm and patient enough to consider Caro's perspective, it also implies a tension between the two modes of knowledge, between therapeutic forms of understanding and wisdom.

The offbeat "crazy wisdom" of the Ya-Yas emerges in the book as an antidote to the professionalization and specialization of contemporary society. Unlike technical forms of knowledge cultivated and monopolized by professional authorities, which are focused upon narrowly delimited spheres, wisdom suggests a broader sensibility, a general conception of *how to live* — and it is this kind of knowledge that regionalist novels often claim to offer. Contexts such as Thornton, Louisiana, by virtue of their unfragmented, anti-modern character, frequently advertise themselves as rare sources of old-fashioned, eccentric lore or guidance, and regionalist authors often seek to transfer the aura of authentic, timeless wisdom that attends these places to their novels. The wisdom offered by regionalist novels is often rooted in traditional practices or holistic crafts, which elude the specialized division of labor that defines industrial and postindustrial society. Vivi for instance passes on to Sidda her perfect swimming stroke, which she has mastered in Thornton's local creek, and which serves, in keeping with the book's ubiquitous aquatic symbolism, as a metaphor for how to maneuver without undue fear or self-consciousness through life's various challenges.

The title, *Divine Secrets of the Ya-Ya Sisterhood*, yields a suggestive ambiguity about the kind of wisdom that the novel makes available to readers. As I have argued, the term "secrets" may refer either to the secrets told or to the secrets preserved by the Ya-Yas—preserved not only from outsiders but from each other. The term can also, however, signify a form of advice—a meaning typically mobilized by self-help books such as *The Secret of the Millionaire Mind*, *The Secret of Happiness*, or that most popular of inspirational manuals, *The Secret*. The irony and brilliance of these books, of course, is that they typically market an obvious platitude, such as "believe in yourself" or "project confidence," as if it were in fact a well-kept secret, unavailable (except by means of the best-selling self-help book that is advertising it) to all those who are striving to succeed or find happiness. What kinds of secrets does Wells's novel contain? Are its most important secrets the ones it refuses to disclose, as Vivi suggests about her scrapbook (247)? Or are its secrets completely obvious, like those that fill the pages of self-help books?

The central inspirational advice that Sidda learns from her mother, which also seems directed at readers, is probably best encapsulated by the following remark made by Vivi: "Do you remember how horrified you were as a little girl when you found the word 'vivisection' in the dictionary? Came running to me in tears, remember? Well, I'm not a Goddamn frog, Sidda. You can't figure me out. *I* can't figure me out. It's *life*, Sidda. You don't figure it out. You just climb up on the beast and *ride*" (47). A moment before this, Vivi declares, "You want to pick *yourself* apart, go right ahead. But you're not going to pick me to pieces" (47). Vivi defines life as precisely that which cannot be apprehended through analysis, and her equation of analysis and vivisection implies that therapy is essentially a deathly process, one that destroys life by attempting to divide it into smaller constituents. Neither the text, nor Vivi, however, denies the value of self-knowledge; both simply prescribe forms of comprehension that preserve a recognition of knowledge's limits, of life's essential obscurity. A quotation from H. L. Mencken constitutes part of the novel's epigraph: "Penetrating so many secrets, we cease to believe in the unknowable. But there it sits, nevertheless, calmly licking its chops" (viii). In two separate instances, Wells evokes the power of blurry vision, in one moment describing Sidda's decision while studying a photo of the Ya-Yas, to put her magnifying glass aside, let her eyes unfocus, and acquiesce to the sensual character of the depicted scene (79), and in another moment, reporting Caro's claim that a jigsaw puzzle is easier to solve when she "blur[s] [her] focus" (293). In deliberate contrast to the procedures of therapy and vivisection — both of which involve attempting to see, with magnified clarity, below the surface to some imagined, onto-logically privileged core, exposing and illuminating the interior essence of a particular phenomenon and dividing it into classifiable parts —Wells asserts a superior, less invasive form of knowledge that respects and thus paradoxically apprehends people and objects in their impenetrable obscu-rity and wholeness.

As it turns out, Vivi's assertion, "you just climb up on the beast and *ride*," which encourages her daughter to stop thinking and simply act, conceals a deeper secret. Sidda eventually uncovers it by remembering the signifi-cance of a tiny key she finds in the scrapbook. The key is a souvenir from a Thornton community event whose central attraction is the chance to ride a circus elephant. In characteristic fashion, Sidda, as a child, freezes at the decisive moment, refuses to mount the elephant, and then experiences in-tense regret over her paralysis, until her mother grants her a second oppor-tunity by bribing the elephant's owner once the event is over. Only late in the novel does Sidda grasp the specific reference of Vivi's remark, "you just climb up on the beast and *ride*," by remembering the incident with the el-ephant. If her mother's advice seems at first insipidly obvious, then its obvi-ousness may best be captured by the expression that cannot help but come to mind in this instance, of the unacknowledged elephant in the room. What this figure for the open secret suggests is that its painfully immense obviousness is precisely what prevents the secret from being disclosed. And the secrets of Wells's novel are, like the elephant in the room, of this dual nature: both obvious and undisclosed, and undisclosed as a consequence of their obviousness. Vivi does, of course, attempt to communicate what she sees as the secret to life rather explicitly to her daughter; but in part because this lesson's discursive formulation seems so obvious, Sidda does not pay it much heed at first. The secret's obviousness, then, prevents its transmis-sion. Vivi may in fact be offering to Sidda an important piece of wisdom, but given its anti-analytical character, its value can be comprehended and realized only by putting it into practice. Sidda comes to grasp the meaning of Vivi's advice precisely when she ceases to read the phrase as a linguistic metaphor for a life-affirming abstraction; she understands it only when she re-situates it within a concrete narrative and recovers its reference to a physical action: climbing onto an actual elephant and riding it.

Throughout *Divine Secrets*, Wells celebrates embodied forms of knowledge. Sidda reflects at one point, "All life, all history happens in the body. I am learning about the woman who carried me inside of hers" (202). And later: "There was nothing to figure out. There was Sidda's heart beating. There was the heart of the planet beating. There was enough time. She was not afraid" (327). In both of these moments, Sidda assigns greater value to the unconscious operations of her body than to the conscious operations of her mind. Her body's spontaneous responsiveness is capable of registering the wisdom of her mother's example more powerfully and demonstratively than her rational faculties. In accordance with her mother's anti-therapeutic sensibility, Sidda rejects analysis, claiming, "there was nothing to figure out," acknowledging parts of herself—bodily, instinctual, empathetic—which resist rational understanding and which function best unfettered by attempts at conscious surveillance or interference. Of course, as the culminating product of the philosophical and structural ambivalences that energize Wells's narrative, Sidda's epiphany is not entirely at odds with the therapeutic paradigm that she is calling into question. The central irony of *Divine Secrets* is that it does not merely depict, but in fact traces in the forward motion of its plot, a therapeutic trajectory while elaborating an anti-therapeutic stance. Sidda is, after all, simply striving to achieve a mode of calm, confident self-acceptance entirely commensurate with the stated goals of most therapeutic programs in the United States. If Sidda requires a therapeutic process in order to embrace her mother's wisdom, then this conclusion is simply further evidence that the therapeutic paradigm has emerged in the United States not merely in opposition to, but also as a compensation for, the local regionalist forms of wisdom and intimacy that it has come to replace.

By celebrating the strange, instinctive intelligence that, in her view, resides within the body, Wells is seeking to establish rationality's limits, identifying a kind of anti-modern wisdom beyond the discursive measures that generally characterize academic or more generally professional modes of assessment and critique. But rather than offer a rigorous argument for the existence of phenomena beyond rational understanding, Wells devotes her energy to underscoring the peculiar aesthetic rewards of limited omniscience — a boldly unfashionable position in the contemporary confessional culture of the United States. People, she suggests, become more compelling when we allow them to preserve their good manners and their secrets, when we believe that they possess inscrutable interior lives, and when our intimacy contains an element of strangeness. Indeed, the same logic seems to govern the relationship between readers and the fictional small-town community of Thornton, Louisiana — an object of yearning and nostalgia apprehended most palpably from outside its borders, from a perspective predicated upon partial knowledge and incomplete access.

Notwithstanding its exuberant tone and life-affirming message, *Divine Secrets*, it turns out, is a wistful, backward-looking book; the communities of readers that it inaugurates depend upon shared nostalgia for a perishing way of life, and one cannot help but feel that these communities are only a partial solution to the insatiable desires that serve as the condition for regionalism's continued viability. The next novel I consider, David Foster Wallace's *Infinite Jest*, seeks to identify forms of solidarity rooted in the present, entirely severed from premodern social structures, and predicated instead upon therapeutic identity categories.

CHAPTER THREE

Infinite Jest and the Recovery of Feeling

NARRATIVES OF ADDICTION are irresistible. The strangely appealing opportunity to observe, imagine, or inhabit vicariously the scenes of pleasure, transgression, abjection, and redemption that these narratives typically unfold has come to function as a substitute gratification capable of replacing the substances whose addictive properties they document. Recognizing this potential, Bill Wilson and Robert Smith, the cofounders of Alcoholics Anonymous (AA), argued that the best method for remaining sober was to engage in a ritualistic exchange of stories about alcoholism. Smith describes his life-saving first encounter with Wilson as follows:

> The question which might naturally come into your mind would be: "What did the man do or say that was different from what others had done or said?" It must be remembered that I had read a great deal and talked to everyone who knew, or thought they knew anything about the subject of alcoholism. But this was a man who had experienced many years of frightful drinking, who had had most all the drunkard's experiences known to man, but who had been cured by the very means I had been trying to employ, that is to say the spiritual approach. He gave me information about the subject of alcoholism which was undoubtedly helpful. *Of far more importance was the fact that he was the first living human with whom I had ever talked, who knew what he was talking about in regard to alcoholism from actual experience. In other words, he talked my language.* He knew all the answers, and certainly not because he had picked them up in his reading.[1]

Of limited use to Smith is "information" about the "subject of alcoholism" — in short, any discourse that attempts to describe but does not originate in "actual experience." His claim that Wilson holds a kind of knowledge that reading alone cannot provide seems to challenge the capacity of language on its own to capture or communicate the truth of alcoholism. And yet, in clarifying his reasons for trusting Wilson, Smith maintains, "*In other words, he talked my language,*" asserting a shared mode of discourse as the basis for their immediate sense of solidarity. His reformulation of "*talking . . . from actual experience*" into "*talk*[ing] *my language*" seems to conflate precisely what the rest of the passage strives to distinguish, that is, "*actual experience*" and "*language,*" but in doing so it recapitulates the transition that AA encourages between experiencing the effects of alcohol firsthand and merely talking about doing so. In order to attract members to the organization, Smith must present the latter, talking, as a radical improvement on the former, drinking, but also as a compensatory surrogate that reproduces, in benign form, the experiences that it is designed to supplant. Narratives of addiction accomplish this seemingly self-contradicting task not only by allowing members to relive, at least imaginatively, drunken dramas from their past, but also by facilitating within the meeting a visceral, indeed intoxicating form of identification between teller and listener. Thus language in AA serves not only to represent, but to produce in its moment of enunciation, the kind of "actual experience" that its members crave.

If narratives of addiction seem to usurp the captivating power of the substances that they depict, then this is a power that works not only upon AA members, but also upon more general audiences, judging by the onslaught of movies, novels, memoirs, and talk-show episodes devoted to the subject. These narratives clearly satisfy a complex set of desires, among them the urge to participate in a cathartic emotional reaction similar to the responses elicited in AA meetings.[2] While the gratifications of these narratives must depend for some consumers precisely upon their own safe distance from the threat of addiction, the temptation and thrill of merely imagined capitulation, abjection, or recovery are based, arguably, on a craving for "actual experience" of the kind that substance abuse is thought to offer and that stories of addiction promise to replicate. But what has conditioned this craving? Why, in other words, might contemporary audiences see themselves as suffering from a dearth of actual experience?

In his critically celebrated experimental, 1,079-page novel, *Infinite Jest*, David Foster Wallace diagnoses a pervasive national malaise, a collective state of jaded ennui in part responsible, in his view, for the tendency to glamorize and romanticize substance abuse as an escape from the banality and sterility of post-capitalist American life.[3] The problem with addiction, in Wallace's view, beyond its obvious hazards, is that it exacerbates the very conditions that it promises to alleviate, namely disaffection, solipsism, and emotional detachment. As a preferable answer to widespread cravings for "actual experience," Wallace proposes the less alluring but ultimately more sustaining forms of empathy, conviction, and emotional solidarity exemplified by Alcoholics Anonymous. Recognizing that many of his readers will likely view this organization's practices and values as unappealingly trite and old-fashioned, Wallace produces a compulsive reading experience designed to simulate the trajectory of addiction in order to overwhelm and oversaturate his readers' desires, exhaust their internal mechanisms of defensive sophistication, and thus prepare them to confront AA as a salutary model for an alternative paradigm refreshingly at odds with their cynical impulses. Like regionalist fiction, *Infinite Jest* responds to feelings of loneliness and isolation produced by a disconnected and privatized American society. But instead of the fantasies of small-town togetherness promoted by Wells, Wallace suggests that pathological identity categories, such as addict, might serve as a foundation for intimacy among strangers. Wallace, of course, is writing for a different kind of audience, a more self-consciously intellectual readership unlikely to entertain fantasies of living in a quaint small town filled with local eccentrics. The therapeutic orientation, however, is even more pronounced in Wallace's highbrow fiction than it is in Wells's regionalist novel. Eschewing the notion that a shared sense of place, whether real or imagined, is necessary to solidify communities, Wallace offers an even more interiorized or psychological mode of affiliation, proposing that his cynical, self-absorbed readers learn to empathize with each other on the basis of their own shared narcissism.

Middle-Class Apathy

Although he frequently claims to be identifying a disorder that transects the entire U.S. population under late-capitalism, Wallace is especially astute in his exploration of the ambivalent relationship between addiction and well-educated, middle-class professionals, that is, his readership. Asked in an interview with Larry McCaffery to characterize his audience, Wallace responded: "I suppose it's people more or less like me, in their twenties and thirties, maybe, with enough experience or good education to have realized that the hard work serious fiction requires of a reader sometimes has a payoff. People who've been raised with U.S. commercial culture and are engaged with it and informed by it and fascinated with it but still hungry for something commercial art can't provide. Yuppies, I guess, and younger intellectuals, whatever" (128). As Wallace acknowledges, his novel is designed for the well-educated or the serious autodidact. Set in an ominously preapocalyptic near-future setting, centered around a drug recovery house and a high school tennis academy, containing a massive cast of characters whose narratives are intertwined in bewildering ways, *Infinite Jest* serves out a barrage of experiments: shifts in time and perspective; multiple jargons; metafictional games; circuitous, logically complex, page-long sentences; and tiny-font endnotes. And the novel suggests that those to whom these strategies appeal are also precisely the ones likely to suffer from the problem that it explores: a combination of emotional detachment and cerebral sophistication — a detachment that, in turn, produces cravings for the intense sensations that substance abuse seems to offer.

Infinite Jest depicts case after case of highly educated, middle-class, typically male characters who are incapable of expressing, accessing, or sustaining modes of affect, including love, sorrow, and joy. Among his examples are Erdedy, the yuppie marijuana addict, who refuses to hug fellow members at a Narcotics Anonymous meeting until an intimidating biker threatens him with physical violence; Geoffrey Day, the junior college professor of "historicity," who relentlessly and comically deconstructs AA's system so as to avoid acknowledging his need for help (272); Hal Incandenza, the precocious, alarmingly well-read tennis star, who satisfies his grief therapist after his father's death by robotically performing the stages of mourning, which he has studied in a textbook; his brother, Orin, who seduces countless women through clever and seductive pretenses of sincerity but departs from each encounter unsatiated; and their father, James, a genius in optics, who makes avant-garde pastiche films largely devoid of any invitation to empathize with the characters that he portrays.

Wallace offers his most comprehensive critique of what he sees as a prevailing reflexive attitude in the United States in his description of Hal:

> Hal, who's empty but not dumb, theorizes privately that what passes for hip cynical transcendence of sentiment is really some kind of fear of being really human, since to be really human (at least as he conceptualizes it) is probably to be unavoidably sentimental and naïve and goo-prone and generally pathetic, is to be in some basic interior way forever infantile, some sort of not-quite-right-looking infant dragging itself anaclitically around the map, with big wet eyes and froggy-soft skin, huge skull, gooey drool. One of the really American things about Hal, probably, is the way he despises what it is he's really lonely for: this hideous internal self, incontinent of sentiment and need, that pulses and writhes just under the hip empty mask, anhedonia. (694–95)

Although the aversion Wallace describes is almost too visceral to bear analysis, strong emotions, in his view, have become indicators of weakness and dependence; hence Americans hide them by means of an ironic, nonchalant posture. Whether or not, in the face of such self-regulation, these emotions persist in subterranean, unacknowledged form remains ambiguous. Wallace seems to corroborate the therapeutic notion, which I explored in the introduction, of the hidden, emotionally damaged inner child.[4] He claims, however, that Hal is "lonely" for this creature, as if he entirely lacks and thus yearns for the inner child that he claims to despise. Hal abstractly posits a need to restrain emotions too unruly to be granted outward expression as the origin of his overriding apathy, but the passage also suggests that this theory is in fact motivated by the urge to avoid acknowledging a more disturbing possibility: his own inner emptiness. The notion of a hidden, unacknowledged inner child in need of constant discipline allows him to lay claim to the status of the human in the face, indeed on the basis, of evidence pointing to his inhumanity, that is, his affectless demeanor. But even if this self-description, which Hal seems to find both embarrassing and valorizing, is merely a fiction, his "loneliness" at least recuperates some purchase on the sentiment that he sees as a condition for personhood. Thus Hal exemplifies the peculiar melodrama of banality that has served as the American middle class's ironic lament in the postwar period.

To be sure, Wallace is not suggesting that banality and boredom represent the only problems middle-class Americans confront. Nor is he dismissing the therapeutic concept of the wounded inner child as merely a self-gratifying fantasy. Although in one ludicrous scene depicting a "men's issues-Men's-Movement type Meeting" (804), which involves "projectile weeping" (806), he satirizes the excesses of self-pity that this concept is capable of promoting, throughout much of *Infinite Jest* he depicts legitimate and severe pathologies suffered by members of the middle class, typically tracing them back to unhealthy childhoods. Physically disabled and genetically deformed infants are ubiquitous in the novel, symbolizing the psychic handicaps that adults carry with them as a consequence of traumatic experiences in their youth.[5] Focusing therapeutically upon forms of domestic abuse, neglect, and dysfunction, Wallace underscores problems that afflict individuals across class and racial boundaries, thus furthering a desire, which he voices in multiple essays and interviews, to portray universal forms of suffering. What he depicts as especially characteristic of middle-class, well-educated Americans, however, is their strategy for dealing with their pain: methods of emotional repression, denial, and self-regulation so effective as to foreclose any awareness of the turbulence that "pulses and writhes just under the hip empty mask."

The attitude that Hal exemplifies is, Wallace notes, emphatically American. The United States, in his depiction, overstimulates its citizens with commodities, shallow forms of entertainment, and manipulative marketing mechanisms, resulting in widespread desensitization and boredom. The most obvious sign that consumer capitalism has colonized new areas of experience in Wallace's dystopian depiction of the early twenty-first century is the sale of the calendar to corporations, so that years are designated as "Year of the Whopper," "Year of the Tucks Medicated Pad," "Year of the Perdue Wonderchicken," and "Year of the Whisper-Quiet Maytag

Dishmaster" (223). The president Johnny Gentle is a former "lounge singer turned teenybopper throb turned B-movie mainstay" (381). Television has been replaced by an endless variety of cartridges all connected to people's individual entertainment units. The United States has entered a union with its northern and southern neighbors called, in a ludicrous pun, O.N.A.N. The cultural landscape depicted in *Infinite Jest*, a grotesque satire of the United States at the end of the twentieth century, fosters a default attitude of blasé irony. Although this affective pose is especially pronounced among the privileged and the educated in the novel, Wallace represents it as a more pervasive condition, suggesting that the relentless deployment of kitsch, pastiche, and self-parody within popular culture has served to democratize this mode of automatic irony, teaching it to generations of Americans, especially to the young and the impressionable.[6]

Alienated from their own lives by their habits of compulsive, ironic self-consciousness, the characters in *Infinite Jest* seek intense sensations in athletic competition, in drug use, and in excessively violent movies, all in hopes of slashing through the layers of numbness that envelop them, thus furthering both their desensitization and their insatiable quest for novel thrills. Substance abuse in particular represents both a revolt against and an extension of the narcissism and banality that, in Wallace's view, pattern the lives of affluent Americans — as one character's memorable, if dreary, predicament exemplifies. Erdedy, a white-collar ad executive, indulges in regular marijuana binges, during which he calls in sick, closes his blinds, refuses to answer the phone, turns on his entertainment unit, masturbates frequently, and eats huge amounts of junk food. Drug use, in Erdedy's case, represents a combination of monotonous routine and yuppie self-gratification.

At one point, Erdedy decides to overindulge in marijuana systematically, as a means of destroying his desire for it.

> This last time, he would smoke the whole 200 grams — 120 grams
> cleaned, de-stemmed — in four days, over an ounce a day, all in tight
> heavy economical one-hitters off a quality virgin bong, an incredible,
> insane amount per day, he'd make it a mission, treating it like a pen-
> ance and behavior modification regimen all at once, he'd smoke his

way through thirty high-grade grams a day. . . . He would smoke it all
even if he didn't want it. Even if it started to make him dizzy and ill.
He would use discipline and persistence and will and make the whole
experience so unpleasant, so debased and debauched and unpleasant, that his behavior would be henceforward modified, he'd never
even want to do it again because the memory of the insane four days
to come would be so firmly, terribly emblazoned in his memory. He'd
cure himself by excess. (22)

The injection of a Protestant ethic into his experience of hedonistic indulgence is a dubious proposition, primarily because it is clear that even this
planned further excess is itself a repetition of a past effort. Attempting to
wrench himself free of his pattern of excessive indulgence by indulging
even more excessively, Erdedy only perpetuates the pattern, and motivates
further efforts at extravagant escape. He is addicted to trying to break his
addiction.

Considering his negotiation with his marijuana source, Erdedy reflects:

This arrangement, very casual, made him anxious, so he'd been even
more casual and said sure, fine, whatever. Thinking back, he was
sure he'd said *whatever*, which in retrospect worried him because it
might have sounded as if he didn't care at all, not at all, so little that
it wouldn't matter if she forgot to get it or call, and once he'd made
the decision to have marijuana in his home one more time it mattered a lot. It mattered a lot. He'd been too casual with the woman, he
should have made her take $1250 from him up front, claiming polite-
ness, claiming he didn't want to inconvenience her financially over
something so trivial and casual. . . . Once he'd been set off inside, it
mattered so much that he was somehow afraid to show how much it
mattered. (19)

Erdedy's casual attitude is a means both of concealing and satisfying a
desperate need. But the tone of the passage is comically flat, ruefully cynical, as if mocking the repeated, slightly defensive claim that his decision
to engage in yet another binge "matter[s] a lot." Whether he is truly in the
midst of a crisis or only fabricating one, whether this scene depicts a casual

problem masquerading as an urgent one or the other way around remains unresolved. At one point during this scene, Erdedy cries for a moment, then stops, and cannot make himself cry any longer. His crisis in fact consists of his inability to determine whether his predicament is a crisis — an inability that the narrative reproduces in its adoption of an equivocally deadpan style designed to capture the pathetic anti-pathos that Erdedy epitomizes and that Wallace sees as the condition of the consumer in late-capitalist America.

Wallace's various articulations of his dissatisfaction with contemporary cultural trends identify a loose, amorphous family of traits and affectations, including irony, world-weariness, nihilism, emotional detachment, self-referentiality, and sadism, which he believes are pervasive, and which certainly pervade his own fiction.[7] In "E Unibus Pluram," he imagines what form an artistic revolt against these tendencies would need to assume: "The next real literary 'rebels' in this country might well emerge as some weird bunch of *anti*-rebels, born oglers who dare somehow to back away from ironic watching, who have the childish gall actually to endorse and instantiate single-entendre principles. Who treat of plain old untrendy human troubles and emotions in U.S. life with reverence and conviction. Who eschew self-consciousness and hip fatigue" (81).

His surmises echo several observations within *Infinite Jest*. One character, Mario, becomes attached to a radio show, because it offers the only earnest voice he can find within a culture of irony and detachment: "Mario'd fallen in love with the first Madame Psychosis programs because he felt like he was listening to someone sad read out loud from yellow letters she'd taken out of a shoebox on a rainy P.M., stuff about heartbreak and people you loved dying and U.S. woe, stuff that was real. It is increasingly hard to find valid art that is about stuff that is real in this way" (592).

The author behind the Madame Psychosis programs, a film student named Joelle van Dyne, appears to share Mario's sensibility. Considering an experimental film, *Pre-Nuptial Agreement of Heaven and Hell*, she decides it is "mordant, sophisticated, campy, hip, cynical, technically mindbending; but cold, amateurish, hidden: no risk of empathy with the Job-like protagonist, whom she felt like the audience was induced to regard like somebody sitting atop a dunk-tank" (740). While this characterization could well describe sections of *Infinite Jest*, Wallace clearly aspires to produce a different kind of art.[8] Explaining in a *Salon* interview with Laura Miller what good fiction, as opposed to excessively avant-garde or commercial work, can accomplish, Wallace remarks, "There's a kind of Ah-ha! Somebody at least for a moment feels about something or sees something the way that I do. It doesn't happen all the time. It's these brief flashes or flames, but I get that sometimes. I feel unalone — intellectually, emotionally, spiritually." The "ah-ha moment," of course, is the term that Oprah Winfrey frequently uses to describe her interpretive epiphanies. And Wallace's claim that reading fiction is a means of mitigating loneliness seems to align his priorities, if not his textual strategies, with those that characterize the therapeutic, middlebrow culture that Winfrey celebrates.

Alcoholics Anonymous

As a model for the aesthetic, affective, and interpretive practices that he would like to promote, Wallace offers a meticulous and exhaustive account of Alcoholics Anonymous, an organization whose emphasis on simplicity, empathy, and faith is likely, he admits in the 1996 *Salon* interview with Laura Miller, to repel many of his readers. "I get the feeling that a lot of us, privileged Americans, as we enter our early thirties, have to find a way to put away childish things and confront stuff about spirituality and values. Probably the AA model isn't the only way to do it, but it seems to me to be one of the most vigorous." AA offers members a tight-knit community of fellow addicts, an opportunity to exchange heart-wrenching stories about their experiences with substances, and a series of simple steps and clichés to help keep them sober.[9] AA functions as an antidote, in the novel, not only to addiction, but also to a more general set of tendencies, in many cases concomitant with addiction, that prevail among the privileged in the United States. The group's rejection of "analysis-paralysis" for instance asserts the limitations of the intellect. Habitual self-analysis is dangerous, according to AA, in part because its members are so skilled at rationalizing their destructive behavior.[10] The problem most addicts have, according to Wallace, is not that they fail to think enough, but that they think too much, about their problem. He remarks: "Most Substance-addicted people are also addicted to thinking, meaning they have a compulsive and unhealthy relationship with their own thinking" (203). Recursive thought patterns are particularly dangerous insofar as they enable addicts to reconsider and disavow their own previous conclusions and decisions, so that their commitments (to get sober, accept responsibility, keep their promises) remain perpetually subject to reinterpretation, and thus perpetually in flux. The experience of the addict, as it is represented by AA, is almost always a downward, self-destructive spiral, a harrowing dialectic of decisions negated by rationalized failures of will, leading to further rationalizations and further decisions — each moment of resolution undermined by the subsequent moment *until* the moment in which the alcoholic joins AA. The organization replaces the protean, ceaselessly self-subverting and self-destructive logic of addiction with a series of clear rules, simple clichés, and straightforward narratives, all with the same rigid moral: total abstinence from substance abuse is the only safe path for the recovering addict.

A corollary to AA's rejection of excessive rational analysis is its belief in the importance of unmasked sentiment. Describing an AA meeting, Wallace observes "Everybody in the audience is aiming for total empathy with the speaker; that way they'll be able to receive the AA message he's here to carry. Empathy, in Boston AA, is called Identification. . . . Identifying, unless you've got a stake in Comparing, isn't very hard to do, here" (345). The world outside of AA, in his depiction, is dominated by a fiercely competitive capitalist paradigm, and by various class, race, and gender boundaries, which disable potential forms of emotional solidarity. Thus, he values AA because it promotes empathy across identity categories and offers a refuge of shared sentiment within a divided, fragmented society. Though professedly apolitical, AA operates according to a vehemently anticapitalist economy; the ordinary rules of exchange are suspended. Wallace observes, "Sobriety in Boston is regarded as less a gift than a sort of cosmic loan. You can't pay the loan back, but you can pay it *forward*, by spreading the message that despite all appearances AA works, spreading this message to the next guy who's tottered in to a meeting" (344). AA does not rely upon the spontaneous, altruistic impulses of its members to promote its non-competitive forms of exchange. Its philosophy is that the best method for remaining sober is to help someone else get sober. Each act of assistance, each gift, distributes its energy backward and forward so that it is impossible to distinguish giver from receiver. AA thus instantiates a pragmatic utopianism whereby every act spreads its value in all directions, and self-interest and generosity become symbiotic partners.

In its commitment to fixed principles, unquestioned pieties, and unmediated empathy, AA, Wallace argues, rejects irony. "The thing is it has to be the truth to really go over, here [in AA]. It can't be a calculated crowd-pleaser, and it has to be the truth unslanted, unfortified. And maximally unironic. An ironist in a Boston AA meeting is a witch in a church. Irony-free zone. Same with sly disingenuous manipulative pseudo-sincerity. Sincerity with an ulterior motive is something these tough ravaged people know and fear, all of them trained to remember the coyly sincere, ironic, self-presenting fortifications they'd had to construct in order to carry on Out There, under the ceaseless neon bottle" (369). Irony is a "fortification"—a mask on the self, a winking sheen on one's language disavowing the truth it would otherwise declare. Drugs too are a fortification, a shield; they offer a basis for disclaiming responsibility for one's behavior. Both drugs and irony, in Wallace's depiction, are artificial supplements that negate the ability to be what Hal terms "really human," injected into one's body or one's words, producing self-division and self-deception, subverting the unity and presence of self upon which sincerity and identification are predicated.

A commonly voiced concern about AA is that it promotes empathy by brainwashing its members. But its apparent disciplinary power, according to Wallace, is merely a reflection or transposition of the extreme threat that lurks outside its borders.

Boston AA's Sergeant at Arms stood *outside* the orderly meeting halls, in that much-invoked Out There where exciting clubs full of good cheer throbbed gaily below lit signs with neon bottles endlessly pouring. AA's patient enforcer was always and everywhere Out There: it stood casually checking its cuticles in the astringent fluorescence of pharmacies that took forged Talwin scrips for a hefty surcharge, in the onionlight through paper shades in the furnished rooms of strung-out nurses who financed their own cages' maintenance with stolen pharmaceutical samples, in the isopropyl reek of the storefront offices of stooped old chain-smoking MD's whose scrip pads were always out and who needed only to hear "pain" and see cash. (359)

The organization could easily fall prey to skepticism, but skepticism — toward relationships, stable principles, and commitments — is often, it holds, what exacerbates, if not causes, addiction. AA offers a series of bromides and rituals as an antidote to the extravagant self-conscious, self-doubting, ironic processes undergirding addiction. Members adopt AA's system not because it can withstand the assaults of their skeptical tendencies, but because they have been exhausted, almost destroyed, by their skeptical tendencies. They embrace the organization not based on their own intellectual criteria, but based on pragmatist criteria supplied by AA: because it seems to work better. Miserable, desperate, drained, they choose against all odds to put their faith in people they barely know and a set of beliefs they can barely swallow because doing so defies everything they have ever valued, and everything they have ever valued has consistently let them down.

Addiction Recovery

Alcoholics Anonymous encapsulates its philosophy with the prescription "Keep it simple," but this is advice that Wallace doggedly refuses to follow. Displays of cleverness, irony, sophistication, and self-referentiality crowd every page of the novel, often derailing the reader's capacity to identify emotionally with the characters, directing attention instead onto the novel's textual devices and experiments, encouraging just the kind of dispassionate, intellectual response that Wallace's unlikely embrace of AA is designed to critique. As critic A. O. Scott points out, Wallace appears to be no less addicted to the aesthetic habits that he claims to find tiresome than his characters are to various substances ("Panic").[11] The correspondence between Wallace and his editor Michael Pietsch confirms Scott's reading: not unlike a smoker or drinker who resorts to disposing of all tempting substances, Wallace describes his effort to accept a particular editorial change as follows: "p. 133 — Poor old FN33 about the grammar exam is cut. I'll also erase it from the back up disk so I can't come back in an hour and put it back in (an enduring hazard, I'm finding)" (Pietsch 26). In another letter Wallace remarks, "I just learned the word 'horology' and was determined to use it at least once," treating words like exotic drugs, which invite recreational experimentation.

Scott compares Wallace's efforts to break his writerly addictions to Erdedy's: "This nameless character's doomed, misguided, yet oddly convincing plan to rid himself of his marijuana habit bears an unmistakable resemblance to Wallace's own repeated attempts to cure himself of his interlocking addictions to irony, metafiction, and other cheap postmodern highs. If I blow my mind on self-consciousness this one last time, Wallace resolves over and over, I'll never go near it again. But he always comes back for more" ("Panic" 42). Wallace of course also aims to blow the reader's mind. If he is in fact addicted to "cheap postmodern highs," he uses these techniques in order to produce, as Frank Cioffi has argued, an addictive experience for his audience. In the near-future setting of the novel, Wallace imagines a video cartridge so fatally addictive that viewers can never tear themselves away from it; the title of this film, significantly, is *Infinite Jest*. Although it is necessary, if only because holding it aloft tires the muscles, to put Wallace's novel down, the title's joke suggests the compulsive effort that *Infinite Jest*, in its sheer length and density, demands. As Amazon customer reviews of the novel testify, the relationship between many readers and *Infinite Jest* is quite similar to the relationship between addicts and their substance; they adore it, they loathe it, they want to stop returning to it, they cannot stop, they cannot understand why they are incapable of stopping, and so forth.[12]

Wallace uses a conventional device to underscore the text's addictive quality; he jumps from one plot line to another, just before major developments occur, so that readers, hooked on several different narratives, are likely to feel at once divided and addicted as they push their way through the text. Moreover, *Infinite Jest* makes the unfolding of its own narrative itself a subject of reflection, as it foregrounds questions about its own persistence. The most obvious example of this strategy is the use of tiny-font endnotes, which interrupt the forward motion of the narrative with seemingly trivial technical data or qualifications, but then frequently disclose crucial information necessary to decipher the plot, at times usurping the role of the primary narrative. Wallace further conflates what is central and what is marginal by periodically introducing within the body of the text fairly extraneous information that would seem to deserve placement in an endnote. For instance, Wallace leaves a central character of the novel, Don Gately, lying on the ground with a gunshot wound he has received defending the Ennet Drug and Alcohol Recovery House against angry Canadian thugs, and shifts focus, offering an audaciously dry technical description of computer equipment: "Year of the Depend Adult Undergarment: Interlace TelEntertainment, 932/1864 R.I.S.C. power-TPs w/ or w/o console, Pink$_2$, post-Primestar D.S.S. dissemination, menus and icons, pixel-free InterNet Fax, tri- and quad-modems w/ adjustable baud, post-Web Dissemination-Grids, screens so high-def you might as well be there, cost-effective couture, all-in-one consoles, Yushityu ceramic nanoprocessors, laser chromatography, Virtual-capable media-cars, fiber-optic pulse, digital encoding, killer apps" (620). In the very moment Wallace taunts the reader's impatient need for further narrative development with a sudden freeze, he invokes the home entertainment unit, the primary agent of addiction in contemporary culture, thus suggesting a continuity between the consumption of mass-media entertainment and the reader's compulsive relationship to *Infinite Jest*. He then waits 190 pages before returning to Gately, alive but languishing in a hospital bed. Ultimately the book frustrates the reader's addictive need for narrative closure; hints of a collision between every major character in the book, whose outcome may determine the fate of the United States, draw the reader toward a climax that never materializes.

When he interrupts the progression of the narrative, rendering it all the more compelling, Wallace highlights the fact, noted by Peter Brooks, that plots are often propelled by efforts to suspend them, and he exposes a similar pattern in addiction. Erdedy, as we remember, is addicted to the very act of pretending/attempting to break his addiction. Present in almost every narrative of addiction are decisions to quit forever, decisions which typically lead to one last binge as a response to the daunting prospect of living sober. Hence the trajectory of addiction is generally sustained by repeated attempts to interrupt its progression. Such efforts at intervention tend to produce an obsessive, self-conscious meditation upon the very course of the addiction, which only exacerbates the problem, leading to further abuse and further reflection. Addiction and metafiction, then, turn out, as Scott notes, to be peculiarly resonant. Readers of *Infinite Jest* are made to confront not only their own addiction to plot, but also the plotted nature of addiction; mutually clarifying continuities emerge between the structure of the reader's experience and the structure of the addict's. By frustrating readerly expectations, by making readers both follow the plot of the novel compulsively and register constantly their own compulsion to follow the plot, Wallace produces an experience that mimics the hyper-self-conscious character of addiction.[13]

Wallace's motive in designing a text that functions as a virtual-addiction apparatus, in my view, is to bring readers into a state of dazzled intellectual fatigue, a state which might prepare them to embrace the salutary simplicity offered by Alcoholics Anonymous. Addicts, according to AA, initially exhilarated by their experiments with substances, slowly destroy everything that matters to them until they "hit bottom" and, in a state of extreme desperation, embrace the organization's seemingly mindless and hackneyed precepts as a last resort method for saving themselves. *Infinite Jest* initiates an analogous process. In order to make readers hit bottom in an intellectual sense, the novel overwhelms them with irony, with dialectical modes of logic, with deconstructive games, with metafictional devices in a seemingly endless process that will, like addiction itself, potentially exhaust them, make them weary of sophistication and ready perhaps to consider adopting the alternative values celebrated by AA. Wallace's assumption is, of course, that AA's emphasis on simplicity and sentiment can become viable for his audience only when it is attached to abundant proofs of intellectual prowess. The complexity of his novel, then, is a necessary element of the heuristic experience I am describing, in order to draw skeptical readers in, to challenge and tire their critical capacities, to push them eventually to accept, as a refreshing departure, a perspective whose banality and simplicity is legitimized only by the arduous intellectual process, the journey through difficulty, required to reach that point. Wallace's strategy is almost exactly the inverse of Toni Morrison's. If Morrison, in other words, slyly employs conventional middlebrow tropes in order to enlist her insecure readers in an engagement with highbrow interpretive difficulties, then Wallace employs highbrow techniques in order to persuade his intellectual readers to try out middlebrow responses. One might call the lesson of his text reverse self-improvement.

Of course those whom Wallace successfully persuades to restrain their skeptical, ironic impulses and take AA's practices seriously will find within the pages of *Infinite Jest* no oasis of uncomplicated sentiment shielded from Wallace's own critical, subversive maneuvers. While the novel, for the most part, reads as an apology for AA, Wallace also subjects the organization to the full interrogative force of his formidable intellectual powers, comically exposing many of its contradictions and shortcomings. If AA strives to foster earnest exchanges, unguarded expressions of feeling, and noninvidious forms of communal identification, its meetings, he observes, are fraught with various modes of artifice, posturing, and self-consciousness. He describes members' "saccharin grins" (350) and the "polyesterishly banal" insights AA helps people to achieve (358). Moreover, new members learn to "Fake It Till You Make It" (369), to repeat clichés they do not believe, to go through the motions of prayer, and to affect devotion to AA's tenets until they actually feel devotion, all of which seem to be institutionalized forms of insincerity. Uttering a slogan whose truth you are not prepared to affirm, after all, would seem to be an exemplary instance of irony.

Wallace signals his ambivalent resistance to AA's program most pointedly in his representation of the stories told by recovering addicts at meetings. These more than any other section of the novel promise to elicit the kind of powerful, empathetic response whose devaluation in contemporary culture Wallace laments. But in almost every instance he compulsively subverts the pathos that these stories might otherwise generate with grotesquely satirical gestures that overtly bear the disruptive mark of the clown — Wallace's own unmistakable fingerprint.[14] One member's narrative about her sexually abusive father turns laughably absurd when she describes his fantasy that her paralyzed, catatonic sister was in fact Raquel Welch. Her father, she recounts, tended to cry out "RAQUEL!" in the middle of his molestations, and eventually found a polyester mask of Raquel Welch to place on her head during his nocturnal visits (370–74). Another member finishes his narrative with a vivid description of the first solid bowel movement he was able to achieve after becoming sober: "The man's red-leather face radiant throughout. Gately and the other White Flaggers fall about, laugh from the gut, a turd that practically had a pulse, an ode to a solid dump; but the lightless eyes of certain palsied back-row newcomers widen with a very private Identification and possible hope, hardly daring to imagine. . . . A certain Message has been Carried" (352).

One could argue of course that such instances serve to fuse Wallace's irony and AA's earnestness so that the pathos becomes a source of comedy, and the comedy a source of pathos — an interpretation that another scene explicitly encourages:

> The next Advanced Basics guy summoned by their gleamingly bald western-wear chairman to speak is dreadfully, transparently unfunny, painfully new but pretending to be at ease, to be an old hand, desperate to amuse and impress them. The guy's got the sort of professional background where he's used to trying to impress gatherings of persons. He's dying to be liked up there. He's performing. The White Flag crowd can see all this. Even the true morons among them see right through this guy. This is not a regular audience. A Boston AA is very sensitive to the presence of ego. When the new guy introduces himself and makes an ironic gesture and says, "I'm told I've been given the Gift of Desperation. I'm looking for the exchange window," it's so clearly unspontaneous, rehearsed — plus commits the subtle but cardinal Message-offense of appearing to deprecate the Program rather than the Self — that just a few polite titters resound, and people shift in their seats with a slight but signal discomfort. (367)

With his self-consciousness, his nervous wit, and his desire to present himself as down-to-earth and likeable, the speaker enacts a sad caricature of Wallace's own writerly tendencies. The speaker introduces certain qualities that violate AA's tacit code, and everyone in the crowd is embarrassed for him, but ironically enough his approach provokes precisely the catharsis AA aims to facilitate. Falsely affecting self-assuredness, the speaker exposes his painful vulnerability, eliciting mass empathy, and "the applause when this guy's done has the relieved feel of a fist unclenching, and their cries of 'Keep Coming!' are so sincere it's almost painful" (368). Remarkably, then, it is the character's excessive self-consciousness that actually promotes empathy. Described with slightly too much mockery to be purely self-congratulatory, this incongruous moment nonetheless represents Wallace's effort to recuperate some of his own propensities, to imagine a zone of reconciliation between AA's insistence on sincerity, empathy, and simplicity and his text's attachment to irony, intellect, and recursivity.

The Author-Protagonist

If the sadly ironic AA member reads as an authorial projection, this is in part a product of Wallace's ubiquitous, cagey presence within the text as a domineering, self-referential narrative consciousness. His tone, characterized by a rueful, dauntingly allusive wit that seems abashed by its own cleverness, permeates the novel's atmosphere rather like an intrusive soundtrack in a movie. Moreover his voice — the combination of overwrought, desultory syntax, obscure, researched diction, and fidgety, compulsive slang — announces itself on every page and intrudes constantly into Wallace's attempts to render the thoughts of his characters, producing insights and observations so inseparable from the style in which they achieve articulation that they always seem far more congruent with the mind of the unidentified narrator than with that of the characters. In some moments, in order to avoid confusion, Wallace is forced to inform the reader that he is introducing free indirect discourse, rendering the character's, rather than the narrator's, perspective:

> Katherine Ann Gompert probably felt that here was yet another psychward M.D. with zero sense of humor. This was probably because she did not understand the strict methodological limits that dictated how literal he, a doctor, had to be with admits on the psych ward. Nor that jokes and sarcasm were here usually too pregnant and fertile with clinical significance not to be taken seriously: sarcasm and jokes were often the bottle in which clinical depressives sent out their most plangent screams for someone to care and help them. The doctor — who by the way wasn't an M.D. yet but a resident, here on a twelve-week psych rotation — indulged in this clinical reverie while the patient made an elaborate show of getting the thin pillow out from under her and leaning it up the tall way against the bare wall behind the bed and slumping back against it, her arms crossed over her breasts. (71)

At another point Wallace apologizes for not remaining within the mind of his character: "This should not be rendered in exposition like this, but Mario Incandenza has a severely limited range of verbatim recall" (82).

Even more self-consciously, Wallace describes the working-class Gately's consciousness as invaded by a foreign, hyperliterate diction that is clearly the narrator's own: "Other terms and words Gately knows he doesn't know from a divot in the sod now come crashing through his head with the same ghastly intrusive force, e.g., ACCIACCATURA and ALEMBIC, LATRO-DECTRUS MACTANS and NEUTRAL DENSITY POINT, CHIARO-SCURO and PROPRIOCEPTION and TESTUDO and ANNULATE and BRICOLAGE and CATALEPT and GERRYMANDER and SCO-POPHILIA and LAERTES" (832). In this passage, Wallace acknowledges what has been glaringly obvious throughout the novel: that the narrator's voice has come to haunt the minds of the characters, usurping their status as the primary actors in the drama, and outshining their particularity with his own irrepressible, self-congratulatory brilliance.[15] Indeed, in some endnotes Wallace admits that the words he has attributed to certain characters are not in fact theirs: "The speaker doesn't actually use the terms *thereon, most assuredly,* or *operant limbic system,* though she really had, before, said *chordate phylum*" (Endnote 142, 1026). In general the endnotes, which frequently gloss, qualify, or extend various observations made by the characters, but never in a manner that is neutral or fully omniscient, suggest a dauntingly well-informed yet insecure narrator who is desperate for attention and not content to allow the action to move forward or the characters to assume center stage without calling attention to his own governing intelligence. If *Infinite Jest* at times disrupts the reader's ability to empathize with the plight of the characters, this is because there is truly only one character in the novel, and it is the narrator.

What to name this narrator? The temptation of course is to call him David Foster Wallace, to imagine that the author is narcissistically drawing attention away from his characters and to himself. Several comments made by Wallace in fact explicitly encourage this reading. In his cleverly titled "Greatly Exaggerated," a review of H. L. Hix's *Morte d'Author,* an academic work on the "death of the author," Wallace remarks: "It's finally hard for me to predict just whom, besides professional critics and hardcore theory-wienies, 226 dense pages on whether the author lives is really going to interest. For those of us civilians who know in our gut that writing is an act of communication between one human being and another, the whole question seems sort of arcane" (144).

In the *Salon* interview, Wallace asserts a similar position, one that de-emphasizes the importance of identifying with fictional characters in favor of connecting with the actual writer: "I don't know what you're thinking or what it's like inside you and you don't know what it's like inside me. In fiction I think we can leap over that wall itself in a certain way. But that's just the first level, because the idea of mental or emotional intimacy with a character is a delusion or contrivance that's set up through art by the writer. There's another level that a piece of fiction is a conversation. There's a relationship set up between the reader and the writer that's very strange and complicated and hard to talk about" (L. Miller, *Salon* 9 March 1998). Intimacy with a fictional character is, Wallace rightly asserts, a "delusion or contrivance," but he seems to believe that the relationship between reader and writer ("between one human being and another") is, though "very strange and complicated," superior to the former and less unreal. Wallace rejects the deconstructionist argument that the author is, no less than the depicted characters, a fictional creature, a fantastical projection of the reader, but his position is difficult either to challenge or to defend insofar as he deliberately avoids articulating it in the sort of logical or theoretical terms that would merit critical engagement, instead deferring to the authority of his "gut."[16] His statements do, however, help to illuminate the basis for his self-referential aesthetic strategies.

In a footnote to his 1999 short story "Octet," Wallace tortuously explores the rationale for metafiction in explaining why he has chosen to present the narrative in the form of pop quizzes addressed to the reader:

> Though it all gets a little complicated, because part of what you want these little Pop Quizzes to do is to break the textual fourth wall and kind of address (or "interrogate") the reader directly, which desire is somehow related to the old "meta"-device desire to puncture some sort of fourth wall of realist pretense, although it seems like the latter is less a puncturing of any sort of real wall and more a puncturing of the

veil of impersonality or effacement around the writer himself, i.e. with the now-tired S.O.P. "meta"-stuff it's more the dramatist himself coming onstage from the wings and reminding you that what's going on is artificial and that the artificer is him (the dramatist) and but that he's at least respectful enough of you as reader/audience to be honest about the fact that he's back there pulling the strings, an "honesty" which personally you've always had the feeling is actually a highly rhetorical sham-honesty that's designed to get you to like him and approve of him (i.e., of the "meta"-type writer) and feel flattered that he apparently thinks you're enough of a grownup to handle being reminded that what you're in the middle of is artificial (like you didn't know that already, like you needed to be reminded of it over and over again as if you were a myopic child who couldn't see what was right in front of you), which more than anything seems to resemble the type of real-world person who tries to manipulate you into liking him by making a big deal of how open and honest and unmanipulative he's being all the time, a type who's even more irritating than the sort of person who tries to manipulate you by just flat-out lying to you, since at least the latter isn't constantly congratulating himself for not doing precisely what the self-congratulation itself ends up doing, viz. not interrogating you or have any sort of interchange or even really *talking* to you but rather just *performing* in some highly self-conscious and manipulative way. (124–25)

The complexities that Wallace underscores here are myriad. According to the narrator of this footnote, whose degree of identification with Wallace is among the issues implicitly raised, metafictional devices are designed not only to remind the reader of the author's role as the contriver behind the artifice, but also to establish the author, in his willingness to acknowledge the fictional status of his narrative, as truthful and trustworthy. The author, in other words, seeks to assert both his own ontologically privileged status as a real human being and his integrity as an honest speaker by placing himself in explicit contrast to the purportedly unreal, unreliable world that he is describing, a world whose artificial character he has obligingly affirmed. The position elaborated here, of course, is considerably more nuanced than Wallace's simple characterization of fiction as an act of communication between two human beings. The author, he acknowledges, merely "resembles" a "real-world person." And, assuming the judgment of this nameless "you" is correct, these metafictional devices fail to achieve their end: the author's supposed honesty, indeed his very presence within the text, will strike the intelligent reader as a performance, no more real, no less fabricated than the fiction that the author is staging, but thereby all the more dangerous and repellent insofar as it denies its status as such.[17] The assertion that realist fiction dupes its readers turns out to be itself a deception intended to buttress the dubious claims to comparably greater sincerity and veracity made by the metafictional author.

The telling premise underlying the positions of both the metafictional author and his debunker is that the categories "honest," "artificial," and "manipulative" can be employed to judge an author based on that author's fictional work in the same way that they are employed to judge an individual based on her or his words and actions — as if the text is the emanation or expression of a personality. This claim of course poses a challenge both to deconstructionist arguments about the death of the author and to the modernist principle forwarded most famously by T. S. Eliot that the author should strive for impersonality. Whether or not the author that readers imagine bears any resemblance to the actual biographical individual responsible for producing the text, the act of reading, in Wallace's conception, is most intellectually and emotionally rewarding when it posits and seeks intimacy with the implied creator. The footnote in "Octet" questions the illusion the author rhetorically perpetrates of his own honest self-revelation by comparing his tactics to those of a "real-world person," a self-conscious manipulator who is starved for approval. Ironically, then, even as he denies the conceit of the text as a means of sympathetic access between author and reader, Wallace's skeptical challenge to the pretenses of the author serves to humanize this figure, asking readers to approach him the way they would another person, positing as a motivation for his self-congratulatory metafictional devices a desire to be liked and trusted that some may treat as a sign of vulnerability familiar enough to merit identification.

The latter, barely hinted interpretation, of course, will likely register, if it does at all, as a cerebral realization. Whether his self-referential devices appear honest or manipulative, they manifestly lack the capacity to inspire the kind of strong emotional responses that Wallace, in moments, evinces a muted yearning to produce.[18] And this in fact may provide the key to understanding his strangely reductive, ostensibly disingenuous claim about *Infinite Jest*, that he "wanted to do something sad" (L. Miller, *Salon* 9 March 1996). The perverse invisible pathos of the novel resides in the gestures that aim, by calling attention to themselves, to arouse the reader's sympathy, but inevitably produce, as the narrator of "Octet" fears, the reverse effect: distrust, irritation, and resistance. The more nakedly human Wallace tries to appear, the more he comes across as artificial. The sadness of *Infinite Jest* consists of its incapacity to express or evoke sadness. This incapacity operates through a compulsive self-undermining, self-reconstituting pattern: Wallace's persona intrudes, thus disrupting the empathy that the illusion of a direct connection with his characters might allow, in order to solicit identification with himself as the author-protagonist; but this gesture, by foregrounding its own manipulative character, appears to disable the very possibility of identification that it is designed to produce, while simultaneously seeking to inspire sympathy on the basis of its own inevitable failure.

Wallace's status as a figure of fascination for his readers was in part the product of a publicity campaign inspired by the enticingly reclusive personalities of writers such as J. D. Salinger and Thomas Pynchon and carefully orchestrated by his publishing company Little, Brown. Step one was to spin *Infinite Jest*'s forbidding heft, which marketing executives decided to present as a sign of its monumental importance, an indication, as Frank Bruni observes, that its young author was the new "wunderkind," the "current 'it' boy of contemporary fiction." Prior to publication, Little, Brown sent out a series of enigmatic postcards to four thousand people in the book-selling industry and other media figures promising a novel that would offer "infinite pleasure" with "infinite style," thus jump-starting its hype while preserving its mystery — a dual gesture perfectly suited to the public persona that the company was about to unveil. More postcards followed offering blurbs from critics and authors. After much anticipatory fanfare, Little, Brown unleashed the star hidden at the center of all the buzz and behind the dazzling displays of wit and erudition on a ten-city book tour, the remarkably awkward and unassuming David Foster Wallace, an unlikely celebrity who repeatedly evinced discomfort about all the attention that he was receiving in interviews. As Bruni puts it, "And Wallace — wittingly or unwittingly — has served [the promotional campaign] well, projecting the perfect measure of aloofness, particularly in his appearance, which flouts conventional vanity in a manner that doth protest perhaps too much." The book jacket author photo reinforces this image; Wallace displays the long hair and bandana of a rock star, but his shy, slightly pained expression is turned away from the camera, as if he is too sensitive to handle the limelight. Indeed the subject of Frank Bruni's *New York Times Magazine* article, which helped to launch the David Foster Wallace mystique and thus supported the Little, Brown publicity campaign, was the author's misgivings about his own publicity.

The idea of a promotional campaign centered around the author's resistance to the promotional campaign reiterates the principle behind his metafictional tactics; these, as Wallace has suggested, can be read as a manipulative plea on the author's part for attention and approval. But the suggestion of an agonized dissatisfaction with these techniques, a suggestion inevitably registered by the techniques themselves, hints that underneath all the ploys, tricks, and gimmicks there is an authentic human being incapable of expressing his need for love and sympathy in any other way. Both the publicity stunts performed by Little, Brown to accompany the release of *Infinite Jest* and the textual experiments deployed by the novel turn the reader's attention to the vulnerable figure of David Foster Wallace, who seems tormented not only by these various artifices of self-promotion but also by the possibility that this purportedly private torment itself might serve as the central means of enhancing his popularity. Sadly, his suicide has served only to intensify the power of his mystique — a development Wallace would likely have greeted with characteristic uneasiness.

There is perhaps no better example of the mode of response that Wallace's fiction seeks to elicit among readers than *New York Times* film critic A. O. Scott's perceptive review ("Panic"). Like Wallace, a thirty-something, intellectual, white son of academics at the time he writes his essay, Scott may well represent Wallace's ideal reader. Throughout the review, Scott is well attuned to Wallace's equivocal desire to pay homage to "'old untrendy human troubles'" and "the virtues of 'reverence and conviction'" ("Panic"

40). More importantly, he seems to recognize that David Foster Wallace is the central character of his own fiction. Recall that Scott interprets Erdedy's predicament as an analogy for the author's, thus foregrounding Wallace's frustrations and struggles as the action most worth attending to. Moreover, though Scott concentrates on Wallace's efforts to manage the aesthetic problems that confront the contemporary experimental novelist, he articulates these efforts in primarily psychological terms — using the fiction to diagnose the dysfunctions of the author. Briefly acknowledging Harold Bloom, he describes Wallace's anxiety in the face of his postmodernist forefathers: "And Wallace has a bad case: anxiety may not be a strong enough word; panic is more like it" (39). The term "panic" accomplishes a picturesque intensification, evoking a condition that extends beyond the parameters of artistic production, inviting readers to imagine a pathological personality trait. His characterization of Wallace's "addiction" to "irony, metafiction, and other cheap postmodern highs" continues to conflate aesthetic and therapeutic dilemmas, treating the fiction as a symptom of the author's psychological problems. Moreover, Scott enacts his identification with Wallace, ventriloquizing his pain in the first person: "If I blow my mind on self-consciousness this one last time, Wallace resolves over and over, I'll never go near it again" (41). Of course Scott's voicing of this resolution is cleverly parodic and largely devoid of sympathy. But, given his characterization of Wallace's compulsively glib tone, Scott's employment of irony here actually demonstrates, uncannily and unwittingly, his identification with the author, even as his critical stance denies this identification and forestalls any betrayal of real feeling for Wallace's plight. This denial of feeling through irony is, according to Scott, precisely the condition that Wallace both describes and exemplifies: the sadness that emerges in the form of its own erasure.[19]

Metafictional Therapy

A question worth asking is whether Wallace's metafictional strategies serve either to support or to challenge the emotive, anti-ironic practices of Alcoholics Anonymous. The condition that the author-protagonist of *Infinite Jest* instantiates — narcissism, ironic nihilism, emotional repression — is pervasive, Wallace implies, among the category of Americans to whom his novel appeals: well-educated, young, self-conscious intellectuals like A. O. Scott. For these readers, the figure of David Foster Wallace becomes an object of identification, an identification in part based on his exemplary failure to evoke pathos. But of course the frustration that accompanies this failure suggests the existence of a vulnerable, painfully concealed interiority, an embarrassing private zone of repressed emotions, a stifled inner child, which registers only through skeptical mockery or winking disavowal. Thus Wallace does, in accord with his urge to promote the humanistic precepts of AA, inspire a kind of therapeutic identification, between reader and author-figure, but it is identification rooted in a shared, impregnable resistance to the unguarded displays of sentiment that AA facilitates and in the necessarily implicit, undisclosed sadness that accompanies this resistance.

"Fiction," Wallace emphatically argues in the *Review* interview with McCaffrey, is "about what it is to be a fucking *human* being" (131). Oddly, though, his work tends to focus on characters whose distance from their own emotions endangers their humanity. Thus, a moment later, he qualifies his initial claim: "If you operate, which most of us do, from the premise that there are things about the contemporary U.S. that make it distinctively hard to be a real human being, then maybe half of fiction's job is to dramatize what it is that makes it tough. The other half is to dramatize the fact that we still *are* human beings, now. Or can be" (131). Being human, for Wallace, is not easy. It is not a quality people automatically possess as a given birthright; it is a precarious state increasingly jeopardized by certain inhospitable conditions and dependent upon mechanisms of cultivation, support, and maintenance. AA teaches its members how to be human by fostering their capacity for empathy, identification, compassion, sincerity, and personal integrity. Toal's claim, based upon her reading of one small section of the novel, that Wallace celebrates a "shapeless" mode of "humanness" in opposition to all disciplinary mechanisms of subject formation, completely ignores Wallace's sympathetic portrayal of AA and the means by which the organization in fact produces and polices a specific kind of humanness (Toal 320). In valorizing AA, Wallace forwards a concept of the human that is normative rather than descriptive — an ideal he believes people need to strive to achieve, a learned state of being rather than an inherited essence. One of the central insights of *Infinite Jest* is that this striving actually defines humanity: there is nothing more human than striving, in the face of formidable obstacles, to be human. Thus Wallace suggests that a measure of dehumanization, at least in the contemporary United States, is in fact a constitutive condition of humanity.[20] And for readers alienated from their own emotions by means of reflexive irony, self-consciousness, and cynicism, Wallace offers the potentially rehumanizing experience of identifying with a figure ensnared in a similar predicament.

Brian McHale contends that a shift from epistemological to ontological concerns marks the transition from modernist to postmodernist fiction. Whereas modernist fiction by authors including Joyce, Conrad, Woolf, and Fitzgerald raises questions about how individuals can access, apprehend, and know the world that they inhabit, postmodernist fiction by authors including Robbe-Grillet, Pynchon, and Barthelme raises questions about what defines or constitutes a world, what properties characterize a fictional world, and what distinguishes the fictional world from the so-called real world. Modernist experiments, McHale observes, frequently underline the limits of any given character's perspective, thus attributing moments of strangeness, contradiction, or hyperbole to the delusions of the character's consciousness; postmodernist experiments, by contrast, attribute these same phenomena to the artificial or textually produced status of the world itself.[21] Wallace's account of postmodernist fiction resembles McHale's, but Wallace de-emphasizes its ontological, in favor of its therapeutic, agenda. He argues that postmodernist tactics are designed to call attention not merely to the fabricated status of the fictional world, but to the role of the fabricator, the self-conscious presence of the generating authorial consciousness, as way of allowing the reader to connect or identify with the author. While, for McHale, modernism testifies to the strangeness of the character's consciousness and postmodernism testifies to the strangeness of the fictional world, for Wallace the latter in fact testifies to the strangeness of the mind that has constructed the fictional world. Though unabashedly narcissistic, the metafictional device, he claims, is a simple plea for empathy.

McHale recognizes that postmodernist fiction inaugurates at least the illusion of the author's return: "It should be obvious by now why postmodernist texts have opened themselves once again to intrusions by the authorial persona. This ontologically amphibious figure, alternately present and absent, embodies the same action of ontological vacillation or 'flicker' that we have observed in other elements of postmodernist poetics. The author, in short, is another tool for the exploration and exploitation of ontology" (202). In McHale's view, such gestures are designed to support a more significant ontological agenda, one that is abstracted ultimately from the personality of the author-figure. Wallace's remarks and his textual strategies, I would argue, turn this formulation on its head, effecting a self-conscious shift of priorities, one that recasts the postmodernist genre, construing ontological games not as the ultimate end, but as a means of furthering a strange form of imagined intimacy between author and reader.[22] In McHale's examples, from writers including Katz, Sukenick, Borges, and Mailer, the author actually appears as a named character within the fiction, and thus seems to straddle the boundary between the real and the fictional world. In *Infinite Jest*, Wallace avoids that particular gimmick, and the author-character exists more as an overbearing narrative presence. Though self-referential, Wallace's persona does not assume the form of a tangible individual whose status as either real or fictional becomes the central object of speculation. As merely a voice, the author-protagonist in *Infinite Jest* identifies himself with the text itself and thereby evades questions about which world, real or fictional, he inhabits.

Wallace's postmodernist devices are designed to perform a function that, in his view, all serious fiction performs, one that Wayne Booth also identifies: to provide companionship to the reader. At times, Wallace's unfashionably earnest account of the tasks that fiction ought to accomplish seems to emulate AA's emphasis on simplicity and its phlegmatic insistence upon demystifying the individual's intellectual fortifications. In the *Review* interview, Wallace remarks:

> I guess a big part of serious fiction's purpose is to give the reader, who like all of us is sort of marooned in her own skull, to give her imaginative access to other selves. Since an ineluctable part of being a human self is suffering, part of what we humans come to art for is an experience of suffering, necessarily a vicarious experience, more like a sort of *generalization* of suffering. Does this make sense? We all suffer alone

in the real world; true empathy's impossible. But if a piece of fiction can allow us imaginatively to identify with characters' pain, we might then also more easily conceive of others identifying with our own. This is nourishing, redemptive; we become less alone inside. It might just be that simple. (McCaffery 127)

Infinite Jest is aligned with the therapeutic paradigm, then, both in its pragmatic aspiration to alleviate the reader's loneliness and in Wallace's effort to humanize or anthropomorphize his text's rhetorical strategies — an effort predicated upon the presumption of the psychological as a space of depth and fascination that can rival the aesthetic or the philosophical. Wallace's intervention does not deny the various problems, pitfalls, and complications that necessarily attend questions about the author's presence or absence; it simply posits that interpretive efforts to engage with a text conceived as the expression of a multifaceted, multilayered personality may well offer greater intellectual and emotional satisfactions than the more impersonal ontological reflections typically associated with experimental fiction. By offering both, by offering middlebrow therapy disguised as highbrow ontology, *Infinite Jest* strives to produce forms of solace, self-recognition, and identification to a self-consciously intellectual readership that might otherwise view such offerings with skepticism and disdain.

Addiction, the central concept of the contemporary twelve-step recovery movement, is also the subject of my next chapter. The book I consider, James Frey's pseudomemoir, *A Million Little Pieces*, however, is more intent than Wallace's book on disavowing self-help culture, which it presents as a threat to masculinity and individuality. Frey nevertheless does seek to appeal to the members of Oprah Winfrey's book club, and his controversial appearances on the show reveal the uncertain and paradoxical role that traditional notions of rugged individualism continue to play within the contemporary therapeutic paradigm.

CHAPTER FOUR

The Pain of Reading *A Million Little Pieces*

THE REVELATION THAT James Frey's best-selling memoir about his recovery from drug and alcohol addiction, *A Million Little Pieces*, contains
multiple lies and exaggerations has evidently undermined its value for
many readers. Oprah Winfrey concluded her punishing interview with
Frey subsequent to the public exposure of his dishonesty with this declaration: "And I believe that the truth matters"—a fitting remark insofar as
an encounter with "the truth" is precisely what *A Million Little Pieces* purports to offer its readers (*Oprah*, 26 January 2006). In fact, both the book's
capacity to inspire visceral forms of credulity and its remarkable implau-
sibility are symptoms of Frey's effort not to describe his life in a truthful
fashion, but instead to deliver something that readers could register as "the
truth." That these two aims might conflict suggests contradictory concepts
of truth within contemporary culture that Frey had been hoping to negotiate for his benefit. "Truth" as the Frey scandal reveals, has come to con-
note not only a neutral correspondence between a statement and a given
state of affairs, but also a particular kind of content, often painful and
grotesque, capable of promoting aesthetic experiences for its consumers
that are paradoxically empowering and uplifting. Both Frey and Winfrey
are attempting to offer their middle-class American audience a tenuous
form of authenticity whose aesthetic, sociological, and ethical valences the
controversy has rendered visible and thus available for analysis.

As Wallace's *Infinite Jest* demonstrates, therapeutic categories, like addict, help individuals escape their sense of isolation, allowing them to rec-

ognize that their problems are shared by others. And yet, at the same time, the language of the interior and the language of pathology often serve as a means of claiming individuality. The memoir genre, now one of the most popular literary forms, in part because of its participation within the confessional culture of the therapeutic paradigm, is especially well suited to dramatize the tension between these two competing impulses; it is supposedly about one specific individual whose uniqueness renders him or her worthy of a memoir, and yet it aims to inspire the identification of mass readerships. If this tension is a structural element of memoirs in general, it is particularly salient in the case of James Frey, given that he brazenly manipulated the content of his book in order to meet the needs of his market. The question of how his fabrications manage to serve both aims — to establish his individuality and to further his status as a broadly representative victim of addiction — is one that I hope to answer in this chapter.

On October 26, 2005, Oprah Winfrey's book club featured *A Million Little Pieces*, and Winfrey devoted most of the episode to lauding Frey for his courage and to scaring the parents in her audience with the idea that, like Frey, their adolescents might too become substance abusers. Shortly thereafter, The Smoking Gun, a Web site that uncovers official documents related to celebrities, discovered that many of Frey's claims about the crimes he committed, his various arrests, and the jail time he served were dramatically exaggerated or simply untrue ("A Million Little Lies"). According to The Smoking Gun, he was never charged with possession of crack cocaine, resisting arrest, assaulting a police officer, or attempting to incite a riot. He served three days rather than three months in a county jail. Overall, he was not the excessively self-destructive, ostracized felon that he claimed to be, but instead a fairly well-liked middle-class youth with a substance abuse problem that was not even severe enough to prevent him from finishing college. Moreover, Frey originally pitched his manuscript as a novel but, prompted by editors at Random House, decided to publish it with modifications as a memoir. In response to The Smoking Gun's exposé, Frey appeared on *Larry King Live*, and Winfrey called in to offer her support, maintaining that "the underlying message of redemption in James Frey's memoir still resonates with me. And I know it resonates with millions of other people." But by January 26, 2006, amid continuing criticism, Winfrey had changed her position, and she hosted a second episode featuring Frey, a senior editor at Random House Nan Talese, and several prominent journalists, during which she lambasted Frey for his dishonesty and Random House for its failure of integrity.[1]

As Timothy Dow Adams, Lynn Domina, Laurie Leach, and Leigh Gilmore have observed, autobiographies and memoirs have long practiced hyperbole and prevarication. Distortion, these scholars argue, is inevitable in the act of describing or narrating oneself in language, and lying can often function as a paradoxical means of self-revelation. While such claims are, in my view, valid, my aim in this chapter is not to defend Frey; I do not seek to assess either the degree of deliberate deception or the moral soundness of Frey's self-depiction. Rather, my purpose is to consider what Frey's text and the controversy surrounding it reveal about the codes and imperatives, particular to contemporary America, that underwrote his efforts to produce the compelling appearance of truth. As Gilmore has contended, the criteria that determine what constitutes the truth in the genre of life writing are continually changing in response to new historical conditions ("Policing Truth"). The question arises, then, what does the Frey controversy reveal about the prevailing truth criteria in the current moment? His ruse, after all, worked in part because it answered to a particular set of pre-existing desires and demands whose underexamined complicity in the controversy I want to consider.

Vicarious Pain

In the January episode, Winfrey observes correctly that many of the scenes in *A Million Little Pieces* seem implausible, and the *Washington Post* columnist Richard Cohen, a guest on the show, asserts that the memoir simply fails to "pass the smell test." But if the book's falsehoods are so brazenly detectable, why were so many readers, including Winfrey, passionately convinced of its truthfulness? Borrowing a term from Comedy Central's *The Colbert Report*, *New York Times* drama critic and op-ed writer Frank Rich claims that *A Million Little Pieces*, though filled with distortions and inaccuracies, possesses the quality of "truthiness."[2] Rich's implication is that a particular aesthetic shapes perceptions of what constitutes the truth, and that some figures, such as Frey, are more concerned with satisfying the demands of this aesthetic, producing the appearance of truth, than they are with offering an accurate representation of the actual world. But what conditions must a work satisfy in order to appear true? In *Literary Power and the Criteria of Truth*, Laura Quinney proposes that widely internalized assumptions about the bleak nature of the truth determine which literary works readers will find to be credible and realistic. The aesthetic power certain texts assume by virtue of their tragic energies compels belief and thereby shapes the very criteria that readers use to assess the truth of other works. "Truthfulness — the grim sound of truth — has its own power of persuasion, and though its floating authority is not that of empirical truth, it cannot but be felt as if it were" (59). Quinney is describing an aesthetic that dates back to the eighteenth century, but she notes that it is even more salient now.[3] Her theory may help to explain why Frey chose to exaggerate the ugly and unpleasant aspects of his experience, or at the very least why these exaggerations served to reinforce, rather than undermine, his book's plausibility.

Perhaps most importantly, Frey's text exemplifies the extraordinary rhetorical power that the form of the confessional currently commands.[4] *A Million Little Pieces* features repeated instances of taking stock, in which both the grisly content and the grammatical form — consisting of simple declarative sentences — impersonate an unflinching confrontation with the facts: "I have a hole in my cheek that has been closed with forty-one stitches. I have a broken nose and I have black swollen eyes. I have an Escort because I am a Patient at a Drug and Alcohol Treatment Center" (62). Largely responsible for Frey's credibility is his willingness to advertise details about himself that are typically treated as a source of shame or embarrassment. His most vivid efforts to obey this principle depict the copious amounts of vomit that he produces every morning while in the recovery center. "The sickness is worse than usual. Thicker, bloodier, more chunks of stomach, more painful" (48). "It is a foul endeavor. I vomit twice and I have to clean my own vomit as well as the spit and the piss and the bloody tissue and the shit" (78). Frey's inclusion of a subject matter that is ordinarily the object of euphemism and evasion signals his revolt against the strategies of concealment that typically envelop everyday bodily practices. His revolt reads as a simple reversal, as a form of de-concealment, so that his scatological descriptions function as an honesty effect, promoting the perception that he is bravely refusing to shield any feature of himself, however disgusting or despicable, from the reader's scrutiny.

Essential to the aesthetics of truth production at least in the eighteenth century, according to Quinney, is the achievement of "fierce impersonality," a fatalistic recognition of the ineluctable forces to which the individual inevitably and tragically succumbs.[5] Frey's strategic deployment of the confessional presupposes an aesthetic no less grim, but one in accord with a twenty-first-century therapeutic paradigm that privileges the personal or the private as the domain where tragedy and truth reside in a mutually sustaining partnership. The scope and content of mimetic focus, in other words, have changed. As the remarkable popularity of the memoir genre suggests, the truth, in its current conception, now manifests itself most forcefully not in the form of grand, cosmic, sublimely impersonal imagery, but rather in depictions of interior, subjective, or bodily pain that is often embarrassingly private. At the same time, Frey's most memorable confessional mantra, that he is an "Alcoholic," a "drug Addict," and a "Criminal" (62, 85, 251), posits an act of self-categorization as the result of introspection. Thus, in characteristic fashion, the apparently inward-turning therapeutic impulse seems necessarily to expand its scale of reference, employing social forms of classification and introducing a depersonalizing taxonomy even as it appears to zero in on the individual consciousness.

Frey's long-winded documentation of his own bodily pain intensifies the truthiness of his narrative in another manner no less effective than his willingness to risk embarrassment. The unlikelihood that Frey has actually regurgitated pieces of his own stomach is less important for his agenda than the impulse to cringe that this image produces. In his memoir, Frey relentlessly deploys the peculiar capacity that descriptions of bodily injury have to provoke sympathetic visceral responses whose intense combination of attraction and aversion toward the described experience constitutes an experience in itself, one that transfers its affective energy to the object of representation, thus endowing it with a factitious aura of reality.

In his memoir, Frey claims that he allows health care professionals to reset his nose, to sew up his cheek, to sand his teeth, and to perform two root canals, all without painkillers, because they are supposedly banned by the drug treatment center. The dental procedures occupy eight pages of the book; the following is a representative passage: "The drill is back on and it is working through the fragment of my left front tooth. It is moving through a thinner, more fragile section of bone, so it works quickly. It shoots grit, makes the hole, penetrates. At the point of penetration, a current shoots through my body that is not pain, or even close to pain, but something infinitely greater" (69).

To this scene, Winfrey responds in a duly fascinated and horrified manner:

Winfrey: Now, James, I cannot let you leave here, 'cause everybody who's reading at home, I think the first reason — first time you start reading and you're like, "Is this real? OK, this isn't a novel." And then you get to the dentist.

Mr. J. Frey: Right.

Winfrey: You get to the dentist, and I'm just saying my friend Gayle has a great fear of going to the dentist. I mean they need to — she needs to be totally drugged to go there. And she called me while she was in the room, she goes, "I cannot read this!" I mean, I never first of all even heard of anybody not having Novocain or anything for a root canal. That is like being crucified.

Mr. J. Frey: It was pretty unpleasant.

Winfrey: No, all — that is all completely true. I don't doubt you, but . . .

Mr. J. Frey: It's — you know, we . . .

Winfrey: Hot, searing fire, hot pain, pain, pain. (26 October 2006)

Winfrey's demonstrative effort to place herself in the dentist's chair and to feel Frey's pain exemplifies the reflexive bodily identification that such descriptions elicit, but she clearly feels incapable of comprehending his experience: "No, all — that is all completely true. I don't doubt you, but . . ." As Winfrey's conflicted reaction reveals, the unavoidable impulse to embody the textually evoked pain through one's own imaginative response functions to substantiate the pain's reality, while the inevitable inadequacy of the response serves only to strengthen conviction in that reality through a troubled sense of the discrepancy between it and the reader's comparatively vague or thin vicarious experience.

While the grotesque content of Frey's narrative promotes its simulation of the truth, certain stylistic features also support this end. The most striking quality of Frey's writing is an oppressive lack of syntactical complexity or variety:

> I get out of bed. Miles is asleep I walk quietly to the Bathroom. I shower and I shave and I brush my teeth. I get dressed and I leave the Room.
>
> I get a cup of coffee and I sit down at a table and I drink the coffee and I smoke cigarettes and I watch the men do their morning Jobs. One cleans the Kitchen, one takes out the garbage, one vacuums the floor. I see a man carrying the supplies for the Group Toilets. (399)

Frey's flat unadorned style, consisting of uniformly structured declarative sentences in the present tense, maintains the pretense that he is simply presenting everything he sees, does, and feels, without deferring to any principles of selection. Though Frey's language often seems, in a paradoxically precious fashion, to flaunt its own sparseness, its rhetorical aim is to send the message that its stylistic organization is less important than the subject matter — that its primary aim is to press ungracefully upon the reader's faculties Frey's direct and disorderly impressions of the drug recovery center, as he first had them, or at least as he remembers them.

Even more radically, Frey generally refrains from using logical terms such as "because," "if," and "therefore," signifying his refusal to impose any conceptual or interpretive schema upon his impulses and perceptions.

> I'm in another white Room and I hate it. I'm in another white robe and I want to tear it to shreds. There is another bed and another desk and another chair and I want to destroy them. There is a window. I want to throw myself through it.
>
> I follow my usual routine. Crawl to the Bathroom. Vomit. Lie on the floor. Vomit. Lie on the floor. Vomit. Lie on the floor. (75)

To pose the question why here would, one can only assume, interrupt the writing's mimetic fidelity to the steady succession of desires, movements, and sensations, which Frey regards as real, unalloyed experience. One peculiar consequence of this stylistic strategy is that Frey's narrative voice never seems to achieve any perspective in relation to his struggles; the truths his text purports to offer do not present themselves as the product of rational reflection upon his past. Any knowledge about the grim character of reality inevitably assumes, for Frey, the form of lived, concrete experience, which is why he employs such exhaustively mimetic strategies in order to impart what he feels to be the truth to his readers — a truth that they can access only by means of a visceral vicarious response.

In his memoir, Frey forwards his own set of aesthetic criteria for determining the truth of other texts. Most important to Frey is whether a particular text "rings true." The Bible does not; neither does Alcoholics Anonymous's Big Book; the *Tao Te Ching* does. "I've read the Bible. It didn't ring true to me" (225). "[The *Tao Te Ching*] still affects me and it still makes sense. It still moves me and it still rings true. That is all that matters. The truth. Does it ring true it does. I can feel it" (201). A text is true if it makes Frey feel a certain way, and that feeling indicates a resonance between the text's tone and his own sensibility. Often his intuitive assessment of whether particular texts, stories, or statements are true presupposes an understanding of the world as fundamentally painful, difficult, and depressing.[6] To explain his disdain for the Bible, Frey remarks: "I think God is something that People use to avoid reality. I think faith allows People to reject what is right in front of our eyes, which is that this thing, this life, this existence, this consciousness, or whatever word you want to use for it, is all we have, and all we'll ever have. I think People have faith because they want and need to believe in something, whatever that something is, because life can be hard and depressing and brutal if you don't" (224). Texts are true, in Frey's view, to the extent that they reflect his pessimistic conception of life — or his idea of *the* truth about the world. Clearly, when Frey declares repeatedly that the truth is all that matters, he is referring to this singular attitudinal truth, this recognition of the world's bleak essence, rather than a commitment to local, factual verifiability.

At times, Frey treats the truth as a quality of experience rather than a property of statements about the world. Describing an encounter with his love interest, Lilly, he remarks: "I don't care what she's done or who she's done it with, I don't care about whatever demons may be in her closet. I care about how she makes me feel and she makes me feel strong and safe and calm and warm and true" (255). Owing to his antitheoretical sensibility, Frey conceives of the truth as an unmediated visceral perception, a direct emotion that is also a means of apprehending the world. Truth for Frey is at once a form of knowledge and an object of knowledge, an affective mode of cognition that collapses the distinction between beliefs or perceptions about the world and the world itself. Frey, in other words, attributes a kind of absolute validity to his own subjective intuitions, as if they both record and exemplify the truth about the world, which is why his primary means of measuring a text's truthfulness is to ask whether it "rings true."

In order for the assertion that certain experiences or feelings are true to be meaningful and not merely tautological, then other experiences or feelings must be untrue. What would it mean for an experience or a feeling to be untrue? Frey never explains the logic that underpins his notion of the truth, but presumably an untrue experience or feeling is one that somehow denies or misrecognizes its own reality. "Truth," in Frey's usage of the term seems to suggest the same meaning that "authenticity" denotes — that is, a state of expressing or realizing one's essence.[7] But since Frey defines reality as painful and hard, certain experiences, certain modes of life are inauthentic insofar as they attempt to disown this reality — a reality from which they can divorce themselves only by means of duplicity or self-deception. And the demographic category that Frey singles out as most prone to engage in this tendency, most prone to live inauthentically, is unsurprisingly his own: the American middle class.

Addiction and the Middle Class

One evening, watching TV, Frey dismisses a sitcom for its lack of realism and proposes what he views as a more convincing alternative: "There is a sitcom about some witty New Yorkers who spend all of their time in one Apartment. One of the men praises the show and he talks about how real it is. The only people I know who spend so much time in one Apartment usually have black plastic taped over the windows and guns in the closet and burn marks on their lips and fingers and huge locks on the doors. They are not witty people, though their paranoia can be amusing. I don't see anything like that on this show, but it is supposedly very real. Maybe I don't know what real is anymore" (212–13). Although the sitcom characters who reside in Manhattan tend to have far nicer apartments and more leisure time than the average New Yorker, Frey's picture of well-armed, strung-out drug addicts holed up in a squalid hideout is no more representative and would likely strike the majority of his middle-class readers as grotesquely unfamiliar. Yet the latter image Frey equates with reality, a judgment whose rhetorical force depends upon a frequently deployed preconception of the real as painful, menacing, gritty, and generally unavailable to the insulated experiences of middle-class Americans. On the one hand, then, Frey suggests that reality is essentially hard, painful, and bleak, but on the other hand, he narrowly identifies that reality with a particular class, projecting the purportedly unhappy truth about life into traumatized regions of urban poverty.

Significantly, Frey defines realism and reality against a representation that foregrounds the affluent middle-class status of its subjects. In his first appearance on *Oprah*, he describes his childhood: "I mean it's 'Leave it to Beaver,' it's Wisteria Lane, it's 'The Brady Bunch.' It's the perfect American life where daughters don't have sex and sons don't do drugs and parents don't fight and it's all a façade." Frey's disdain for his middle-class background represents only the latest installment in a history of American writers, dating back to David Riesman, William Whyte, and C. Wright Mills in the 1950s, who complain that suburban existence is inauthentic. In *Sincerity and Authenticity*, Lionel Trilling remarks that contemporary conceptualizations of authenticity tend to align it with "roughness" or "hardness," in opposition to bourgeois lifestyles; and he registers the widespread perception that members of the American middle class are doomed to lead inauthentic lives.[8] For Trilling, suffering is a necessary condition for authenticity. To suffer is to experience a "sentiment of being" (146), to apprehend in a palpable way, the painful and essential reality of one's own existence. And this of course is generally understood to be a lonely, antisocial experience. Thus, according to some critics, a central function of middle-class suburbia, with its material comforts, its soothing social rituals, and its tacitly enforced evasions, is to thwart authentic experiences.

Such perceptions, which have spread into the popular consciousness, create a conundrum for members of the middle class. To seek authenticity, they must disavow bourgeois lifestyles, but such disavowals necessarily jeopardize their claim upon "authenticity", insofar as the term is also understood to characterize those who acknowledge and embrace what they truly are. If they flee their middle-class status, middle-class subjects render themselves ineligible to attain the authenticity that they are chasing. To deal with this problem, James Frey depicts himself as revolting against his suburban background, but he simultaneously recasts this environment as more fraught with hidden risk and pain than is generally acknowledged, thus imagining such efforts at revolt to be a hidden, constitutive element of suburban life. His pejorative characterization of his hometown's picturesque conformity to suburban clichés, in other words, extends only to its outward appearance: "it's all a façade." Frey's description, while unflattering, exemplifies a ubiquitous strategy in contemporary American culture for valorizing middle-class existence; his approach makes the supposed inauthenticity of the suburban lifestyle into an alibi that both disguises and protects within its duplicitous structure a *deeper authenticity*. Just below the well-manicured surface, suburbanites too experience conflict, self-destruction, and violence, and thereby have some access to the essential reality of life — as he imagines it.[9]

The most clichéd, but inexhaustibly alluring gateway to suffering and authenticity for the American middle class in the past few decades has been drug use, due in part to its hyperbolic demonization by the media.[10] Frey has craftily mined the imagery of the drug addict in order to construct the rhetorically potent persona of a tormented but tough, street-smart survivor who has confronted reality in its cruelest, least disguised incarnation and emerged eager to share his wisdom about the world. Hard drugs, especially, offer a transgression of normative middle-class boundaries not only because of their potentially destructive capacities, but also because of widely accepted associations between them and nonwhite urban poor populations, which Frey strategically invokes. In his memoir, his parents react to his confession that he is a recovering crack addict with the observation that they think of crack as a "ghetto drug" (263). On *Oprah*, he revisits the site of his teenage drug use: "This street was lined with hookers and drug dealers. You'd see pimps on the corners"; and he describes his dealer, Freddie, who referred to Frey as "White Boy James" (248): "Freddie was a friend. I remember the first time I met him, I was like, 'I can't believe how lucky I am.' It was like winning the lottery or something. You know, he'd just pull up, park on that grass right there and go in the house. He'd walk across the street and get us whatever we needed. You know, there were coke dealers around the corner" (*Oprah*, 26 October 2005). Striving to appear remorseful, Frey cannot repress his self-congratulatory impulses; he advertises his intimacy with such neighborhoods as a source of street credibility.

If hard drugs such as crack and heroin frequently function in the United States as a metonym for the black inner city, their complex symbolic energy stems largely from their mobility, their perceived capacity to proliferate within other kinds of spaces. An onscreen graphic during Frey's October 2005 appearance on *Oprah* ominously reveals: "JAMES FOUND ALCOHOL AND DRUGS LESS THAN A MILE AWAY" from his home, suggesting a frightening proximity between the lower-class world of pimps and pushers that Frey visits and the middle-class world of staid decorum that his parents inhabit. The drama of such revelations depends both upon an assumed incongruity and upon subterranean relays between the two contexts. Winfrey announces at the show's opening: "Look at this sweet nine-year-old midwestern boy. What was about to happen to him nobody would have guessed." But a moment later she adds, "He could be your son," suggesting, in accord with the hysterical rhetoric of the war on drugs, that drugs are an insistent threat capable of invading middle-class enclaves and bringing with them all of the danger and disorder perceived as endemic to their purportedly inner-city origins. Later in the show, just after discussing Frey's hatred for suburbia, Winfrey asks him a question designed to alarm her middle-class viewers: "Do you think a lot of parents are in denial about what's going on with their kids . . . ?" He responds, "Absolutely." Their exchange exemplifies the perception of illicit substances as the open secret of suburbia; they are utterly foreign, and at the same time they are disturbingly ubiquitous.

Winfrey's ostensibly shocking exposure of drug use in places like Frey's hometown betrays, in the form of a denial, a systematically overlooked insight about the intimate relations between drugs and the middle class. First of all, as we saw with Wallace, members of the middle class have historically been deeply involved in the circulation and consumption of drugs.[11] Secondly, and more importantly, drug dealing and drug use can be understood as merely an extreme realization of the middle class's values in late-capitalist America, with its emphasis on compulsive consumption, instant gratification, incessantly novel, visceral thrills, and quick, easy profits.[12] To be sure, drugs are a destructive presence within poor urban areas, but the relentless identification of drugs with such contexts in popular representations is also a means for the middle class to disavow its own close relations with drugs. And this symbolic projection outward enables certain individuals, such as Frey, to imagine drug use as a method for escaping from the confines of middle-class existence and making contact with what they see as reality, as the bleak but bracing truth about the world, whose power derives from its relative inaccessibility. Frey's text and his appearance on *Oprah* mobilize several powerful myths — the myth of suburbia as an unreal place,[13] the myth of the ghetto as an all-too-real embodiment of the painful truth, and the myth of drug use as a dangerous and heroic transgression of middle-class norms — in order to constitute both a barrier and a doorway between middle-class lifestyles and a romanticized version of the real. In warning readers that Frey could be one of their kids, and by suggesting that parents are in denial, Winfrey aims to exhilarate as well as frighten her audience; she posits addiction and delinquency as pervasive possibilities, weighty dangers constitutive of middle-class identity, and thereby works to satisfy her viewers' desire for some claim, however distant and mediated, upon authenticity.

Authenticity and Masculinity

Possibly even more important to Frey than his authenticity is his masculinity, whose fragile status his histrionics incessantly betray. At the recovery center, he starts fights, mocks fellow patients with homophobic insults, and describes his struggle to beat his addiction in a language borrowed from televised sports. While in popular conceptions drug and alcohol addiction affects gender identity equivocally, in some cases understood as a masculine rejection of conventions and a heroic confrontation with reality, in other cases understood as an emasculating surrender of agency and bodily control, Frey generally emphasizes the first set of associations, maintaining the more serious the addiction, the manlier the addict.[14] In fact, he divides the male patients at the recovery center into two categories: "One group is made up of the Hardcore. They are the heaviest users and the truly fucked up. The other group is made up of the Wussies. They are the functional and the potentially saved. The Hardcore make fun of the Wussies and tell them they don't belong here. The Wussies don't respond with words, but with looks that say thank God I'm not one of you. Ed and Ted and John sit among the Hardcore, Roy and his friend Warren and the Bald Man sit with the Wussies" (88). The Hardcore addicts that he lists are working class, while the Wussies tend to be middle class, but Frey sits with the Hardcore addicts; thus the supposed severity of his addiction enables him to transcend the potentially emasculating effects of his sheltered middle-class existence.[15]

If Frey is keen to assert his masculinity, he also works to reconcile these tactics with the middlebrow protocols of Oprah Winfrey's women-centered sphere. Winfrey has her own set of strategies for validating the experiences of her viewers in keeping with the therapeutic paradigm, which involve the foregrounding and staging of psychological or emotional problems, frequently severed from a specific sociological context. By constituting affective pain as the most difficult and fundamental reality that people can encounter — as a kind of deracinated, decontextualized psychological currency — Winfrey enables her middle-class viewers to treat their own struggles as commensurate with those of other less economically and politically empowered communities, and thus as legitimate forms of suffering.[16] The need to satisfy Winfrey's therapeutic imperatives without relinquishing his masculinity is obviously responsible for one unconvincing remark Frey makes during his first appearance on the show: "People say, 'How did you do that with your teeth?' and there's a way I always respond is physical pain is physical pain and it is what it is, and it fades very quickly, and I would much rather have my teeth drilled again than have my heart broken again, and I would much rather deal with physical pain of any kind than emotional pain of any kind." In his memoir too, Frey works to reconcile his hypermasculine self-representations with the therapeutic paradigm, remarking multiple times that expressions of vulnerability, especially crying, can be signifiers of masculinity, but generally coupling these gestures with chivalric attitudes and actions vis-à-vis the women who inspire these emotive responses.

The alliance between Frey's masculine, street-hardened version of authenticity and *Oprah*'s women-oriented realm of affect and empathy turns out unsurprisingly to be tenuous, and after discovering his various falsifications, Winfrey complains especially about Frey's efforts to appear manly. During his January 26, 2006, appearance on the show, she asks him: "So all of those encounters where there are the big fights and chairs and you're Mr. Bravado Tough Guy. Were you making that up, or was that your idea of who you were?" And then in the same episode, responding to his supposed dental procedure, she remarks, "So why? Was that to make yourself look like a big __ because you know what? It worked." Winfrey's reaction here indicates not only her sense of betrayal but also the imperfect fit between the gendered registers that Frey and she occupy, and, concomitantly, tensions between their strategies for producing the resonance of truth.[17]

To a degree, Frey's and Winfrey's strategies conform respectively to the norms long held to characterize male and female autobiography. Academics have frequently observed that male authors tend to stress their individuality, while female authors tend to stress their relationship to others.[18] Recently, however, scholars such as Nancy K. Miller and Leigh Gilmore (in *The Limits of Autobiography*) have challenged these dichotomies, asserting that the self necessarily emerges as relational and representative rather than autonomous and unique in the life writing of both men and women. Indeed, their claim is partially true even of Frey — given his eagerness to encourage identification from his readers, a tendency perfectly in accord with Winfrey's own strategies. When Frey describes his struggles in the recovery center or when Winfrey's guests discuss their psychological problems, the audience is expected to inhabit the depicted experience in order to assess whether or not these representations feel true. But Winfrey more than Frey depends upon the foregrounding of actual resemblances between subjects and viewers.[19] Her audience members, in other words, believe in the reality of her guests' problems to the extent that they have experienced similar difficulties. Such goals and practices resemble those that tend to prevail within various women's groups in the United States and that have their roots in the feminist consciousness-raising practices of the 1970s.[20] Frey employs a different strategy, more in line with the individualist protocols of male autobiography as it has been traditionally conceived. In a competitive fashion, he predicates his memoir's truth upon the radically individuating extremity of the experiences that it depicts. The distinction here, it should be noted, is not rigid or absolute. Like Frey, Winfrey frequently employs sensationalized or exoticized images of the truth whose rhetorical power depends upon their grotesque character.[21] But more often she emphasizes commonalties; what she presents as true is that which is immediately recognizable to her viewers, that which seems to resemble their own daily struggles and challenges.

The aesthetics of the truth embraced by Frey automatically render the status of his memoir rather precarious. Precisely the same qualities that initially provoked belief in the truthfulness of Frey's memoir seem just as easily to provoke disbelief and skepticism. Anderson Cooper, one of the journalists invited to appear in the January episode, remarks, "Because the book has seemed so honest and raw, who knows what's real and what's not?" *A Million Little Pieces* seems raw because it hyperbolizes Frey's pain; its depiction of extreme suffering functions, as I have argued, as a reality effect. But insofar as Frey exoticizes the truth, severing it too definitively from the imagery of everyday middle-class life and aligning it with depictions of excessively sordid, abject misery, he runs the risk of undermining his readers' belief. As Winfrey observes during Frey's second appearance on the show, "one of the reasons why we're all so taken with the book is because it feels and reads so sensationally that it — it — you you can't believe that all of this happened to one person." Readers reject the book's truth, then, for the same reason that they once accepted it — because it describes a predicament far beyond anything they have ever experienced. That which once seemed hyper-real suddenly seems unreal. The tendency of middle-class individuals to view reality and authenticity, in contradictory fashion, as both radically removed from and yet obscurely available to their own experience, enables this dramatic reversal.

Frey's posture of extreme authenticity obviously depends to no small degree upon belief in the literal, factual truth of his memoir. The discovery that Frey deliberately fabricated certain details prompted accusations that he had broken a contract between author and reader — which raises the question of what exactly he promised but failed to provide.[22] What, in other words, do readers stand to gain from the particular contract instantiated in the memoir genre? Why does it matter to them whether or not the events described actually happened? In the January episode, Winfrey suggests why she feels betrayed: "And I have to tell you, James, that when I was reading that book and I get to the last page and Lily has hung herself and you arrived, you know, the day that she hang — was — was hung, and I couldn't even believe it. I'm, like, gasping. I'm calling people, like, 'Oh my God, this happened.'" The experience that Winfrey emphasizes is not the one described by the memoir, but the experience that *she herself had* in response to it, which was so intense that it seems to have involved, in its "gasping," a sympathetic re-enactment of the suicide depicted in the text. One might even conclude that the event's reality does not matter insofar as it is supplanted as the focus of attention by Winfrey's own apparently visceral response to it. If, in other words, memoirs are designed to bring readers into contact with some painful reality, then Winfrey has at least succeeded in encountering the painful reality of her own emotions. But her comments also assert that her response was predicated upon the belief that this experience "happened" to someone.

Although on her book club Winfrey has repeatedly shown herself capable of treating fictional characters as if they were real people, apparently the certitude that the suffering described was experienced by an actual person, and not just a fictional character, intensifies and adds a legitimizing concreteness to her own empathetic bodily response. In acknowledging his fabrications, then, Frey has foreclosed the peculiar, self-validating pleasure of suffering alongside him. To put it a slightly different way, the inevitably inadequate identification that Frey's narrative inspires acquires a satisfying poignancy only insofar as readers can posit an actual experience beyond their own imaginative reach, which they heroically try but ultimately fail to imagine and relive. Absent this actual untouchable object, their pained sympathy cannot help but feel self-indulgent.

Fictions of Agency

One might think that Frey's status as a role model for other addicts would entail a heavy responsibility toward the factual truth. Interestingly enough, however, Frey invokes this status to turn attention away from the accuracy of his memoir. On *Larry King Live*, after admitting that he had altered certain aspects, Frey declares, "As I said, the essential truth of the book, which is about drug and alcohol addiction is there. I couldn't have written about what I write about if I hadn't gone through it. You know, the emotional truth is there." He adds, "I hope the emotional truth of the book resonate [sic] with [readers]." Moments later, Winfrey, calling into the show, corroborates Frey's arguments, claiming that the facts are less important than the "underlying message of redemption," which "still resonates with me" and still "resonates with millions of other people." What matters most, Frey and Winfrey maintain, is not whether the events the book describes actually happened, but whether readers can relate to them. To say that *A Million Little Pieces* is true in this more literary sense of the term is to suggest that it captures some essential truth applicable to people and situations beyond those depicted in the text; Frey maintains that whether or not his book accurately represents the particular events of his life, it nevertheless reveals the reality of addiction, as it is experienced by many people and especially by many readers.

Frey's contention that his memoir depicts broadly representative experiences is peculiar, however, given his competitive celebration of his own individuality. Nobody, he brags, has taken as many drugs as he has. His doctor reports to him, "I have never seen so much and such extensive damage in someone so young" (92). And while in the recovery center, he repudiates all given models for achieving sobriety, rejecting the disease concept of addiction and refusing to participate in Alcoholics Anonymous. His counselor tells him, "In all of my experience, I have never seen anyone stay sober and survive in the long term using anything but AA and the Twelve steps" (222)—a dubious statement given research suggesting that many addicts can recover outside of Alcoholics Anonymous, and a statement which Frey includes presumably to underscore his image as heroic nonconformist.[23] Later she tells him: "The odds of someone with your substance abuse history staying sober without tremendous amounts of support, both in AA and therapy, be it Individual therapy or Group therapy, are a million to one. A million to one at best" (410).

So committed is Frey to a belief in his own agency, that he practically denies the influence of any factors over his addiction other than his own individual will. In the book, his parents suggest that a genetic predisposition combined with the trauma of intensely painful ear infections as an infant may be responsible for his subsequent feelings of rage and his need to abuse substances. But he refuses fully to accept this explanation:

> I try to decide if I am willing to accept genetics and ear infections as an explanation for twenty-three years of chaos. . . .
>
> I look up. My Parents are watching me, Joanne is watching me. They are waiting for a response. I take a breath and I speak.
>
> It's an interesting theory. It probably holds some weight. I can accept it for what I feel it is, which is a possibility. I won't accept it as a root cause, because I think it's a cop-out, and because I don't think it does me any good to accept anything other than myself and my own weakness as a root cause. I did everything I did. I made the decisions to do it all. (306)

Notice that ethical imperatives predicated upon a priori assumptions about individual agency govern Frey's assessment of his parents' explanation. He questions their theory not because it fails to offer a plausible account of the facts, but only because he believes that it would be irresponsible, "a cop-out," to substitute ear infections for his own weakness of the will as the cause of his addiction. In other words, his ethics dictate his analysis of the facts rather than the other way around. Like many conservatives in the United States, Frey is so invested in a rhetoric of individual responsibility that he employs that very rhetoric as a foundation for its own legitimacy: it would be irresponsible, he claims, to deny his own responsibility.[24]

Unfettered and unswayed in Frey's conception by all external factors, his will serves as the final basis and cause of all of his actions — a conclusion that helps him maintain a fiction of almost total autonomy. The will, as Valverde has noted, is a peculiar, hybrid concept; it eludes neat categorization within the mind-body dichotomy; it straddles medical and ethical paradigms, and historically it has proved fairly inaccessible to scientific theorization (2–4). To accept Frey's account of his own will is to deny its susceptibility to external causality, but this approach, whose aim is to preserve the conceptual viability of freedom and individual responsibility, also renders his impulses and actions impervious to explanation or analysis. Frey has great difficulty understanding himself: "I close my eyes and I take a deep breath and I think about my life and how I ended up this way. I think about the ruin, devastation and wreckage I have caused to myself and to others. I think about self-hatred and self-loathing. I think about how and why and what happened and the thoughts come easily, but the answers don't" (25–26). Frey's circular insistence upon his will's own self-mobilizing, self-creating status precludes any capacity to identify what has influenced or shaped the tendencies of that will. Indeed, his belief in his individual agency may account for the dearth of logical terms in the narrative; "because," "thus," and "therefore" would imply that his actions are the consequences of outside pressures — and this possibility Frey refuses to admit.

Frey's rejection of external causality entails a refusal to admit that his behavior is accountable in terms of logical or predictable trajectories and thus would seem to undermine any basis for asserting its relevance to other people and other scenarios. If each decision he makes is the product of nothing more than his own inexplicable, monadic will, then it would be impossible for him to embody patterns of action based upon norms of causality that are applicable to anyone else. Thus any claim that Frey's narrative, while factually inaccurate, nevertheless delivers the essential truth about addiction, to which his readers can relate, contradicts Frey's own embrace of radical individuality.

To be sure, Americans tend to identify themselves with exceptional figures: the "million to one" odds of remaining sober that Frey describes seem to foreground him as the *one* with whom *millions* of people can identify. Frey's status as role model for millions of Americans depends upon the pervasive faith in self-improvement and self-salvation rooted in the ever-resilient ideology of American individualism.[25] One of the central tasks of the therapeutic paradigm and its most outspoken advocate, Oprah Winfrey, is to reconcile seemingly disempowering pathological identity categories popular within the twelve-step recovery movement, such as addict and codependent, with this ideology.[26] That *A Million Little Pieces* is remarkably serviceable to that end partly explains how it became a selection for the book club. Frey's short-lived success depended upon two significant offerings: he provided his middle-class readers an image of an abject, defamiliarized reality, an embodiment of the painful but cathartic truth as one of the constitutive possibilities of their own existence—a source of both fear and self-valorization. And he abetted fantasies of individual will at once responsible for and capable of overcoming the grim reality he described. Hence, life, in Frey's depiction, is universally painful, difficult, and risky enough to be meaningful and authentic, even for those who enjoy the comforts of middle-class existence, and at the same time it is not beyond the control of the individual.

But given the improbability of Frey's story, the idea that it actually did happen to someone, to an individual, seems to be a necessary condition for its capacity to support the delusions of extraordinary willpower that its consumers may entertain about themselves. Once the factual truth of the story falls prey to skepticism, then Frey ceases to be a single living individual and becomes nothing more than a fiction, an embodiment of a widely shared fantasy deliberately designed to appeal to millions of readers. But the realization that they, the readers, are merely identifying with a cleverly deployed collective fantasy vitiates the very conceit of individuality that motivates the act of identification in the first place. Like many therapeutic strategies, Frey's broadly appealing singularity depends upon its capacity to mask itself as the instantiation of collective desire. The book's unlikely factual truth alone can sanction and support its dubious symbolic, representative truth. The two in fact need to play a strange game of mutual reinforcement and mutual mystification: readers accept the book's representative truth on the basis of its factual truth, believing that its depiction of exceptional willpower, since it is true for Frey, could be true for them, while simultaneously emphasizing the local, factual truth that it is actually true only for one person, in order to conceal from themselves its status as the symbol of generic aspirations.

Remarkably, Winfrey actually succeeds where Frey fails by producing a narrative out of his failure. Of course the story that she stages is about not just his failure, but that of the entire publishing industry. Inviting Nan Talese onto the show and interrogating her about whether Doubleday fact-checked *A Million Little Pieces*, Winfrey calls attention to the larger institutional mechanisms involved in the production of memoirs and responsible for guaranteeing the validity of the genre's truth claims. Such a gesture would seem to complicate Winfrey's efforts to understand the scandal as the consequence of an individual moral error. But even as she includes the editors at Doubleday as an object of her outrage, Winfrey continues to employ the language of individual responsibility, echoing Frey's own ideological assumptions, seeking someone to blame rather than viewing the controversy as the product of a more widespread cultural situation. The journalists on the show share Winfrey's indignation. Maureen Dowd disdainfully observes, "It's just very disappointing that the publishing house doesn't care; they're counting their money." Such comments, which attempt to portray Doubleday as a greedy corporate Goliath, disregard the beleaguered state of the industry, the severe constraints within which it operates, and its dim financial prospects. Given their dwindling number of readers and narrow profit margins, it is somewhat understandable that publishing houses would attempt to force certain books, whose contents do not precisely meet the requisite truth criteria, into the category of memoir — a genre, as *Publishers Weekly* editor Sarah Nelson grudgingly notes, more likely to attract readers than fiction (5). Moreover, it is also unsurprising that most publishing houses refrain from hiring fact-checkers for their memoirs, since such measures would only diminish whatever meager profits they and the majority of their authors are capable of achieving. But Winfrey and her absurdly lucrative production company, Harpo, opt not to present this more complicated picture in part because, like Frey, they want to tell a good story — and a good story, as they conceive it, whether true or false, requires individual agents responsible for the triumphs and catastrophes that they experience.

Winfrey, no less than Frey, is attempting to stage authenticity, but her strategies prove to be more effective and sustainable than those he deploys in his memoir. Repeatedly observing during his second appearance that the interview is live, Winfrey facilitates an encounter between her audience and the painful reality of Frey's uncomfortable confession. He stutters, he hedges, he grimaces, and all throughout the audience has the sense that something real is happening, an authentic display of emotion, which is why Frank Rich comments, "I think it's amazing television." But if Winfrey is able to enact the painful truth as an embodied developing reality, she does so, unlike Frey, by defining reality as fundamentally psychological rather than material or sociological. In her analysis of Winfrey's strategies, Eva

Illouz maintains, "What enables such narratives to develop under our own eyes is the use of a therapeutic language in which talking about one's problems constitutes an event in and of itself" (39).[27] Watching guests such as Frey think aloud, evince emotion, and discuss their difficulties, viewers are led to believe that they are directly observing and participating emotionally in significant moments and developments in the lives of real people. Frey ends his awkward second appearance by claiming that returning to the show has helped him in the process of becoming "a better person." This, as journalist Virginia Heffernan wryly observes, is his only gesture during the episode to win any measure of Winfrey's approval. It has been a hard hour, but Frey will be stronger because of it. Indeed his brief moment of redemptive self-improvement serves as a reminder that the most popular and convincing efforts to reconcile the vision of a painful, weighty, ineluctable reality and the American ideology of unlimited individual agency tend to happen within the therapeutic register that Winfrey celebrates.

Some viewers may continue to believe, despite Winfrey's powers of persuasion, that the reality constituted within therapeutic culture is attenuated or incomplete. Indeed the concern voiced by Frey that the experience of the American middle class is excessively insulated and thus detached from reality is evident, remarkably enough, in the subgenre typically dedicated to dramatizing the struggles of this demographic: contemporary women's fiction. The efforts of one novelist within this canon, Anita Shreve, to reconceive the suburban private sphere so as to rescue it from banality is the subject of my next chapter.

CHAPTER FIVE

The Politics of Interiority in *The Pilot's Wife*

ALTHOUGH OCCASIONALLY called upon to perform certain emeritus functions, the omniscient narrator has mostly retired from the scene of contemporary U.S. fiction. In the place of this appealingly wise but problematic figure emerges an array of speakers no less ignorant, prejudiced, and confused than the reader. First-person narrators, of course, have a long history of unreliability, but now even most third-person narrators, at least within American mainstream literary fiction, report the action of the novel almost entirely from the standpoint of the character or characters through free indirect discourse. A modernist innovation originally, the refusal of omniscience has become a fixed principle, especially within middlebrow fiction — a development that has allowed the subjective perspective of particular characters to assume paramount importance and individual psychology to emerge as the ontological center of the fictional world.

Women's fiction, a prominent category within the middlebrow genre, typically aims to foster identification with a sympathetic female protagonist and, according to many critics, focuses therapeutically on personal or domestic struggles to the exclusion of social or political issues. For the most part, however, dismissive attitudes have impeded a truly nuanced understanding of what functions and agendas the therapeutically inflected conventions of this subgenre serve and what meanings they are capable of accommodating. Women's fiction, I intend to argue, renders visible a family of increasingly prevalent needs, anxieties, and modes of affect, which has come to represent, for middle-class Americans, not only a way of relating to political struggle, but also a central, valorized site of political struggle in itself.

In this chapter, I examine one particular work, *The Pilot's Wife* by Anita Shreve, an Oprah's Book Club selection about the efforts of a widowed pilot's wife to make sense of the plane crash that killed her husband.[1] Undeniably psychological in its emphasis, Shreve's text nevertheless demonstrates, like Frey's memoir, the capacity of individual-centered, therapeutic discourse to describe larger social formations and class anxieties through the depiction of a single character's conventional interiority. Even more vividly than *A Million Little Pieces*, however, *The Pilot's Wife* reveals how psychological terms can activate not only social but also political meanings; her text exemplifies the ways in which the private sphere depends for its significance and value upon power struggles purportedly outside its boundaries. Instead of retreating from politics, *The Pilot's Wife* works actively to politicize the private sphere in a systematic fashion, cataloging the ways in which the husband's secret affiliation with the Irish Republican Army has shaped the protagonist's family dynamics. By the end of the novel, Shreve succeeds at endowing all of the psychological impulses, physical gestures, conversations, and memories that usually constitute intimate familial relations with the dramatic valences and affective energies of high-stakes political conflict.

Published in 1998, *The Pilot's Wife* turns out to be remarkably prescient in its insinuation of political terror into the domestic sphere. This appropriation and proliferation of the political serves psychological needs particular to the protagonist and the category of middle-class women she represents, and in so doing anticipates the Bush administration's post-9/11 rhetoric. A careful analysis of Shreve's text reveals a psychological realm ripe for the kind of politicization that Bush's War on Terror so shrewdly enacted.

Joyce's Middlebrow Legacy

If middlebrow protagonists' enviable status as unimpeachable targets of collective empathy occasionally inspires readers to imagine themselves novelized, or, more ambitiously, to imagine novelizing themselves, then apparently James Joyce is partly to blame. In *Dubliners, Portrait of the Artist as a*

Young Man, and some parts of *Ulysses*, he pays his characters the equivocal compliment of rendering their thoughts and activities in the mode of discourse they themselves would use if they were composing the text, a strategy Hugh Kenner has named the Uncle Charles Principle, after the character by that name in *Portrait of the Artist* (Kenner 15–18). Uncle Charles, a self-important rhetorician learned in the conventions of certain pretentious nineteenth-century novels, does not merely go to the outhouse; he "repairs" to the outhouse (62). Lily, the overworked serving girl in "The Dead," is "literally run off her feet," though one can assume that Joyce, were he to write in his own idiom, would never misuse "literally" as a synonym for its opposite, "figuratively" (175). What distinguishes the Uncle Charles Principle from traditional modes of free indirect discourse, which also try to evoke the subjectivity of the characters they describe, is Joyce's imitation of the received idiom used by his characters. Most admirable in Joyce, according to Kenner, is his awareness of how the inherited modes of rhetoric that his characters employ shape and delimit their experience. "To wonder what 'literally' may mean," Kenner remarks in discussing the opening sentence of "The Dead," "is the fear of the Word and the beginning of reading" (15). Interestingly enough, Kenner himself never does speculate what "literally" might mean in this context except to observe that Joyce is parodying the exhausted Lily, adding insult to an injury not nearly as grotesque as Lily's self-dramatization would insist. To Lily, however, "literally" obviously means more than simply its antonym, "figuratively." When detached from Joyce's modernist irony, the declaration that she has been "literally run off her feet" refuses the figurative, or metaphorical, character of her expression and seeks to focus attention on the object of representation, in this case Lily's pain, rather than its rhetorical formulation.

The narrator of Anita Shreve's *The Pilot's Wife* also misuses the term "literally," and, as in Joyce, it hyperbolizes the disabling effects of heavy labor. Describing Kathryn, the widowed pilot's wife, and her grandmother Julia boxing and wrapping Christmas gifts ordered from Julia's store, the narrator observes: "Julia had been determined to fill the Christmas rush orders from the shop. Privately, Kathryn had thought this misguided effort might kill her grandmother, but Kathryn could not dissuade Julia from her sense of duty. And so the two of them, with Mattie helping sporadically, had spent several long nights boxing and packing and wrapping and ticking off names and addresses from a list. And in its own way, Kathryn thought, the work had been mildly therapeutic. Julia and she had slept when they literally could no longer see, and thus they had avoided the insomnia that might have been their fate" (141). The labor does not kill Julia as Kathryn fears; it just blinds them both—literally. Given that these two characters do not actually surrender their capacity to see after wrapping presents, one must conclude that someone here is misusing the term "literally." Is this the narrator's mistake, or is it Kathryn's? The passage, written in free indirect discourse, obviously evokes Kathryn's consciousness, and it may exemplify the Uncle Charles Principle, especially given that Kathryn misuses "literally" in spoken dialogue, demonstrating her susceptibility to this linguistic error (127). Nevertheless, I would argue that Shreve is not parodying her character's idiom in the same way that Joyce parodies Lily's. While "The Dead" attends mostly to the everyday banalities that its characters hopelessly aim to elude through their rhetorical exaggerations, *The Pilot's Wife* depicts a situation of extreme distress: a woman's husband has just died in a transatlantic plane crash. Protocols of tact in the face of bereavement, upon which Shreve solemnly insists, prohibit ironic attitudes toward Kathryn on the part of the narrator or the reader. Furthermore, if one must deny the embodiment of Kathryn's exaggeration demanded by the term "literally" and conclude that her condition is less extreme than blindness, then the text anticipates only relief from the reader upon witnessing her unspectacular complaints, backlit by the tragedy of her husband's death.

The irony of Shreve's distinctly nonironic text is that, like many novels in its genre, it uses the Uncle Charles Principle not to parody or mock the protagonist, but in fact to perform and to elicit sympathy for her. *The Pilot's Wife* is written almost entirely in free indirect discourse, exclusively from Kathryn's perspective without a single statement of authorial wisdom or entry into another character's consciousness. And it all seems to be written in Kathryn's voice. In certain moments, she actively assumes the narrator's function. "The camera slid back to the old man and moved in close to his face. He looked shocky around the eyes, and his mouth was hanging open, as though it was hard for him to breathe. Kathryn watched him on the television, and she thought: That is what I look like now. Gray in the face. The eyes staring out at something that isn't even there. The mouth loose like that of a hooked fish" (11). The style she deploys in her self-description is identical to the overall style of the book. Both rely upon brief, sparsely ornamented sentences or phrases in uninflated Standard English; periodic moments of understated poetry through slightly surprising combinations of commonplace words; casually elegant, if sometimes hackneyed, metaphors; and a restrained suggestion of some profundity just beyond the text's expressive capacity—all of which aspire to a tasteful wedding between everyday consciousness and novelistic lyricism.

If Kathryn's thoughts sometimes assume a novelistic idiom, the novelistic idiom often seems to imitate the structure of her thoughts, as in this description of a brawl between her and her husband.

> She climbs the stairs to Jack's office and stands silently with her glass of wine, leaning against the doorjamb. She has no articulate dialogue, just truncated thoughts, unfinished sentences. Phrases of frustration.
> Perhaps she has had too much to drink. (102)

Keen to articulate Kathryn's inarticulateness, the text imitates her fractured thoughts, offering a pair of phrases followed by a sentence fragment. The language appears, for a moment, to break down, as the narration performs a kind of sympathetic identification with Kathryn at her most unseemly.[2] But the text does not entirely surrender its poise or its formality; the aim here is not to accentuate satirically the protagonist's drunk and disheveled condition but to dignify her emotional pain in a characteristically muted fashion. Significantly, this passage, with its "unfinished sentences" and "phrases of frustration," is as far as the text ever goes in calling attention to its own language, and even here the syntactical subversion is extremely inconspicuous in order to maintain focus upon Kathryn's psychological state. The Uncle Charles Principle, in the absence of authorial irony, insists upon the primacy of the represented subject over the means of representation, in order to provide a fantasy of direct, unmediated access to the character's consciousness.

Subjective Knowledge

If Kathryn makes a claim upon the reader's sympathy in *The Pilot's Wife*, one important basis for this claim is an assumption of widely shared uncertainties about knowledge. Starting with the very first moment of the text, when Kathryn, lying literally in the dark, hears a knocking of unclear significance on the door, *The Pilot's Wife* dramatizes her confrontation with her own ignorance. First she discovers that her husband has been in a plane crash in a region of Ireland that she admits she cannot locate on a map. Over the course of the novel, she learns in piecemeal fashion that her Irish mother-in-law is not, as her husband Jack had informed her, actually dead; that Jack was not in his hotel room the night before the crash; that during their marriage he had also illicitly married an Irish woman living in Britain; that he had conceived two children with her; that he was working for the IRA covertly; and, finally, that Robert, the union representative and her new love interest, had been secretly hoping to uncover the IRA conspiracy all along. These perpetual reminders of her incorrigibly deficient knowledge lead her to ask the question, voiced already once by her daughter, "How do you ever know that you know a person?" (158).

With this question, Shreve universalizes epistemological insecurity, suggesting that it is a general condition. Her premise is not surprising. It registers the well-documented continuation in the postwar period of historical developments that originally precipitated the widespread sense of uncertainty evoked by modernist authors, including bureaucratization, proliferation of media, and the explosion of new specialized forms of knowledge and technical expertise, all of which have led to an overwhelming sense of individual bewilderment and the need for compensation through various kinds of retreat to the domestic, private, or subjective realm.[3] One crucial difference between Shreve and her modernist precursors is that, while modernist laments often seem anguished in confronting limitations on knowledge, Shreve treats this condition as inevitable and offers an awareness of its inevitability as a therapeutic alibi for her characters' inadequacies.[4] While Kathryn is troubled at times by how much she does not know, *The Pilot's Wife* maintains that ignorance is humanizing and thus desirable. As a demonstration of this, Shreve details the encounter between Kathryn and her husband's other wife, Muire. Muire knows everything about Kathryn's life, while Kathryn knows nothing about Muire's, and Kathryn continually remarks to herself upon this discrepancy. But Muire comes across as "cool" or "even cold" (220), and her superiority of knowledge consequently wins her no sympathy, whereas Kathryn's lack of knowledge seems to be the very condition for her reception as a warm, likeable human being.

Although Kathryn is surrounded by individuals, including family members, who conceal their secrets and mislead her, the text suggests that Kathryn is not without resources for discovering the truth. Upon first hearing an unconfirmed account of the crash offered by a fisherman, Kathryn decides, simply because she can picture the images he describes, that it must be true. Throughout the narrative, she experiences a series of what Shreve calls "moment[s] of knowledge" (18), in which she intuits major pieces of information based primarily on an emotion or mental image prior to any empirical confirmation. She guesses that the stranger at the door is there to tell her about a plane crash, that there was a bomb on her husband's plane, that her husband did not in fact commit suicide as some have been alleging, and that a first name written on a scrap of paper refers to Robert's mistress. Of course, Kathryn's intuitions have been wrong before, and egregiously so, but once she finds herself trapped in a concentrated and visceral relationship with her own emotions, brought about by grief, then her guesses, surmises, and visions seem to acquire an unshakeable grasp on reality. By endowing Kathryn with unfailingly accurate intuitions, Shreve implies that her character has access to a supremely reliable, yet wholly subjective source of knowledge through an intimacy with her own affective impulses. This somewhat dubious proposition, which celebrates "the hunch" and asserts an obscure correlation between psychological pain and epistemological potency, clearly represents a compensation for and a consequence of various exclusions from more public, socially constituted forms of information.

The subjective, then, becomes the realm in which truth resides, if one has attained a sufficiently intense familiarity with it. Furthermore, *The Pilot's Wife* seems to privilege not only truths that emanate from the subjective, but also truths *about* the subjective. Individual consciousness functions in the novel as the central truth capable of accounting for all other phenomena.

In trying to determine what caused her husband to become involved with the IRA, Kathryn considers a variety of possibilities, and even reads books about the Irish troubles, but the explanations she produces are psychological rather than political per se. "What baffled her now, though, was not the reason for such a conflict, but Jack's participation in it, a reality she could barely absorb" (264). She wonders, "Had he believed in the cause, or had he been drawn to its seeming authenticity? She could see the appeal of that, the instant meaning given to life" (264–65). With even greater assurance, she decides that the psychodynamics of Jack's family must be responsible for his participation: "Of course, it would have been the mother, Kathryn thought. A desire to recapture the mother he'd been denied" (266).

Middle-Class Psychology

According to Fredric Jameson, the psychological realm has become a site of apparent depth, meaning, and complexity that enables fantasies of escape from a fragmented, alienating, market-centered social landscape. But the emphasis on the psychological and on the concomitant notion of privacy, in his view, helps to produce this atomized world, and to preclude our capacity to imagine or construct collective forms of existence (*Political* 221–22). Moreover numerous scholars, political thinkers, and journalists have contended that the magnification of the psychological through various therapeutic techniques supports the position of the privileged in the United States by de-emphasizing and obscuring the consequences of invidious divisions based on class, race, and culture, asserting that what truly defines people are the features of their inner selves, underneath all of the purportedly inessential sociological trappings.[5] In many ways, *The Pilot's Wife* and women's fiction in general, with their emphasis on women's domestic dramas, exemplify these tendencies. Kathryn, for instance, understands her struggles primarily in psychological terms, and she occasionally imagines herself as exemplifying broad universal truths about human nature, thus ignoring her own sociological specificity. In describing Kathryn's growing intimacy with the union representative Robert, Shreve writes, "She studied him and added a small detail to a portrait that had been forming since the day he'd entered her house. It was what one did with people, Kathryn thought, form portraits, fill in missing brushstrokes, wait for form and color to materialize" (172). But if the text treats Kathryn as an example of what "one" does, as a kind of everyperson, or everywoman, it also codes her unmistakably as middle class, in part precisely through its avowal of her psychological propensities. When Kathryn imagines the possibility of her daughter's death, she maintains that it would be "literally unbearable." This second misuse of the term "literally" establishes narrow limits for what kinds of pain Kathryn ought to be capable of withstanding, which coincide with an insulated middle-class existence unaccustomed to the miseries borne by members of other classes with depressing frequency. Later in the novel, when Kathryn is forced to see herself through the critical eyes of her husband's other wife, she acknowledges somewhat reluctantly that "she, of course, lived in what might be described as a suburb" (221).

Moreover, the novel's effort to provide a direct evocation of Kathryn's private thoughts seems to depend entirely upon her conformity to middle-class norms. Notice the assumptions that the novel's opening relies upon in describing her interiority:

She heard a knocking, and then a dog barking. Her dream left her, skittering behind a closing door. It had been a good dream, warm and close, and she minded. She fought the waking. It was dark in the small bedroom, with no light yet behind the shades. She reached for the lamp, fumbled her way up the brass, and she was thinking, *What? What?*

The lit room alarmed her, the wrongness of it, like an emergency room lit at midnight. She thought in quick succession: Mattie. Then, Jack. Then, Neighbor. Then, Car accident. But Mattie was in bed, wasn't she? Kathryn had seen her to bed, had watched her walk down the hall and through a door, the door shutting with a firmness that was just short of a slam, enough to make a statement but not provoke a reprimand. (3)

The passage demonstrates how very few hints are necessary to conjure the details of conventional suburban domesticity. Jack, the reader is invited to assume, is her husband, and Mattie her passively rebellious teenage daughter. The neighbor is a fellow resident of her affluent suburb, where barking dogs and occasional car accidents represent the only danger to peace and harmony. Kathryn's singular terror acquires significance only against this background of stability, prosperity, and privacy, which the reader can infer wholesale, in all of its economic and social dimensions. While she emphasizes Kathryn's psychological responses, Shreve relies upon interpretive assumptions about her social position to fill in the context, enabling the narrative to offer an economical evocation of Kathryn's consciousness with all of the mental shorthand that a character in her situation would be likely to use: "Mattie. Then, Jack. Then, Neighbor. Then, Car accident." No cumbersome exposition explaining what all of these names signify interrupts the fluid transcription of Kathryn's private thoughts. Her submission to middle-class social codes, in other words, renders her interiority representable.[6] Of course, not all readers will interpret Kathryn primarily or fundamentally as an embodiment of middle-class status, but in order simply to follow the narrative, to fill in the informational gaps, the "missing brushstrokes," they must at least register certain facts about her class position and social context.

Notwithstanding the novel's therapeutic assumption that the psychological is the privileged realm of individuality, Kathryn's own psychological tendencies turn out to be remarkably conventional — which may account for the repeated complaints made by customers on Amazon that the book is excessively clichéd.[7] No laboratory of idiosyncratic concoctions, Kathryn's mind, even when glimpsed in its least public, most inward manifestations, lacks a single element or pretense of originality, eccentricity, or novelty. Her ponderous march through the textbook stages of grief stimulates excitement only when it collides with various revelations about her husband's plane crash. Often her consciousness seems designed solely to produce uncritical platitudes about its own submission to generalities. Surprised by all of the press attention after the plane crash, she wonders, "How could she possibly be the focus of so much attention, she who had lived the most ordinary of lives under the most ordinary of circumstances?" (109).

Shreve's assiduous erasure of any truly individuating characteristics emphasizes Kathryn's role as broadly representative of a particular, if somewhat loosely defined, sociological type — the very category of readers *The Pilot's Wife* aims to address: middle-class, college-educated, suburban women.[8] At one point Shreve even notes that Kathyrn generally reads "fiction written by women, usually contemporary novels" (176), as if to make it utterly clear that her protagonist is designed to be a stand-in for Shreve's own readers. Obviously all fictional characters, however idiosyncratic, function to a degree as types, but, more than other authors, Shreve seems actively to avoid any gestures that would create a sense of her protagonist's uniqueness. Kathryn is manifestly a representative of a large class, an undifferentiated target of collective projection, a hypothetical measure of what all of Shreve's readers would do if confronted with a similarly catastrophic event. The novel might appear to be depicting one particular individual's response to a particular scenario, but it is obviously describing a set of generic psychological responses characteristic of a larger demographic category to a situation that represents a source of widespread, class-inflected anxiety. Many readers, of course, would not agree with this interpretation of the text, and most would not choose to articulate their understanding of it in the manner that I have. Yet the act of identification with the protagonist presupposes that the character is not merely an individual, but a figure for a shared body of psychological tendencies invested in a broadly resonant social dilemma. This claim is not, of course, all that controversial; it simply suggests that the psychological, ostensibly individual-centered discourse of the middlebrow novel has a fairly accessible social, or perhaps even sociological, valence, which critical scholarship on the left tends to obscure.

The Invasion of the Political

If Kathryn is less a person than she is a representative of generic psychological tendencies, what exactly does she represent? I would argue that from the first moment of the novel, when a knocking on the door disrupts her sleep, Kathryn embodies the middle-class struggle for privacy. Robert, who does his best to shield Kathryn from the press after the plane crash, describes his job:

> "I like to think of myself as forming a cocoon around the family,"
> he said, "insulating them from the outside world."
> "Which has so grotesquely intruded," she said.
> "Which has so grotesquely intruded." (53)

Though the outside world may assume multiple forms and enter the domestic sphere in a variety of ways, what troubles Kathryn the most, and what is revealed only after all of the other secrets in the novel have come out, is the presence, in her home, of the political — the very thing against which her privacy is supposedly defined. Shocked by her husband's clandestine IRA association, Kathryn wonders, "Had [her] life been invaded in ways she'd never noticed?" (266). Though its evocation of military conflict is certainly appropriate, the term "invade" connotes an action too direct, forceful, and obvious to describe the surreptitious manner in which her husband's political commitments have infiltrated and shaped their domestic interactions. The political does not exactly smash loudly through her front door; it gradually unmasks itself until Kathryn discovers that it has been there all along.

The deliberately frightening image of the political mobilized by *The Pilot's Wife* invites comparison to Carl Schmitt's equally frightening understanding of the political as a mode of struggle that radically and dangerously divides people into friends and enemies who are ultimately willing, if necessary, to destroy each other. While Schmitt maintains that conspicuous markers identify the political enemy and estrange him from the group to which one belongs, Kathryn comes to the startling realization that her own husband was, before his death, a stranger, a member of a militant organization whose tactics and ideology pose a violent challenge to the middle-class suburban values that she upholds. She remembers his willingness during their arguments to "escalate hostilities," a phrase that implies, in light of her discoveries, a new set of disturbing possibilities well outside the conventional limits of nonviolent marital friction.

The revelations that emerge after the death of Kathryn's husband radically undermine her capacity to comprehend or categorize him. The ostensibly inviolable boundaries of the domestic sphere against the intrusions of the political depend upon the stability and knowability of friend-enemy groupings; there can be no strangers disguised as friends, no potential enemies within the safe circle of the family. Thus Kathryn's defining and most humanizingly representative trait, her epistemological uncertainty, encapsulated by the question "[H]ow do you ever know that you know a person?" (158), entails irresolvable anxieties about the possibility of political conflict inside her home.[9] Her discovery of her husband's IRA activities ultimately endows, retrospectively, all of their quotidian rituals, minor quarrels, and failures of communication with political significance. The first time around, Kathryn reads these difficulties, innocently enough, as symptoms of a normal marriage; her perfectly plausible yet entirely mistaken interpretation constitutes a frightening, if thrilling, warning to the reader, attaching incipient political pathos to the most everyday details of domestic life—whose true character an obscure future may one day unmask. Kathryn characterizes her memories of her husband as "mines in a field, waiting to detonate" (169). As the novel progresses, she comes to view more and more of her existence through political or military metaphors, observing that her grandmother "moved through the house with the stolid presence of a relief worker in an emergency zone" (30), and later remarking upon her "distinct sense that they [she and her family] were involved in a war, that they were all in danger of becoming battle casualties" (73).

Friend-enemy indeterminacy recurs in a variety of contexts in the novel. Jack, it turns out, was himself betrayed by the supposed IRA members who gave him a package to deliver; it contained a bomb unbeknownst to him, and his friends who gave it to him were actually enemies, members of a loyalist paramilitary group. Robert, Kathryn's helper throughout her grieving process and potential lover, has been motivated by a secret agenda: to uncover the ring of IRA members working for his airline. Upon discovering this, Kathryn takes abrupt leave of him, remarking accusingly, "I trusted you," suggesting that he is no different from her husband—yet another stranger masquerading as a friend. Muire, Jack's other wife, comes to Kathryn in what could be read as a gesture of friendship, on the basis of the shared blood between their children, and tells her about Jack's IRA affiliations, but Muire does not realize that Kathryn is actually her enemy, or at least unwittingly allied with her enemy. Hence Muire's confession, heedlessly offered in front of Robert, puts her in danger of incarceration. Finally, Kathryn creates the condition for estrangement between her and her daughter, Mattie, keeping secret all she knows about her husband's other family in Ireland.

The existence of secrets is what destabilizes given friend or enemy categories, as Kathryn has learned from both Jack and Robert. Indeed she acknowledges a connection between her strategy for dealing with Mattie and Robert's strategy for dealing with her: "She realized that Robert, too, had gambled. As she was doing now with Mattie. Not revealing something she might" (292). What are the stakes of such a gamble? At a minimum, Kathryn has injected an element of unknowability into the family, as her husband did before, creating latent divisions that keep open the question of potential political escalation within the supposedly apolitical space of the domestic sphere. This is not to say that by keeping a secret from her daughter, Kathryn turns her into a political enemy. But the parallel the text draws between the secretive behavior of Jack and Robert toward Kathryn and Kathryn's secretive behavior toward Mattie appropriates the tension, pathos, and uncertainty embedded in Jack's political activities and injects them into the private dynamics of Kathryn's relationship with her daughter.

The Pilot's Wife appears to offer a salutary reminder that the measures members of the middle class take to protect the domestic sphere from the intrusions of the outside world and from the dangers of politics are, themselves, completely political in character. But Shreve's strategy actually serves to camouflage the crucial political act that Kathryn has committed, drowning the specificity of her actual political involvement inside an inescapable ocean of diffuse political pathos. Though devoid of explicit intention, Kathryn's actions appear to lead indirectly to the capture of Muire and her associates within the IRA — an organization whose radical nationalist ideology is at odds with Kathryn's bourgeois values. But the text abstains, perhaps deliberately, from explaining how exactly these developments unfold, thus obscuring whatever responsibility Kathryn might bear for their outcome. And she herself denies any direct conflict between her and the IRA or any complicity between her and the forces that would quell this organization.

> Now there was again a cease-fire. It was possible that one day there would be a resolution, although Kathryn didn't think it would happen soon.
>
> But it was not for her to say. It was not her war. (285)

Although she reads about the Irish troubles, she refuses to take sides, refuses any acknowledgment of her own involvement. Kathryn's implicit argument is that, while the IRA is engaging in political struggle, she is simply trying to lead an ordinary life safely shielded from the cross fire. Thus she disavows the political character of her desire for privacy and the way it functions, necessarily, as one agenda within a field of competing interests and ideological aims.

Shreve abets Kathryn's denial of her political relationship with the IRA, not by effacing her investment in politics per se but by multiplying the hints, signs, and possibilities of latent political drama within her everyday life. The inadequacy of knowledge that Shreve insists upon as a general condition seems to defer any certainty regarding friend or enemy categories. In effect, *The Pilot's Wife* naturalizes the political, discovers its origins and its dangers just about everywhere—an agenda confirmed by the repeated use of military imagery to describe the ocean that abuts Kathryn's house. Shreve describes its color as "gunmetal blue" (271) and later observes, "the sun had popped, a detonation on the sea, and the water had turned, for a few glorious minutes, a flat rippling turquoise, reflecting the mackerel pattern of the neon. It was the paradoxical beauty of a nuclear bomb, she had thought, or of a fire aboard a ship" (284). Shreve's politicization of the domestic sphere obviously owes a debt to the second-wave feminist movement's compelling deconstruction of the personal-political binary.[10] But *The Pilot's Wife* does not offer or invite a feminist analysis of Kathryn's marital problems; it does not make any explicit connections between her complaints about her husband and their respective gender roles. Instead, it simply appropriates the vague but potent modes of drama and affect that attend violent political conflicts and inserts them into Kathryn's private existence in a way that obscures the particularity of her most significant political act vis-à-vis the IRA. In other words, the text's strategy of proliferating and internalizing ominously unfocused political anxieties makes it somewhat harder to recognize that Kathryn does have an easily definable and locatable political enemy: anyone or anything that actively works to undermine the privacy of her family as well as the middle-class structures that support it.

Political Therapy

A question obviously worth considering is why Shreve saturates the domestic space with quasipolitical tension. What purpose does this serve? Is it not, after all, a collective fantasy of the middle class that the home remain a private, apolitical space? To answer these questions, it is necessary to return for a moment to Kathryn's defining trait: her banality. Given her lack of eccentricity, wit, and unpredictability, Kathryn is in great danger of being a completely uninteresting character. But she has nevertheless inspired enough fascination and sympathy to make *The Pilot's Wife* a best seller. Kathryn accomplishes this not because of any intrinsic properties, but because of her proximity to political conflict, which serves to enliven her quotidian existence. Shreve's novel is in fact a response to the flip side of the middle class's intense desire for privacy, safety, and security: its equally intense anxieties regarding the banality, boredom, and conformity that seem to accompany the fulfillment of its desires.

Shreve's tendency to represent the private sphere as imperiled by obscure but potentially deadly threats has rendered her work somewhat resistant to classification. Her purportedly careful attention to style and character psychology has led many critics to classify her writing as "literary," while her sensational plotlines, composed of catastrophic accidents, festering secrets, and steamy seduction scenes, cause others to treat her work as lowbrow genre fiction. Indeed, as several savvy readers have recognized, she has strategically positioned herself in between these categories. Jocelyn Mc-Clurg concludes that her books are "Harlequins for the high-minded" (McClurg 4d; Mobilio 10). In discussing Shreve's novel *Fortune's Rocks*, Albert Mobilio suggests that she "classes up her soap opera," but "no matter what highbrow atmospherics are deployed, this is still a novel in which 'the sea continually licks the pink and silver sand,' and the presiding spirit is that of Fabio, not Henry James."[11] Shreve herself has contributed to uncertainty about her status. Discussing in an interview her fondness for Wharton's *Ethan Frome*, which several of her novels reference, she remarks, "I consider it a nearly perfect novel. It's a framed story and contains within it the delicate thread of literary suspense" (Papinchak 29). Coupling the terms "literary" and "suspense," Shreve treats Wharton as a model for the hybrid fiction she seeks to produce, thus employing a canonical figure to support her claim that an exciting, plot-driven narrative can be a constitutive element of a great literary work.

By branding herself in this ambivalent fashion, Shreve appeals to several different categories of readers, especially to those middlebrow audiences who want the elevating satisfactions of serious literature but without relinquishing the pleasures of a page-turner. But as a "literary" author, she does not offer readers pure thrillers; the action is typically muted, offstage, or incipient, a hovering threat worthy of attention primarily for the psychological repercussions that it produces. This tendency to translate various struggles — economic, bodily, political — into therapeutic challenges not only allows Shreve to avoid being pigeonholed as a writer of genre fiction; it also serves as an antidote to banality, allowing her readers to imagine that the perversely satisfying feelings of uncertainty and fear precipitated by her novels put them in contact with real, substantial, character-building hardship. Or as critic Tom Shone notes, in discussing Shreve, "The promise of trauma takes on a rather inviting glow; readers slip into these books as they would into a warm bath" (34).

Shreve finds a therapeutic solution to middle-class boredom in her appropriation of the political, which apparently offers automatic access to drama, individuality, mystery, and even psychological depth. A quick glance at Kathryn and her husband, Jack, confirms this claim. Compared to Kathryn, whose conscious political investments are fairly limited, Jack comes across as an intriguing, multidimensional character. While Kathryn uses the phrases "aggressively sterile" and "spectacularly dull" to describe her Methodist church and public school education, she imagines Jack's Catholic upbringing — which ultimately helps to motivate his political commitments — as colorful, rich, and mysterious (143–44). It is Jack who cultivates a knowledge of somewhat obscure artists. It is Jack who springs upon Kathryn a series of surprises, including the sudden purchase of a house overlooking the ocean where they first consummated their love and a harrowing but exhilarating flight in a stunt plane. It is Jack who throws a fully functional computer down a staircase in a moment of marital frustration. And it is Jack who responds to the joking innuendoes of marital infidelity made by an annoying fellow guest at a suburban picnic by remarking, "I try to screw around as much as I possibly can" — the one instance of bona fide irony in the entire text (198). With his passions, quirks, and ambiguities, Jack embodies a surprising correlation between political involvement and roundness of character.

Jack's ironical quip is more memorable than anything Kathryn utters partially because it refuses direct disclosure of his private thoughts or the truth about his extramarital activities. Its power lies in its tonal illegibility — enabling a reading of his character as paradoxical and multilayered. Jack is intriguing because he is capable of keeping a secret, and his reticence invites speculation, which projects psychological depth into his interior. Jack's secrecy, it should be noted, is motivated by his political commitments, and at the same time secrecy produces what could be read as further political tension inside his family, through its destabilization of clear friend or enemy categories. The connections between Jack's apparent characterological complexity, his secrecy, and his political involvement betray an ambivalence within middlebrow culture about the way it tends to conceive of psychological depth. Kathryn, after all, is supposed to be the most fully developed character in the text, and yet Shreve's efforts to offer an unadulterated intimacy with her interior thoughts, through free indirect discourse and the Uncle Charles Principle, actually flatten Kathryn, reduce her to a cliché. Significantly, the psychological transparency exemplified by Shreve's nonironic use of the Uncle Charles Principle mimics the confessional, personal modes of disclosure enabled and safeguarded by the private sphere and its purportedly secure removal from overt political struggles. It is in the safety of the home, the therapeutic paradigm suggests, that we can inhabit and express our true, deep, interior selves. But *The Pilot's Wife* reveals the latent middle-class anxiety that complete detachment from the intrigues and uncertainties of political conflict and enclosure within a private sphere of unmediated honesty and trust actually vacate the self, rendering it fully transparent and unredeemably dull. Jack avoids this hazard through his unremitting secrecy and his concomitant investment in politics. Interestingly enough, the deployment of the Uncle Charles Principle in *The Pilot's Wife* serves contradictory ends. It seems to abet fantasies of a purely apolitical, private realm through its imitation of intimate confessional practices. At the same time, however, it invites the uncertainties and ambiguities that promote political pathos through its eschewal of omniscience and its incapacity to categorize characters, even husbands and wives, unequivocally as friends or enemies.

Despite Jack's compelling opacity, many readers will of course remain committed to Kathryn as the truly important and central character within the text, the one worthy of identification. But she is able to sustain interest only because of her relationship to Jack and her reluctant involvement in his political commitments. The narrative structure in fact supports the idea that Jack is the more intriguing of the two.[12] Kathryn emerges as fully, transparently knowable in the first few pages, and her actions and decisions never produce any surprises. By contrast, readers learn progressively more about Jack as the story proceeds through a series of flashbacks, with each chapter offering new and unexpected pieces of information about him; and the very movement of the novel is motivated by the gradual excavation of his character. Ultimately, by means of deception and betrayal, Jack, in a way, transfers his depth, complexity, and allure to Kathryn, enabling her to play the role of protagonist successfully. And, by the end of the novel, she seems actively, if nervously, to embrace this transference, deciding to keep a secret from her daughter, mimicking the gesture that initially invited political drama into the family, and taking the first step toward becoming an actual character. Shreve's strategy here is a clever response to the contradictory desires among middlebrow readers. On the one hand, she validates Kathryn's intense urge to maintain the privacy and security of the domestic sphere; on the other hand, she enables her protagonist to elude the self-nullifying effects of total immersion in that sphere by preserving a haunting sense of her proximity to the political and its attendant affective energies, via her relationship to her husband.

Given that political drama emerges in the novel as a condition for personhood, Shreve offers readers the fantasy, or nightmare, of a fully politicized domestic sphere. Although *The Pilot's Wife* depicts an extreme scenario, the effect of Kathryn's eventual knowledge is to invest, retroactively, all of the ostensibly mundane conflicts between her and her husband with a kind of teleological political significance. The novel, then, poses the question to readers: What unknown political attachments, commitments, or causes might intrude, or might have already intruded, upon your home life in order to shape its purportedly private dynamics? The function of this unsettling question, I would maintain, is paradoxically therapeutic, a means of mitigating the banality and validating the anxieties and challenges of middle-class existence. Thus *The Pilot's Wife* registers both the epistemological uncertainties and the subjective rewards that attend political involvement.

Kathryn's status as an object of identification and a figure for a particular demographic's shared inclinations entails that her ambivalent relationship to the political epitomizes a widespread attitude within the suburban middle class in the United States. And while this sensibility, as *The Pilot's Wife* demonstrates, clearly predates 9/11, the Bush administration's War on Terror rendered it more explicit, particularly among the so-called security moms who presumably constitute a significant portion of Shreve's readership. In President Bush's famous speech, delivered to a joint meeting of Congress on September 20, 2001, several statements bear further scrutiny vis-à-vis the ambiguous boundary between the private and the political that I have been exploring. Addressing the question of how Americans ought to respond to the attack on 9/11, Bush declares, "I ask you to live your lives and hug your children. I know many citizens have fears tonight and I ask you to be calm and resolute, even in the face of a continuing threat" ("President Bush's Address"). The War on Terror, as described by Bush, seems to represent a profound, if self-concealing, politicization of everyday life. Insofar as the "terrorists kill not merely to end lives but to disrupt and end a way of life," simply the act of leading one's private life and caring for one's children constitutes, according to Bush, a potent response to radical terrorism. As in *The Pilot's Wife*, the domestic sphere becomes both valorized and diffusely threatened, an object of anxiously protective measures and a space of unlikely heroism that is invested paradoxically in maintaining a fidelity to unheroic everydayness.

In his memorable formulation, "fear and freedom are at war," Bush conflates the political and the therapeutic even further. His argument is that terrorists aim to control or inflict damage upon not only physical territory or material resources, but also the collective emotional life of American citizens. To the extent that people feel fear, the terrorists have achieved a victory—an argument well encapsulated by the tendency to describe the conflict with Al-Qaeda as the "War on Terror" rather than the "War on Terrorism." The private emotions of American citizens, then, become not only a way of responding to political struggle, but the very tools and objects of political struggle. Americans are thereby empowered to believe that their affective responses, along with their quotidian domestic routines, participate in the collective political battle against terrorism. But defeating terror, according to Bush, involves securing and inhabiting a space that is removed from the hazards of political conflict and the intense modes of affect that such conflict would inevitably inspire. Thus the private sphere functions as a crucial site of resistance to terrorism and serves national interests only insofar as it is perceived to exist safely beyond the reach of terrorism. The Bush administration seems to insist, in other words, that Americans experience the private sphere as both the most vitally political and the most impermeably apolitical place in America. And it is to just this kind of bipolar domestic existence that Kathryn returns at the end of *The Pilot's Wife*.

To be sure, these contradictory conceptions of the private sphere originate in the rhetoric of the cold war and the widespread fear of totalitarianism, but I would argue that the United States has witnessed a subtle shift in the past decade, one that exemplifies the current hegemony of the therapeutic.[13] While cold war rhetoric warned about the threats to domestic privacy and subjective autonomy posed by the specter of a communist state, Americans typically understood the war as a conflict between competing ideologies. Articulations of the War on Terror by contrast frequently invoke a confrontation of opposed affective dispositions or psychological states, as evidenced by the regularly quoted statement from Al-Qaeda: "You love life and we love death," or by constant attributions of mental instability or insanity to Jihadists among American politicians and journalists.

In the years following 9/11, the intensified investment of the personal in the War on Terror became less pronounced, as increasing numbers of Americans dissociated themselves from the Bush administration's rhetoric. But the popularity of *The Pilot's Wife* indicates that the president was simply drawing upon a pre-existing and persistent need within the suburban middle class, which looks to fiction, in the absence of more spectacularly public outlets, for satisfaction. Many works within the middlebrow genre feature structures similar to *The Pilot's Wife*, dramatizing various threats, political or otherwise, to the privacy of the domestic sphere and evoking the strange mix of fear and desire that these threats inspire. It is important to keep in mind, of course, that alliances between the political and the therapeutic frequently instantiated in the middlebrow genre need not function in the same way or serve the same destructive ends as the Bush administration's call for privatized modes of patriotism. The mobilizing idea at the center of *The Pilot's Wife* that involvement in political struggle adds depth and meaning to domestic life is a promising one, insofar as that political struggle is not defensively and paradoxically aimed at re-securing the self-enclosure of the private realm. The Schmittian notion, which Shreve deploys, of the political as the encounter with the enemy is partially responsible for this urge to exhaust all political enthusiasm defending the boundaries of the domestic. A less apocalyptic conception, one that stresses the encounter with the stranger rather than with the enemy and negotiations over differences rather than potentially fatal violence, might productively align itself with the therapeutic in order to serve progressive ends, but only if the latter concept of political struggle does not relinquish the aura of heroism and self-validation that typically attends more dangerous struggles — an aura well captured by Shreve in her depiction of Kathryn's involuntary confrontation with the IRA.

Of equal importance is the recognition, suggested by *The Pilot's Wife*, that ostensibly personal modes of affect and psychological urges are constitutive of larger political struggles. Ideally, this insight can help to broaden our conception of the public sphere and identify novel forms of political participation disregarded by both traditional and progressive models of engaged citizenship.[14] In his presidential campaign, Obama's appeal to emotions shared across ideological, ethnic, and class boundaries, through his invocation of hope, exemplifies an effort to enact political change through the deployment of a psychological vocabulary. As we will see in the chapter that follows on Khaled Hosseini's *The Kite Runner*, this utopian belief that a recognition of affective commonality can overcome various ethnic and ideological divisions is pervasive among American readers. While Obama has obviously recognized that tapping into this belief can inspire political involvement among disaffected voters, it also poses hazards, as many critics and scholars have noted. Assertions of an already existing emotional unity may in some cases serve as merely a convenient cover for a failure to enact concrete policies that actually reduce invidious divisions and disparities among Americans.[15] What these various cases appear to demonstrate, then, is that the therapeutic and the political have the potential to gain enormous resources from each other, but only if their increasing interpenetration re-energizes, without obscuring or disabling, the virtues that are distinctive to each category.

CHAPTER SIX

Reading *The Kite Runner* in America

THE EFFUSIVE CUSTOMER reviews of Khaled Hosseini's *The Kite Runner* posted on Amazon often register surprise: Many Americans were initially reluctant to read what they perceived to be "foreign" fiction.[1] Their short-lived resistance and their subsequent enthusiasm raise an important question. What does this novel, largely about Afghanistan, offer American readers? Why did so many not merely purchase the book but skip work, ignore children, and delay sleep to finish it, and why did they then proceed to recommend it to everyone they knew, making *The Kite Runner* a massive best seller without the help of any large-scale promotional mechanisms?[2]

One Amazon customer explains the book's appeal thus: "It is foreign in language at times, in metaphor some of the time, and in detail of situation almost all the time. But at its core it is more deeply human than any book I've read this year. Loss, grief, betrayal, honor, guilt, self-contempt, love, redemption — these cross nationalities and ethnicities and if anyone doubted that I challenge them to hold those same doubts after reading this novel. Hosseini has fashioned his characters and situations into sharp drillpoints that bore inside the reader and leave him/her gasping in pain and pleasure" (B. Capossere). As an invitation to read *The Kite Runner*, the reviewer promises a sadomasochistic experience. Though slightly more graphic than the average, this review is an exemplary measure of the visceral, intimate, sometimes painful relations between book and reader that *The Kite Runner* enables and consumers seek.[3] In this chapter, I examine Hosseini's novel and some of the hundreds of responses to it on Amazon — a remarkable source of information about contemporary readers, which has thus far received scant scholarly attention — to produce a better understanding of how Americans' therapeutic interpretive framework responds to "foreign" fiction. Paradoxically, it turns out, the book's perceived transcendence, its ability to cross the borders between nationalities and ethnicities seems to depend for American readers on its palpable evocation of its unfamiliar setting. In this chapter, then, we return full circle to the central hope of Toni Morrison's *Paradise*: the possibility of identifying with strangers — a possibility whose realization is arguably the defining project of therapeutic discourse, and one that appears, both for Morrison and for many readers on Amazon, to be inseparable from utopian aspirations.

Using Amazon to understand the tastes and interpretive tendencies of contemporary American readers is no less fraught with perils than using Oprah's Book Club for the same purpose. But it is important to recognize that the two are very different forums. While no direct profit motive seems to dictate the book choices Winfrey makes or the way she presents novels, Amazon is an enterprise specifically designed to sell books and other products. And yet, unlike the content presented on Oprah's Book Club, the Amazon customer reviews are entirely uncensored and unpackaged; they are an unmediated reflection of how readers feel and think about certain books often immediately after reading them, and thus instantiate the interpretive experience of Americans more transparently than most other available media. To be sure, the chance to read and write Amazon customer reviews will appeal to a particular subset of the population, and thus what one discovers on Amazon may not be exactly what one would find in a random survey. But the latter would produce its own distortions, and so Amazon may be as useful an archive of contemporary reader responses as one might hope to locate. It is also important to recognize, of course, that this venue shapes as well as reflects the tastes and inclinations of particular readers, since online visitors inevitably find themselves influenced by the reviews they discover there. But this phenomenon, the formation of an interpretive and affective consensus, is something that obviously happens in less visible ways outside of Amazon; the latter, then, merely provides a legible record of this process. Indeed, the customer reviews suggest that the chance to participate in this process, to influence and feel part of a shared literary experience, is what draws many readers to sites such as Amazon and to high-profile best sellers such as *The Kite Runner*. And while I recognize that this particular urge will characterize only a segment of the American reading public, I hope to shed light on why involvement in the development of a collective sensibility might be broadly appealing, especially given the current political climate.

Written in English and designed for an American audience, Hosseini's novel tells the story of Amir, the narrator, who lives with his wealthy father in Kabul. As Pashtuns, the dominant ethnicity in Afghanistan, they have two servants, Ali and Hassan, who are Hazaras, members of an underprivileged minority ethnicity. Although Amir and Hassan are close friends, Amir fails to defend Hassan from being raped by neighborhood bullies in a racist attack. Amir's guilt, in conjunction with his resentment toward Hassan for winning the affection of Amir's distant father, leads Amir to frame Hassan for a petty crime, causing the two servants to depart from the household. Following this, the Soviets invade, Amir and his father immigrate to the United States, Amir marries another Afghan immigrant, his father dies of cancer, and eventually Amir is summoned back to Afghanistan by an old family friend, where he discovers that Hassan is actually his half-brother. But Hassan has been shot by the Taliban, leaving behind an orphan boy named Sohrab. Amir rescues this boy from Assef, the sadistic pedophile who had raped Hassan and who is now a Taliban official. In the process, Amir seeks to atone for his betrayal of Hassan.

Through its evocation of everyday life in Afghanistan and its frequent use of Farsi vocabulary, *The Kite Runner* foregrounds its foreignness. According to David Damrosch, Lawrence Venuti, and Pascale Casanova, works that originate in or depict cultures foreign to their readerships inevitably negotiate two antithetical hazards. One is that readers will exoticize the text, reducing the complexity of the foreign culture to an embodiment of tantalizing inscrutability.[4] The converse danger is that readers will domesticate the text, reading it narcissistically in order to discover attitudes and values that resemble their own. As an alternative to these two approaches, Damrosch recommends a mode of reading that accommodates both the sense of familiarity and the sense of foreignness that such texts inspire. "The issue is to stay alive to the works' real difference from us without trapping them within their original context or subordinating them entirely to our own immediate moment and needs. An emphasis on universality can be a powerful aid in protecting the work from either of these extremes, so long as this universality isn't created by a process of stripping away much of what is really distinctive about the work" (135). Damrosch's advice is aimed primarily at scholars and students confronting world literature in an academic context. His commitment to establishing the professional rigor of cross-cultural interpretation, best encapsulated by his remark that "the specter of amateurism haunts comparative literature today" (284), betrays a lack of confidence in the ability of nonacademic audiences to interpret literary representations of foreignness. But, as the Amazon reviews demonstrate, the flexible, self-aware responsiveness to the intersections and incompatibilities between the readers' culture and the represented foreign culture that Damrosch prescribes to professors and students also characterizes the complex cultural work performed, in a somewhat different register, by *The Kite Runner* and by many of its readers in settings outside the university. The reviews frequently suggest dialectical modes of identification that simultaneously foreground and disavow the alterity of the characters and their culture — and it is the crucial interplay between these seemingly contradictory responses that I aim to examine.

The Kite Runner's resonance in the United States is obviously inseparable from Afghanistan's role in the War on Terror, but the politics of cross-cultural identification turn out, in this case, to be fairly complex, heterogeneous, and unpredictable. In the latter half of this essay, I consider the multiple relations between the American reception of *The Kite Runner* and attitudes toward Islam and the U.S. military presence in the Middle East and central Asia. Overall the book has encouraged increased tolerance and sympathy for Muslims.[5] At the same time, however, certain sections of the text, most notably its depictions of the Taliban, lend tacit support for a neoconservative vision of the United States' interventionist prerogatives. But a majority of reviews disregard *The Kite Runner*'s political valences altogether and in fact several praise it for eschewing any strong political position.[6] Frequently such comments suggest, if not a rejection of the U.S. War on Terror, then a utopian yearning for an alternative, nonpolitical solution to current international conflicts — one predicated on humanistic, affective connections of compassion and identification.

Universal Appeal

Judging by the approximately one thousand reviews of *The Kite Runner* submitted between June 4, 2003, and January 1, 2006, Amazon customers, many of whom belong to book clubs, are motivated to read and write online reviews not only by a desire to share recommendations with like-minded readers but also by an urge to participate in a public forum dedicated to debating the question of what constitutes good literature.[7] A major topic among reviewers is whether *The Kite Runner*'s subject matter, Afghanistan, is responsible for the novel's success. Notwithstanding their initial resistance to the foreign setting, many appreciate Hosseini's novel for offering a digestible history of Afghanistan from the 1970s to the present and for describing some of the country's cultural, social, and religious practices.[8] Other readers, however, assert that the book is popular only because it portrays a country that is front-page news.[9] Eager to forestall these criticisms, reviewers repeatedly maintain that *The Kite Runner* is about not just Afghanistan but also universal human themes, such as guilt, friendship, fatherhood, and forgiveness, and is therefore a classic.[10]

The attention of academic scholarship, in the past few decades, to the cultural and ideological specificity of literary works has obviously challenged the conception of great literature as a repository of universal truths. But, rather than treat the attribution of universality as inherently, indeed *universally*, wrongheaded, it is important to understand this attribution as responsive to a particular set of political circumstances. The category of the universal, as Damrosch notes, has served many different purposes throughout history (135–39). In claiming that *The Kite Runner* treats themes that underscore our shared humanity, readers are often resisting the onslaught of exoticizing, disparaging conceptions of the Islamic world famously lamented by Edward Said and all the more pervasive now.[11] One reviewer remarks, "We 'European Americans' have so little knowledge of that part of the world (we seem to only want to destroy it) that this picture of pre Soviet Afghanistan is a must read for those in the US that think that anyone from South Asia or the Mideast are a bunch of nuts and terrorists" (Megan Brizzolara). Though potentially problematic, assertions of a shared humanity represent what might be called "strategic universalism" —in response to an approach that constitutes ethnic stereotypes as exhaustively definitive and invidiously divides the West and Islam into polarized categories.[12] Thus, one reviewer writes, "A moving coming of age tale that brings us face to face with the reality and beauty of not only the Muslim world but the universality of our common humanity, passions and frailties. Not for the ideologically blinded" (George R. Odell). The rhetoric of universality here reads as a contingently necessary rejoinder to a dehumanizing ideology.

Some reviews that express this kind of sentiment betray undercurrents of ambivalence. According to one, "[Hosseini] says, in effect, here is a story about people in my land of origin. Yes, they are people of Afghanistan, but they are simply people, too, who are much like us" (Bruce Stern). Although insistent upon the characters' humanity, the reviewer asserts a tension, underscored by his use of the word "too," between the category "people of Afghanistan" and the category "simply people" as if Afghans' humanity were guaranteed as a precultural status but also jeopardized by their Afghan nationality. At the same time, he demonstrates his sincere effort to transcend cultural divisions by actively identifying with Hosseini, *voicing* Hosseini's perspective in the first person, declaring that Afghanistan is "my land of origin." A sentence later, however, he quickly, if inconspicuously, repositions himself, identifying with the privileged "us"— that is, American readers — who may be willing to grant personhood to Afghans, but only insofar as they resemble Americans.

As other reviews demonstrate, however, claims about the characters' humanity need not require a negation of their cultural specificity. "From the bigger-than-life father to whom sin at its root is lies, to the son's guilt based on cowardice, to the servants' quiet display of self-confident, natural morality/dignity this novel shows the sin-guilt-belief problem to be universal. In this novel it is played out in an Islamic/Afghani/American stage— the uncommon Afghani backdrop while particularizing the specifics of the story, only adds to the recognition that the problem is universal" (M. J. Smith). Though privileging the American context as normal in opposition to the "uncommon Afghani backdrop," the reviewer's comment insists on a complex understanding of universality. A particular problem is universal only if it emerges in a heterogeneous array of contexts; perceptions of universality, then, require a sensitivity toward difference. In order to be more than simply the apprehension of an abstraction, the recognition of universality requires "specifics." These unfamiliar particulars about Afghanistan add something to this recognition that the reviewer does not name; they lend it concrete substance so that the perception of universality in this articulation can be practically identified with the close apprehension of locally embedded details. In contradistinction to the straw-man conception of universality as a product of insufficiently contextualized interpretive approaches, readers' assertions of universality in this case seem to be the product of empathy energized dialectically by the tensions and contradictions that they are required to negotiate in their efforts to identify with characters who inhabit a culture that they find radically different from their own.

One reviewer remarks: "The author's use of description put me along side him in the pages — I could almost tast [sic] the pommegranite [sic], smell the kabobs cooking, hear the jagged noise of the bazzars [sic], inhale the smoke and dust and ashes. But most importantly, I learned something. Or at least revisited something I've already learned. For me, this is the mark of a great book — that I am removed from my own little patch of universe and submerged in another world altogether and, for all its strangeness, its unfamiliarity, I recongnize [sic] myself, my humanity, in its story" (J. Olcott). It is easy to see why the reviewer finds *The Kite Runner* so satisfying. Her experience enables a sense of her own subjectivity as globally mobile or infinitely capacious, and thus despite the text's "strangeness" and "unfamiliarity," she identifies with the story, feeling as if she embodies humanity in all its heterogeneous manifestations. While scholars such as Elizabeth Barnes argue that sympathy tends to be either too provincial or too homogenizing to serve as a basis for politics, the sympathy articulated by reviewers of *The Kite Runner* often synthesizes a sense of sameness and a sense of otherness, exemplifying a fertile tension, which mediates both their perceptions of the represented foreign characters and, at least in the moment of reading, their perceptions of themselves.

Although readers' imaginative efforts are in part responsible for this defamiliarizing experience of identification, it is an effect that Hosseini clearly aims to produce. Amir describes a typical scene from his childhood as follows: "We chased the *Kochi*, the nomads who passed through Kabul on their way to the mountains of the north. We would hear their caravans approaching our neighborhood, the mewling of their sheep, the *baa*ing of their goats, the jingle of bells around their camels' necks. We'd run outside to watch the caravan plod through our street, men with dusty, weather-beaten faces and women dressed in long, colorful shawls, beads, and silver bracelets around their wrists and ankles. We hurled pebbles at their goats. We squirted water on their mules" (26). Through its glaringly orientalist imagery, the passage allows American readers to enjoy Afghanistan from a comfortable distance, as tourists, but by placing them in an outsider's position it facilitates their identification with Amir, who occupies a similar position in relation to the nomads. Even as it appears to traffic in stereotypes, with its caravans, its camels, and its colorful shawls, the passage reveals some of Afghanistan's complexity, underlining distinctions between the nomads, who have preserved their indigenous culture, and Amir, who watches them with hostile curiosity and spends his afternoons viewing American westerns and drinking Coca-Cola. But if Amir is more Americanized than other segments of Afghan society, he also expresses a profound affection for Kabul's local culture — its bazaars, its cuisine, its language — and as an adult he becomes a practicing Muslim. Indeed, his act of bowing to Mecca and uttering a desperate, half-remembered prayer while doctors struggle to revive his nephew, Sohrab, after a suicide attempt represents one of the most emotionally potent moments in the text. In that scene, Amir's hesitant approach to his inherited religion stands in marked, perhaps deliberate, contrast to the stereotypical image of the fanatical Muslim. With his divided attachments and his hybrid identity, Amir offers a portrayal of Afghanistan that preserves the well-nigh kitschy allure of its perceived foreignness but simultaneously renders its specific cultural practices emotionally resonant for American readers. Moreover his narrative of sin and redemption conforms to both Christian and Muslim concepts of salvation, and it is thus well designed to inspire the kinds of identification, capable of accommodating difference, that its readers consistently describe.

Generally speaking, reviewers characterize the experience of identification as an intensely emotional one; they feel what they believe the characters are feeling: "We feel (and feel for) Amir's hunger for a cold father's love, Hassan's pure and deadly devotion" (Dolly A. Berthelot). Although some readers identify shared values, principles, or concepts, many emphasize emotion as that which transcends socially constituted boundaries: the book "proves that human emotions such as love, loss, betrayal, and hope are timeless and can be found anywhere, regardless of class or culture" (Stephanie Henry). Another reviewer breathlessly reports: "Not knowing anything much about Afghanistan I simply wasn't interested and was afraid it would be about people I could not in any way relate to. How wrong and stupid I was! Oh my. Not only am I now fascinated by Afghanistan and want to learn as much as possible about the country and peoples but if you are a human with a beating heart you will find the themes in this book are universal: love, betrayal, redemption" (Elspeth). Affect, it would seem, wields an almost unquestionable authority. The very faculty for apprehending the universality of certain themes is, according to this reader, the "beating heart." Hence, emotion serves as an instance of cross-cultural continuity and as the means of apprehending and assessing its own unifying character. For many readers, the universal appears to be nothing other than the name for this overwhelming feeling of empathy. And to deny the validity of such feelings or the broad conclusions they support is to raise suspicions about one's humanity. Thus, articulations of affective humanism instantiate a mildly coercive rhetorical power, but in acknowledging this power, I do not mean to dismiss either their validity or the global mimetic purchase of the emotions they invoke. While such contentions mobilize styles of judgment alien to academic modes of inquiry, they merit consideration by all kinds of readers, especially given their obvious, if underexamined, persuasive potency. It is likely that many academics will confront this dilemma in the classroom; the challenge that professors who introduce *The Kite Runner* to their students face, in my view, is to bring these affective negotiations with cultural difference into a critical, mutually invigorating dialogue with the more dispassionate and scholarly strategies, such as the kind that Damrosch demonstrates, without automatically privileging one approach over the other.

Masochism

Given the many harrowing incidents in the novel, identification with its characters can be rather upsetting, even unpleasant. And this raises an important question. What is the appeal of an empathetic experience so powerful that it becomes painful?[13] Amazon reviewers proudly announce that the book made them cry, made them nauseated, made them lose sleep, made them feel beaten up — all of which suggest an intense bodily form of identification with Amir.[14] "There were times I hated reading this book. I went days feeling physcially [sic] sick from the story" (M. Schijvens). "The emotions are so deep and raw, I can't really go into it. This book is filled with such unspeakable sadness. Amir's guilt turned me into an insomniac . . . I was Amir. I felt all the pain and betrayal . . . I was Hassan. I was destroyed, elated, torn in two by the powerful emotions in this book" (Lover of books). One reviewer refers to *The Kite Runner* as "pure CPR!" (Book Maven), a comment that treats vicarious suffering as a revitalizing experience for readers who are in some way emotionally deadened and thus dangerously excluded from a full participation in humanity, a normative category predicated upon affective capacity.

The Kite Runner depicts a peculiar form of suffering, apparently quite commensurate with the needs of many Americans, which defers the catharsis typically provoked by narratives focused on the heroic martyrdom of innocent or helpless victims. That is, it explores the guilt of those who are responsible for or complicit with the victimization of others. As one reviewer puts it: "While reading this book I wished to scream at the characters in the book, wished to tell them that they were making the wrong decision. But then I looked into myself and realized that I would have made the same wrong decision. At that point my hatred was toward myself. This book was moving, so much so that as one of the reviews on the back of the book puts it, it is 'excruciating' to read" (Mark L. Harris). Identifying with a character who falls prey to pettiness, cowardice, and selfishness can be painfully disconcerting. Having watched Hassan get raped without intervening and having then banished his best friend from his home — an act he thinks is indirectly responsible for Hassan's death — Amir is desperate for something apparently many readers also crave: forgiveness.

The second half of the novel depicts Amir's agonizing effort to atone for his crimes, including a near-fatal confrontation with Assef. Amir laughs uncontrollably during the attack, an indication that this punishment is satisfying a deep need. And Hosseini does his best, through an array of tactics, which a few skeptics on Amazon deem "manipulative," to allow readers to experience Amir's suffering vicariously.[15] An urge to inflict emotional pain upon the reader seems to motivate some of the more devastating moments in the text, including Hassan's rape, his execution by Taliban soldiers, and Sohrab's attempted suicide. Apparently the pain of the reading experience allows people to appropriate a measure of atonement for themselves, in relation to their own sense of guilt. One reviewer dramatically observes, "Passages from this book will burn themselves into your heart, breaking it and then putting it back together piece by piece" (K. Kuehl), asserting that *The Kite Runner* wounds readers in order to heal them. Another describes the peace we feel in "releasing our hidden demons" and hopes that, in reading *The Kite Runner*, "you will find inner peace within its pages" (Iles Fan). A third describes the book as initiating a therapeutic process: "The author brilliantly lets us feel the paralysis of fear, then the paralysis of guilt and then finally embark on the road to recovery of both relationship with others and acceptance of ourselves" (Kent Holland).

Identification with Amir, then, performs a complex psychological function. Readers empathize with his suffering and reinforce their belief in their own humanity through an amplification of their emotional economy and a renewed perception of their capacity for compassion. But readers also identify with Amir's status as victimizer, and they are thus reminded of their own mistakes and transgressions. The pain of the reading experience — a mix of guilt-saturated discomfort, embarrassed self-recognition, and visceral compassion — enables them to imagine themselves partaking in Amir's difficult process of atonement. Even many of those reviewers who do not claim that they directly feel Amir's pain take from the book a reactivated belief that their own flaws and weaknesses are defining features of their humanity and thus deserving of forgiveness.[16]

If Amir embodies universal humanity, his crime and its consequences are completely bound up with the particulars of Afghanistan's turbulent history. Partially responsible for Amir's actions toward Hassan are the ethnically determined social roles they have been assigned—roles that, in a sense, *require* Hassan to suffer stoically for Amir. Though disturbing, their master-servant dynamic is not something that Amir can be expected as a boy to understand fully or overcome. At the same time, his choices' devastating repercussions, in part the product of global historical developments, including the Soviet invasion, the civil war, and the Taliban's seizure of power, magnify the meaning of his crime, rendering it at once painfully irrevocable and yet brilliantly legible in its demands for some act of penitence.[17] This, then, is an ideal crime to elicit identification: it is deeply awful, but deeply forgivable, and thus perfectly structured to produce a simulation of valorizing atonement for those whose shortcomings, mistakes, and breaches of ethics fail to acquire such dramatic proportions.

It is important to note that readers do not just imaginatively inhabit Amir's experiences in escapist fashion; they use the novel to recast and disambiguate their own experiences. "I think everyone will see a little bit of themselves or people they know in this remarkable story" (Teacher). "For any child that has treated a friend spitefully, that has acted cowardly, that yearns for the approval of an indifferent parent, that has a sin to expiate, it carries a simple emotional truth" (A New York Reader). The act of identifying with Amir enables readers to appropriate the historically and culturally bound energies attached to Amir's actions and thereby view their own failings as commensurately consequential, clear, and tragic—as both larger in significance and more deserving of forgiveness than these readers may have previously conceived. Afghanistan's sublimely ruinous history has everything to do with this dramatizing, clarifying, and purifying effect, and therefore Amir's culturally specific identity is no less important than its dialectical counterpart, the narrative's perceived transcendence, in eliciting a therapeutic process of identification from readers. Thus, while quick to claim that Amir's story resonates beyond his time and place, reviewers also frequently describe the power Afghanistan, as a setting, exerts over their responses. "I feel like The Kite Runner opened my mind, and desposited me directly into Afganistan" (Tim A.). "I could smell the lamb kabob, and feel the essence of a society so different than our own" (beachlvr). Imaginatively inhabiting a foreign country, readers recognize themselves in an exotically tinged image of suffering humanity that entails the possibility of meaningful atonement—a psychological effect that may account for readers' eagerness to treat the book as universal.

The therapeutic power of the book, then, seems to require perceptions of its dense local texture combined with a sense of its grand universal scope. A common observation is that *The Kite Runner* offers a revealing look at a completely unfamiliar culture and that it nevertheless tells an essentially human story, to which any reader can relate.[18] "In fact the book provides wonderfully vivid descriptions of the locations and cultures of Afghanistan and its people. However, the story here is about the power of friendship and our ability to overcome our weaknesses and prevail over adversity. These themes are universal and will speak to readers of any culture" (Andrew W. Johns). The frequent proximity of these two apparently disparate observations suggests that they are not opposed but instead constitutive of each other and that perhaps the *however* that typically conjoins them ought to be replaced with *therefore*. American readers, in other words, identify with Amir and conceive of him as a universal figure not only *in spite* but also *because* of the particularizing character of his Afghan identity. Amir enables readers to project themselves, through a combination of narcissism and dislocation, into a foreign identity, facilitating their discovery of recognizable values and feelings in what they perceive to be an extremely inhospitable context as a test case of an idealistic hypothesis about human commonality. Identification with Amir's accessible foreignness thus serves to substantiate an otherwise pallidly theoretical understanding of universality, lending it an immediate, defamiliarizing embodiment while simultaneously allowing readers to make a personal claim upon the pain and tragedy that they associate with Afghanistan for a therapeutic process of self-dramatization and self-forgiveness.

One other important basis for the seemingly spontaneous experience of cross-cultural empathy among readers has been Riverhead's low-key marketing approach—in part a product of initially restrained expectations about the book's sales. The popularity of *The Kite Runner*, according to Wyatt, was something of a surprise; word-of-mouth recommendations and consumer-driven forums like book clubs and the Amazon customer reviews were largely responsible for the novel's sales. Many reviews characterize the book as an unexpected discovery. A first-time author with no name recognition, a foreigner writing about Afghanistan for a market that tends to favor domestic settings in an anti-Muslim climate, Khaled Hosseini seems an unlikely star. But this of course has eventually come to work in his book's favor. As we saw with Wells's *Divine Secrets of the Ya-Ya Sisterhood*'s grassroots Ya-Ya clubs and with Wallace's antipublicity publicity campaign, a key ingredient of the purportedly human experience of empathy, the feeling of a special, even private connection with the character or author that novels generate, is the sense that such responses are not the target of corporate manipulation or market research and are thus specific to the individual reader. A central feature of the promotional strategy employed by publishing houses hoping to produce this effect, then, is necessarily to conceal or underplay their own promotional strategies.

Victims and Monsters

The Amazon customer reviews describe a family of affective responses, including sympathy, compassion, empathy, and identification, all of which seem to function as demonstrative proofs of humanity. Interestingly enough, however, the central figure of the reader's identification, Amir, who is generally understood to be the most realistic, most human character in the book, is overwhelmed by anxieties regarding his own humanity. As a young boy, he writes a story about a character whose tears turn into pearls. Greedy for the wealth he can generate, the man eventually murders his wife to make himself cry (30–31). If the reviews of *The Kite Runner* are any indication, tears are a sought-after commodity.[19] But, as Amir's story suggests, they require victims and thus place us in an uneasy, even guilty relationship to those suffering subjects who enable us to experience our own humanity. Amir feels intense sympathy for his half-brother, Hassan, whose ethnicity makes him a tragic victim in Afghan society. To sympathize with a victim and not be one, however, a person must, as Lauren Berlant has observed, occupy a position of privilege and superiority vis-à-vis the victim ("Compassion" and "Poor Eliza"). Hassan, whose innocent, bewildered face Amir compares to that of a sacrificial lamb, suffers dehumanization so that Amir can be human, and the compassion Amir feels for Hassan is accompanied by the anxiety that he himself may be Hassan's victimizer — a status that would paradoxically endanger his own claim to humanity. Remembering a dream Hassan once described about a monster lurking at the bottom of a lake, Amir responds, "I wanted to tell them all that *I* was the snake in the grass, the monster in the lake" (105). What ultimately saves Amir from the status of monster and preserves his humanity is his unremitting sense of guilt. Throughout his life, Amir is tormented, indeed victimized, by the sense that he is a victimizer. And in fact it is his guilt that renders him, for many Amazon reviewers, such a sympathetic, human figure.[20] The readiness to identify with his dilemma betrays something about the guilty conscience of American readers and their need for vicarious experiences that reaffirm their humanity, a status that exists in a complex relation of emotionally fraught mutual dependence with that very sense of guilt. To be human, in other words, is to be guilty, but the form this guilt inevitably assumes, painfully enough, is a festering question about one's humanity.

The truly inhuman character, the monster, is the one who claims to suffer no guilt for his crimes: Assef, the outlandishly evil neighborhood bully and Taliban official. Characterizing his involvement in the ethnic cleansing of Hazaras, Assef declares, "You don't know the meaning of the word 'liberating' until you've done that, stood in a roomful of targets, let the bullets fly, free of guilt and remorse, knowing you are virtuous, good, and decent" (277). Although at one point Amir dreams that Assef tells him, "We're the same, you and I" (307), one of Assef's primary functions in the text is to embody a form of monstrosity against which Amir's guilt-ridden humanity can be defined. Amir sympathizes with Hassan, and in moments he equates himself with Assef, but his status as human depends on his uncomfortable position somewhere in between the roles of victimizer and victim, capable of identifying with both but never truly being either. One reviewer observes, "The main problem in my mind is that there is little character development at all except for the narrator Amir. The good are only good, while the evil are only evil. The good is likened to the lamb about to be sacrificed, while the evil thinks Hitler is a good guy" (kattepus).

Amir, of course, is also the voice and embodiment of Afghanistan for American readers, and his role is to humanize a country that has been viewed reductively in the American media at times as a vicious monster and at times as a sacrificial lamb. In particular, Hosseini is intent upon defining not only Amir but also his country against the monstrosity that Assef instantiates as the book's primary representative of the Taliban. Many customers, who otherwise loved *The Kite Runner*, express puzzlement and irritation with Assef's one-dimensional characterization and with his implausible reappearance as a Taliban official.[21] Assef's excessively evil, entirely unbelievable character seems to inhabit a literary genre separate from that of the rest of the book or an ontological order separate from that of the daily life of Afghanistan, which Hosseini tries to portray in all of its complexity — but this aesthetic inconsistency may be the point. Assef functions as a contrived vehicle designed to characterize the Taliban as an instance of ahistorical evil with no real connection with the rest of Afghanistan. Assef is half-German and from a young age professes an admiration for Hitler; thus Assef's brutality, and by extension the Taliban's, Hosseini suggests, do not originate in anything indigenous or unique to Afghan culture or, for that matter, to Islam.

It is perfectly understandable that Hosseini would want to sever his readers' perceptions of Afghanistan from their views of the Taliban, whose radical ideology does not reflect the beliefs or cultural traditions of a majority of Afghans, but his rhetoric seems in moments to simplify and elide the historical complexity of his country.[22] One reviewer complains, "Hosseini has the skills but not the courage nor the empathy/sympathy to portray the Taliban as historical, sociological, economic, modern creations. Discounting his own skills, he characterizes the Taliban in the easiest way — as simple, cartoonish, evil. He thereby does nothing to enlighten us" (Chai Trek). Of course, one could argue that this customer has approached the novel with misplaced expectations; capturing the Taliban's "historical, sociological, and economic" dimensions may be beyond the purview of a work of fiction. The reason that his or her concerns are worth entertaining, however, is that many readers seem to approach *The Kite Runner* either as an accurate record of Afghanistan's recent history or as a preferable substitute for such a record — more valuable than nonfiction precisely for its humanizing function. But Hosseini's text performs this function by means of some dangerous misrepresentations — most notably, an unrealistic, demonizing portrait of the Taliban, which, at least in certain moments, de-emphasizes the historical conditions that help to account for their emergence.[23] It is extremely unlikely, for instance, that Assef, the son of upper-middle-class parents living in Kabul, would have joined the Taliban, given that they won their recruits during the 1990s primarily from the rural impoverished refugees dependent on the charity of the madrasas in Peshawar and that they generally installed their own members when occupying a city (Rashid). Although in other moments in the text Hosseini describes the brutal Soviet invasion, the civil war between rival mujahedin, and the unbearable poverty that led people to welcome the Taliban for their ability to restore order to the country, his treatment of Assef seems to downplay the multiple conditions responsible for the Taliban's appeal, instead positing a monstrous appetite for violence as the primary motive for supporting or participating in the group's activities.

The Kite Runner's depiction of the Taliban appears to lend support for the U.S. invasion of Afghanistan. And yet, while some readers have drawn this conclusion, others have interpreted the novel as fundamentally at odds with Bush's War on Terror. It is possible, of course, to conclude that *The Kite Runner* provides evidence in favor of the decision to invade Afghanistan but does not endorse the Bush administration's overall approach to foreign policy or the war in Iraq. What is remarkable about Hosseini's novel, however, is its capacity to appeal to readers who understand it as categorically supporting a neoconservative interventionist philosophy and to those who understand it as categorically opposing this position, while also earning praise among many for apparently avoiding a determinate political stance altogether. How do the novel's rhetorical postures structure and delimit its interpretations so as to give the heterogeneous range of responses their particular shape? *The Kite Runner*'s popularity can be understood, I would argue, as a product of its responsiveness to geo-therapeutic needs shared by readers on both sides of the ideological spectrum. Encouraging Americans' belief that they are human — that is, imperfect but nonetheless compassionate and benign — is evidently a function with widespread appeal. But Hosseini's concept of the human is malleable enough to serve competing political agendas, each of which accents this concept in its own characteristic way.

Bolstered by an abundance of textual evidence, those on Amazon who interpret the book as supporting Bush's overall foreign policy outnumber those who read it as rejecting his policy by approximately two to one. The Afghanistan Amir remembers inhabiting as a child, an idealized product of his nostalgia, is fairly permissive and thus ostensibly ripe for American-style democracy. One reader, equating Afghanistan in the 1970s with the United States now, remarks: "Being the wife of a career soldier who has spent time in the Middle East, I have to say that this book really made me realize what we are fighting for. . . . the life that these people used to have, the life that we Americans take for granted everyday" (B. Udy). Although the Bush administration's War on Terror seems to have produced largely negative perceptions of Islam,[24] its interventionist approach, as this review points out, depends in its most idealistic articulations on the assertion of common human urges — most notably, a desire for freedom — that ought, in its view, to render the people of Islamic nations amenable to the United States' democratizing mission. For some readers, then, Hosseini's effort to underscore commonalities between Afghans and Americans lends support for this mission.[25]

Bush's supposedly inclusive conception of humanity, of course, requires the demonization of certain people — alleged terrorists, who define humanity by standing outside its normative limits — a tactic not unlike *The Kite Runner*'s. Commenting on Assef to his nephew, Amir declares, "Your father was a good man. But that's what I'm trying to tell you, Sohrab jan. That there are bad people in this world, and sometimes bad people stay bad. Sometimes you have to stand up to them" (319). Humanity in *The Kite Runner* acquires a definitive status by opposing itself to monstrosity, but Hosseini equivocates in his efforts to locate monstrosity, in some moments underscoring its tense intimacy with humanity, characterizing it as a potential that exists in everyone, and in other moments exoticizing it, identifying it with unambiguously "bad" people like Assef and, more generally, the Taliban. For Amir, exorcizing his own inner monstrosity and affirming his humanity consist of confronting and defeating the external monstrosity that he identifies with the radically evil Assef — an imperative resonant with the quasi-messianic zeal of Bush's neoconservatism. Amir's primary source of guilt, after all, is his *failure to intervene* when Assef, unwittingly training to assume duties as a Taliban official, brutalizes Hassan. Perhaps inspired by the novel's repudiation of passivity, one customer remarks," "Anyone who doubts the need to stamp out terrorism should read this book" (P. Newton). Another reviewer reaches a similar conclusion about the novel's politics. "And I thought his handling of September 11 was just irresponsible. He mentions the event itself, but then there's no mention at all of the fallout in Afghan communities in the US. Nothing about the people hiding in their homes because people who appeared Middle Eastern were harrassed, assaulted, or sometimes killed. No mention of the outrage American Afghans felt at the abrupt change in US policy towards Afghanistan or the subsequent war. Nothing. I have to wonder, cynically, if he purposely left this out because he knew how many of his American audience he would piss off if he appeared 'un-American' and I just don't have much respect for that" (Jennifer M-R). Whether or not deliberate calculations motivated the omissions detailed by this reviewer, it is undeniable that Amir, who never reports any encounters with racism in his new country of residence, depicts the United States as a remarkably hospitable place for Muslims.

Those who read the book as opposed to Bush's policies are vague but passionate in their justifications.[26] One reader, referring to *The Kite Runner* as "afghani reality therapy," remarks: "The novel contains an eloquent and moving picture of afghanistan before and during the taliban period seen through the eyes of afghanis, some who stayed and some who left. This portrait is so valuable that it should be required reading for those who choose to interfere in afghanistan's (and iraq's) affairs. (Fat chance, I'm afraid)" (Christopher G. Kenber). Another, asserting a slightly different stance, declares, "I am horrified & disheartened as an American that we have not done more for these amazing compassionate, generous people & country" (Rone Prinz). While it is unclear what exactly the reviewer wants the United States to do, he or she opposes the current administration's actions, describing Afghans as the victims of "this so called 'war on terrorism.'" Though not in full agreement — one recommending nonintervention, the other recommending the opposite — both reviewers assume that unsympathetic, dehumanizing attitudes toward Muslims in the Middle East and central Asia, rather than benevolent motives, have underwritten support for Bush's military incursions, and they believe that Hosseini's novel may change these attitudes.

While *The Kite Runner* offers few overt challenges to the Bush administration's neoconservative philosophy, it nevertheless provides a complex form of emotional comfort to readers who are disturbed by their own country's actions and thus less inclined to disavow and exoticize the monstrosity that, according to Amir, incessantly threatens humanity. For Americans "horrified and disheartened" by the United States' War on Terror, Hosseini offers a recuperative narrative that identifies humanity, through Amir, precisely with sin and guilt, thus allowing readers to feel human as a consequence of their struggle to cope with the worry that they, as American citizens, are among the victimizers. At the same time, the novel allows readers to engage in visceral experiences of compassion and sympathy for Hosseini's Afghan characters, who serve perhaps as symbolic surrogates for all the Muslims the United States is bombing, detaining, or racially profiling, and thus licenses these readers to distinguish themselves from the status of victimizer, with which they may identify in light of the Bush administration's prosecution of the War on Terror. The reading of *The Kite Runner* can be understood, then, as an act of collective atonement for those Americans who are troubled by their country's treatment of Muslims abroad and at home. This effect may also include, in a slightly different way, readers on the right who understand their painful empathy with the book's characters not as atonement, but as a vindicating reminder, in the face of criticism, that they are compassionate, good human beings whose politics are fundamentally well intentioned.

For American readers wearied by the regular doses of bad news about the U.S. occupation of Iraq and Afghanistan, the novel offers a third option: fantasies of escape from political divisions altogether (see note 6). Several readers express relief that *The Kite Runner* is not overtly political. Perhaps relatedly, many maintain that Assef, owing to his unrealistic characterization, interferes with the book's otherwise moving narrative. Readers consequently were inclined to focus their attention and their emotional investments elsewhere — away from the ideological function that Assef performs. Their appreciation of the ostensibly nonpolitical aspects of the book suggests an unspoken frustration with, perhaps even repudiation of, the polarizing rhetoric that posits a global conflict between Islam and the West and may reflect a desire to transcend ideological and ethnic divisions through an affective experience that underscores our shared, though culturally differentiated, humanity. While it may be impossible to resolve violent international conflicts, it is possible at least to "*feel right*," as Harriet Beecher Stowe famously advised Americans distraught by slavery. Jane Tompkins maintains that a twentieth-century masculine sensibility would dismiss Stowe's solution as inadequate or naïve ("Sentimental Power" 132–33), but present-day readers, both male and female, seem dissatisfied enough with the results of conventional military and political mechanisms to imagine sentiment as a more promising basis for overcoming cultural conflicts.[27]

One review in particular exemplifies this political exhaustion:

> While it's impossible to completely avoid, I try not to comment too much upon the political background and the impact it has on the story line (which is major one) only because Americans will turn around and say ignorant comments, such as "see, we are helping to save the Afghans (referencing the recent bombing of Aghanistan)," which is, in my view, incorrect (I'll spare you the elaboration) and takes away from the true potential of this book (although this view in itself may provide for yet another metaphor; how the Afghans first perceived the Taliban arrival with joy, and the eventual consequences of such events). True redemption can only be found within the soul, and for each person redemption requires a separate definition and asking price. This book carries within it a whirlwind of human emotions, and a universal link to what we are intrinsically — connected. Any thought of separateness is created within the mind. Amir compartmentalized his connections with Hassan for [a] variety of personal and sociocultural reasons, and as a consequence, he consistently experienced cognitive dissonance. When he was finally able to confront himself with the Truth he realized that there always was a very real connection between himself and Hassan. (Roy Munson)

The reviewer adopts an exasperated, resigned tone in expressing his decision to abstain from initiating a political debate — "I'll spare you the elaboration" — and then changes focus to highlight what he sees as the "true potential" of the novel, at which point his terms become quasi-religious and psychological. His review performs an act of self-censorship, as if the intrinsic connectedness that exists between people is capable of becoming manifest only through a deliberate eschewal of politics. At the same time, his combative tone seems oddly to belie his utopian vision of a unified humanity.

Possibly inspiring the reader's response is a similarly idealistic but equally qualified observation Amir makes about his relationship with Hassan:

> Because history isn't easy to overcome. Neither is religion. In the end, I was a Pashtun and he was a Hazara, I was Sunni and he was Shi'a, and nothing was ever going to change that. Nothing.
>
> But we were kids who had learned to crawl together, and no history, ethnicity, society, or religion was going to change that either. (25)

Ultimately the claim that he and Hassan are capable of transcending the invidious cultural categories that divide them turns out, as Amir fears, to be a fantasy whose failure is the tragedy of the novel. By the end, Hassan is dead, killed by the Taliban in their campaign of ethnic cleansing, and his son, Sohrab, traumatized and mute after a failed suicide attempt, remains almost entirely unresponsive to Amir's efforts to help him. The one half-smile that Amir is finally able to elicit from Sohrab in the novel's final moment of restrained optimism does not, as Amir recognizes, "make everything all right" (371). Ironically, however, readers often perceive their intense emotional responses to the novel to be elevating enough to bolster utopian aspirations. "Through this novel, you will perhaps begin to understand what has been done to Afghani people and find compassion in your heart for them. You will also witness the inhumanity and cruelty that life can deliver and the power of love and compassion that always wins in the end" (Michelle E.). If not in the tragic narrative itself, then in their own compassionate reaction to it, many readers find a self-validating basis for hope — one that posits their participation in a purportedly universal and unifying affective response as a nonpolitical solution to the ethnic hierarchies and antagonisms that the novel, in order to elicit this response, presents as painfully intractable.

According to many Amazon reviews, when political efforts not only fail to promote peace and happiness but exacerbate conflicts between people, our emotional pain in the face of this failure exemplifies our shared humanity, reminding us that we are all the same underneath our divisive cultural, national, and ideological groupings. Oddly, even as this sentimental humanism appears to reject politics, it seems to require political failure as a provocation for the reparative work that it promises to perform. A tensely intimate relationship of dependence and disavowal, then, binds politics and sentimental humanism together and, given this tight fit, it might be worth considering whether the two are truly as mutually exclusive as they sometimes appear. Affect, after all, does not function outside the realm of politics altogether — even if it often derives its authority and influence from its ostensibly apolitical status. Of course the frequently repeated claims that we, as human beings, all have the same feelings, hopes, and desires typically underwrite either too impossibly much or too insubstantially little political change, imagining on the one hand a world in which we miraculously get past our superficial differences and unite on the basis of our common emotions, or declaring on the other hand that this unity already exists, that we are already "intrinsically connected" by virtue of being human, even if we inevitably *appear* divided. Both visions, according to some critics, assign too much significance to shared sentiment and not enough to the less immediately validating work of organizing, debating, and negotiating in order to resolve various conflicts and reduce oppression and inequality. Or to put it more polemically, many would say that it is not sufficient merely to "feel right," though doing so certainly feels *good*.

I would agree that feelings are not sufficient, but I would also maintain that they are not negligible either. At the very least, identification with *The Kite Runner*'s protagonist has inspired greater empathy for a population that many Americans, by their own admission, heretofore viewed with suspicion and incomprehension. And identification has performed this function in many cases not in spite of but on the basis of the very cultural differences that threaten to thwart its operation. Whether and how this widespread change in disposition has influenced the political views of Americans and their willingness to support or challenge their country's policies is obviously an important question. Ironically, it may be possible to measure the actual political efficacy and concrete repercussions of cross-cultural empathy only by disregarding the utopian promise of unity that so many readers ascribe to it and by recognizing instead the particular and more limited goals, policies, and ideologies that it is capable of advancing.

CONCLUSION

IF PSYCHOLOGICAL DISCOURSE functions as the basis for individualism, as the means of ascribing to each and every person a unique and private interior life, it has also come to serve, especially in recent years, as a powerful leveler, one that asserts a common humanity across various cultural, racial, economic, and political categories. But as a tool, the therapeutic has largely answered the needs of particular groups, most notably the middle and upper classes in the United States.[1] This segment of the population obviously enjoys an anomalous measure of prosperity, security, and stability relative to the rest of the world — a condition which some observers have characterized as at odds with reality. But an emphasis on the psychological diminishes the importance of these tangible discrepancies, foregrounding instead an elusive register of experience that resists ready quantification or invidious comparison, thus allowing well-off Americans to believe that they too are participating in the drama of the human condition. As a narrative device available to novelists, the language of the interior has become indispensable for providing urgency and consequence, especially to those texts set within middle-class American contexts. Even when no material hardships or hazards loom, psychological troubles, including dread, anxiety, depression, and boredom, weigh upon the characters, providing them with problems that need to be solved, tragedies that need to be averted, and burdens that need to be heroically shouldered.

Of course novels that dwell too restrictively on the interior, the private, or the personal run the risk of appearing narcissistic, of exemplifying the "banality of pseudo-self-awareness," which Christopher Lasch famously attributed to Americans in the 1970s. In order to function effectively, the machinery of the narrative typically requires other elements — class or racial tension, the specter of violence, and so forth — which it can recast as constituents of a psychological dilemma. In many instances, the therapeutic orientation of contemporary fiction underscores the drama and uncertainty produced by the mere threat of a potential difficulty, placing subjective anxieties on equal footing with whatever concrete event or development they obsessively anticipate. James Frey, for instance, depicts the brutal effects that drug addiction can produce, but his memoir and his appearance on *Oprah* present his predicament as a ubiquitous danger, a problem that all of his readers must confront, at least in the form of an inescapable possibility. Likewise, readers of *The Pilot's Wife* may feel their private world, as a result of their reading, haunted by the ever-present danger of political terrorism. Such gestures help to valorize the lives of readers, allowing the subjective premonitions, worries, and misgivings that attend the possibility of a crisis to acquire an aura of significance.

This is not to say, of course, that all middle-class problems are the specious products of rhetorical inflation. Several scholars have argued that the therapeutic paradigm represents a response — whether effective or not — to substantive difficulties. As Micki McGee notes in her analysis of self-help books, the American middle class has become economically more insecure in the past twenty-five years. Its real income has diminished as inequality between the rich and the poor has grown; competition for white-collar positions has increased as many companies and industries have moved overseas; and workers, generally speaking, run a serious risk of losing their jobs, losing their benefits, and losing their middle-class status altogether. Therapeutic discourses obviously aim to help Americans manage these and other problems. But they also enable individuals to fit their various hardships, whether real, potential, or only imagined, into a meaningful narrative, one that constitutes them as beleaguered yet resilient, as worthy of sympathy yet capable of claiming agency. In a worldwide market where various discourses of suffering and victimization compete for legitimacy as sources, paradoxically, of glamour and empowerment, the therapeutic's prolific production of dysfunctions and pathologies has certainly served the purposes of middle-class Americans.[2]

Especially remarkable about the therapeutic paradigm, according to many scholars, is its capacity to resituate and reconstitute all variety of phenomena, including crime, religion, war, and poverty, within its own terms. The most common academic response to this development is to argue that we now misrepresent difficulties with structural, economic, or political origins as individual or personal, treating grievances as if they were the result of private psychological maladies rather than the symptoms of an unjust system.[3] I have sought to establish that this conception of the therapeutic is reductive, that it deliberately disregards the social character and social purchase of therapeutic discourse. I would, however, maintain that whether we employ a primarily economic, political, ethical, or therapeutic lens will influence the way we view and understand particular problems, and which dimensions of these problems we are capable of apprehending. A conspicuous feature of the psychological emphasis exhibited by many of the novels that I have considered, for instance, is a difficulty in unequivocally identifying an external, concrete cause or origin of suffering. Diffuse, amorphous troubles emerge both within and outside the private worlds that the characters inhabit through tortuous webs of external temptation and internal complicity, and fester and proliferate in the absence of a single responsible agent or enemy. Therapeutic fiction, in short, is remarkably devoid of overt moralism. Even *The Kite Runner* qualifies its division of the world into good guys and bad guys with constant reminders of the potential monstrosity that resides within each individual.

The therapeutic emphasis of contemporary fiction *internalizes* problems, prioritizing their multiple psychic manifestations, ascribing to them causes rooted in the dysfunctional dynamics of the family or the pathological impulses of the characters, and magnifying their affective consequences. Two related historical developments have encouraged these tendencies. The first is the steady expansion of market capitalism and its tendency to displace, conceal, or mitigate ideological and cultural conflicts via the false utopian promise of free trade and the global cooperation that it supposedly promotes. As conspicuous enemies have decreased, most notably with the end of the cold war, threats to America's security and prosperity have appeared to become less concrete, less unified, less locatable. Of the two major dangers that I have considered in this book, drugs and terrorism, responses to the former typically implicate moral or psychological weakness as often as they blame networks of distribution or the countries that produce drugs, while responses to the latter, most notably the very designation "War on Terror," identify a subjective mode of affect rather than a unified external organization as the primary enemy. The second major development concomitant with the growth of the therapeutic in recent years is the effort to privatize the American social landscape through the stigmatization and underfunding of public institutions and services and the construction of ever more decentralized and sprawling technoburbs. Americans have become in the past few decades, as Robert Putnam has documented, less civically engaged, less communally focused, and more concerned with their private, personal lives.

Of course neither communities nor the desire for them has disappeared. Observers have accused therapeutic culture of abetting Americans' inward-looking, self-indulgent impulses. Though some therapeutic practices and texts do foster these impulses, others, as I have argued, perform exactly the opposite function; they support the development of ad hoc, improvised, often largely invisible communities outside the private sphere, capable of surviving within a fragmented, atomistic society. The great number of self-help and recovery groups as well as middlebrow book clubs all testify to the power of psychological discourse to bring people together. But I would maintain that self-help books and novels provide the basis for even more attenuated, intangible communities based not on the organized gathering of individuals within a single place, but on disaggregated solidarities of affect — composed of ostensibly private feelings whose satisfactions derive in part from the sense that others are responding in the same way. As reader responses to Wells's *Divine Secrets* demonstrate, such elusive formations may well be compensations for a lack of long-standing, tight-knit affiliations, and they are often unified by the feelings of sadness, loneliness, and disconnection that this lack produces.[4] Psychological discourse's capacity to perform such functions depends, obviously, upon the veiled but enormous scope of reference that its terms command, especially when they appear in best-selling texts, so that they designate anxieties, yearnings, complaints, and self-conceptions shared by large segments of society, precisely by *appearing* to speak about and speak to the isolated individual.[5]

A central question of this book has been, how broad or inclusive is the sympathy that therapeutic fiction is capable of generating? The psychological descriptions of *The Pilot's Wife*, for instance, address a specific and somewhat narrow demographic category, namely white, educated, middle-class suburban women, while eliciting sympathy for a figure who falls into the same category. Moreover Shreve's novel approves of the desire to enclose the private sphere against unwanted intrusions; it treats gatekeeping as heroic. But as the Amazon responses to *The Kite Runner* demonstrate, identification and the psychological humanism that it mobilizes do not always entail such a restrictive orientation. Assertions of affective commonality across cultural and ethnic categories in those reviews evince a yearning among Americans to see themselves as part of an unbounded, global humanity. This yearning, in search of similarity, also necessitates a capacity to confront difference.[6]

To be sure, some reviews of *The Kite Runner* reveal a willed inability to acknowledge the specific historical and cultural conditions that shape the protagonist's experience. Hence these responses demonstrate the risk that psychological identification, while appearing to reach beyond the boundaries of what is culturally familiar, in fact colonizes and domesticates alterity, narcissistically ignoring or distorting that which is unknown or incomprehensible. But as the diversity of reactions posted on Amazon suggests, identification does not operate only in this narrow manner. For many readers the cultural difference and the dramatic history that Amir experiences are precisely what energize their acts of identification. The text offers a test of their imaginative and empathetic capacities: by proving themselves capable of inhabiting Amir's perspective they reaffirm their own humanity.

At the very least, the Amazon reviews demonstrate that an awareness of the cultural and historical specificity embedded in a character's experience can coexist rather comfortably with cross-cultural identification and feelings of shared humanity. Scholarly arguments frequently frame the two perspectives as mutually exclusive, at times endorsing a version of identity politics that scoffs at notions of universality, dismissing the ability of individuals within a privileged demographic category to understand the experience of those at the margins.[7] And critics may be correct in asserting a contradiction or tension between the urge to identify with characters and the urge to acknowledge difference; but nonacademic readers are apparently able to manage this contradiction, negotiating effortlessly, if sometimes unthinkingly, between the two urges, each of which is necessary, I would argue, in different circumstances to manage the complicated social challenges that a multiethnic and globalized America produces. Perhaps responsible for readers' untroubled capacity to perform this particular oscillation is the manifestly affective character of their interpretive experience —a state of responsiveness that can eschew the logical imperative to decide between two incongruous perspectives.

If *The Kite Runner* reviews demonstrate that perceptions of alterity need not preclude identification, Toni Morrison's *Paradise* seeks to translate this condition of mutual accommodation into a far more radical and paradoxical unity. While other works, such as Wells's *Divine Secrets* and Wallace's *Infinite Jest*, celebrate the kindness of strangers, Morrison's text invites readers to identify with characters on the very basis of their strangeness, to identify precisely with the strangeness of her strange characters. In an effort to conceive of a truly inclusive utopian sphere, her novel *Paradise* strives to inspire sympathy for that which resists assimilation, for that which remains profoundly opaque, unknown, illegible. The recognizable middlebrow trope that she uses, namely a narrative about troubled women who acquire self-esteem by joining a community of fellow misfits, provokes the therapeutic response that Oprah's Book Club typically encourages, but the text employs a series of tactics designed to frustrate this response, as if to test how middlebrow readers will respond to a set of characters who insistently resist recognition or comprehension. Arguably, Morrison is challenging the insularity of the private sphere and the exclusions it promotes, demanding the cultivation of more robust forms of sympathy capable of flourishing not just in the sheltered realm of the familiar and the intimate, but in the public sphere, defined as a space that facilitates the encounter with the stranger.

Morrison's ideals are antithetical to those affirmed in *The Pilot's Wife*, which is also an Oprah's Book Club selection. The latter novel's sympathetic portrayal of a woman's efforts to re-secure her home against the intrusions of the outside world identifies happiness with insularity and privacy, while equating the stranger with the enemy. The only explicitly political activity that the text depicts bears the threat, in Schmittian fashion, of extreme violence; the public world appears dangerous and untrustworthy. Shreve's perspective may reflect more closely that of Winfrey's viewers than Morrison's. The episode devoted to *Paradise* garnered the lowest ratings of any Oprah's Book Club episode in history, suggesting that readers may not be prepared for the hermeneutic work that Morrison sees as necessary to construct an inclusive utopian sphere. But even Shreve's book acknowledges that the possible presence of strangers is necessary to endow the otherwise vapid private sphere with excitement, meaning, and narrative energy. Moreover, some among Winfrey's audience did finish and appreciate *Paradise*, and not by discarding or repudiating the interpretive framework that they typically employ in engaging with Oprah's Book Club selections. That framework in fact proved crucial. Readers' thwarted desires and determination in the face of difficulty were constitutive of the lesson *Paradise* sought to teach them. Hence Morrison's tactics presuppose the belief that the therapeutic interpretive inclinations of middlebrow readers do not in themselves bar, but can under pressure nurture, the utopian possibilities that she hopes to inaugurate.

Considering Morrison's ambitious agenda, one might ask: What, after all, can contemporary novels accomplish? What influence do they exert upon the public sphere? I have sought to demonstrate that the novel's psychological discourse, its language of the interior, helps to promote forms of recognition, identification, and sympathy among strangers living without the support of stable local communities and the habits, institutions, and intimacies that these communities typically encourage. The psychological humanism mobilized by novels and other therapeutic forms thus serves to familiarize the world outside the private sphere, partially divesting it of its foreign, threatening, or hostile aspects, enabling strangers to engage and negotiate with each other in good faith, instantiating public modes of awareness and sociability founded upon perceptions of emotional commonality. Feelings, rather than values, ideas, or principles, are, according to readers, what unite people. Almost all of the novels I have considered have prioritized and celebrated affect, equating it with humanness, privileging it above dispassionate or rational modes of thought and communication, and striving to provoke intense empathy for the characters and their troubles.

The concrete ideological functions served by the cultivation of empathy and the assumption of emotional commonality remain, to the uneasiness of some observers, unpredictable and indeterminate. Critics on the left have argued that the sentimental novel tends to promote a dangerous belief in strong emotions as an adequate response to suffering and injustice, thus forestalling more concrete political measures, while allowing those who experience these emotions to feel they are virtuous and humane people.[8] In short, these critics are unwilling to attribute value to empathy insofar as it fails, in their view, to motivate direct, collective political action aimed at changing the structures responsible for society's problems. Some of the texts that I have examined do in fact produce effects that resist such direct programmatic utility. The group that *Infinite Jest* represents as a model for reawakening its intellectual readers' emotional capacities, Alcoholics Anonymous, explicitly refuses to endorse any political position or camp, for fear that doing so would discourage certain individuals from joining the group and thereby undermine its goal of total inclusivity. Moreover, many view empathy as an apolitical emotion, one that promotes connections between individuals without reference to their ideological affiliations. And yet, as the responses to *The Kite Runner* demonstrate, the experience of cross-cultural identification can unify people around specific political stances, ranging from the progressive to the neoconservative. But this flexibility too is suspect; it seems to suggest that empathy and other emotions are merely serviceable, subject to manipulation, and thus a way of enlisting people's support for particular leaders or programs against the better judgment of their rational faculties.[9]

Both the worry that empathy is too removed from organized collective struggle and the converse fear that it can be too easily co-opted by any given ideological enterprise assess the importance of affect by looking only at the consequences that empathy is capable of producing within the traditional political sphere and thus ignore it as a significant, semiautonomous phenomenon in its own right. The evidence that a particular emotion, such as compassion, can support a range of seemingly contradictory political positions indicates its independence, its refusal to be permanently subordinated to a particular position or program. But if feelings defy determinate political designations, they are not therefore entirely private or personal. Rather, they are always responsive to, productive of, and embodied through a variety of social practices. The efforts of Wells, Wallace, or Hosseini to promote an emotional readiness, a quickening of sympathetic responsiveness in their readers are not guaranteed to serve a specific political party or agenda, but they do alter the social world. The feelings that *The Kite Runner* has generated, for instance, are likely to achieve expression through a multitude of everyday gestures, choices, and actions, which can be seen as an uncoordinated but collective transformation. Political movements aimed at structural, legislative, institutional changes are organized cooperative efforts, designed to channel their participants' acts and feelings into explicit social transformation. By contrast, the affective community that therapeutic fiction can promote is always in part imaginary, a projection of the reader's private desires whose actualization depends upon the spontaneous belief of individuals in a shared fantasy. Though more significant than scholars generally acknowledge, emotional responses are, of course, never enough. Indeed, this inadequacy is a structural feature of the therapeutic, which makes promises that it cannot keep and thereby reproduces the conditions that demand its further operation. The quintessential therapeutic gesture, offered by novels and self-help books alike, to insist that you are not alone in your hidden pain, equates the cathartic recognition of shared suffering with its triumphant cure. Such a tantalizing utopian formula will inevitably produce not only solace and hope but also disappointment.

NOTES

Introduction

1. This is in fact what Joel Pfister sees as therapeutic discourse's central function, which he describes in his essay, "Glamorizing the Psychological."

2. The most important critic to make this claim is Frederic Jameson, who repeatedly laments the psychological emphasis of twentieth-century fiction in *The Political Unconscious*. Richard Ohmann has also argued that, in its efforts to serve the interests of the professional managerial class, successful contemporary American fiction tends to focus on "individual consciousness" and private life to the exclusion of political issues (210). In her exploration of postwar best sellers, *The American Dream*, Elizabeth Long notes the emphasis on personal psychology in contemporary fiction, though she contends that this emphasis need not preclude the articulation of political and sociological insights.

3. Numerous sociologists have pointed to the various social purposes that literature serves. In *Book Clubs*, for instance, Elizabeth Long attempts to debunk the myth of the "solitary reader" (2), pointing to the community-building function of literature.

4. See Dwight Macdonald; Leslie Fiedler, "The Middle Against Both Ends"; John Guillory, "The Ordeal of Middlebrow Culture."

5. For a history of the origins of middlebrow culture in the United States, see Joan Shelley Rubin. See also Janice Radway, *Feeling* and Kenneth Davis.

6. See Macdonald, *Against the American Grain*; Fiedler, "The Middle Against Both Ends."

7. Thomas Schaub captures this perceived narrowness succinctly: "When analysts of the cold war in the United States write of a 'consensus' culture, they mean that a collaboration of business, government, and labor established a dominant center which either saw no need for extreme or divisive positions or actively worked to suppress them" (137).

8. David Riesman, with his description of the "other-directed" individual, and William Whyte, with his analysis of the "organization man," were the two most famous critics to make this claim. C. Wright Mills reached similarly troubling conclusions.

9. The editors of *Partisan Review* opened the symposium with the statement: "Politically, there is a recognition that the kind of democracy which exists in America has an intrinsic and positive value: it is not merely a capitalist myth but a reality which must be defended against Russian totalitarianism. The cultural consequences are bound to be far-reaching and complex, but some of them have already become apparent. For better or worse, most writers no longer accept alienation as the artist's fate in America; on the contrary, they want very much to be a part of American life." See *Partisan Review* 19.3 (1952): 284.

10. See Albert Greco et al.; Rahlee Hughes, 12; Greco, "Shaping the Future."

11. See Hughes, 13; Andre Schriffin, 123; Jim Milliot, 8.

12. In understanding these trends, I am indebted to Joelle Delbourgo, a literary agent who kindly agreed to be interviewed. See also John Tebbel; Schriffin; Jason Epstein.

13. See Hughes; Tatiana Hutton.

14. The most famous examples of reader-response criticism are Stanley Fish and Wolfgang Iser. See also Jane Tompkins's edited collection: *Reader-Response Criticism*.

15. Her arguments about middlebrow readers appear in "The Book-of-The-Month Club and the General Reader" and *A Feeling for Books*. See also Andrew Ross; Susan Bordo.

16. For some good examples of work that has participated in and/or reflected upon this debate, see Robert McChesney; Nicholas Garnham; Lawrence Grossberg; Michael Berúbé.

17. For some critical texts that have tried to characterize different facets of the American middle class in the past fifty years, see Catherine Jurca; Mary Pattillo-McCoy; Barbara Ehrenreich; T. J. Jackson Lears; Christopher Lasch; Scott Donaldson; John Galbraith; Whyte; A. C. Spectorsky; Mills; Riesman.

18. Both Elizabeth Long (in *The American Dream*) and Ohmann assert the centrality and influence of professional middle-class audiences within the American literary scene.

19. See for instance Elizabeth Long, *The American Dream*, 48. See also "Over One-Third," *Harris Poll*.

20. See Caleb Crain; Mary Chapman and Glenn Hendler; Milette Shamir and Jennifer Travis.

21. Rita Felski makes a similar point in "After Suspicion."

22. Cecilia Farr and Jaime Harker observe that Oprah's Book Club often brings the two (emotion and intellect) into dialogue: "While critics have suggested that focusing on emotional (or, in Farr's formulation, empathetic) response is to be immersed in a therapeutic, as opposed to a literary, environment, Oprah's Book Club regularly uses novels as a way to link emotion and intellect. Indeed, the very no-

tion that these two are mutually exclusive modes is part of an Enlightenment inheritance that feminists have long critiqued for its gendered assumptions" (3–4).

23. Cindy Weinstein in her work on nineteenth-century American literature convincingly argues for the need to focus on the particular context in which a sentimental response arises, rather than subscribing to categorical judgments.

24. In their introduction to *The Oprah Phenomenon*, Jennifer Harris and Elwood Watson observe that Winfrey herself is often instrumental in facilitating these connections. "That Winfrey manages to position herself within a black cultural context that acknowledges the historical forces of racism (as Morrison's books do, for instance) without alienating her majority white viewers is telling. It speaks to the way Winfrey creates the opportunity for sympathetic identification across a variety of differences, including racial differences" (13–14).

25. See Radway, "The Book-of-The-Month-Club and the General Reader," 535; Elizabeth Long, "Textual Interpretation as Collective Action," 117.

26. Pierre Bourdieu of course was one of the first scholars to consider how culture functions as a form of capital, allowing individuals to lay claim to a particular class status.

27. See *Cultural Capital*. See also Pfister, "Glamorizing the Psychological."

28. For an example of recent academic work that aims at reconsidering and recuperating the concept of the "literary," see Marjorie Perloff's *PMLA* "Presidential Address 2006," in which she poses the question "Why *is* the 'merely' literary so suspect today?" (655). See also Marjorie Levinson.

29. In his analysis of Oprah's Book Club, Kevin Quirk reaches a similar conclusion: "Careful examination of Book Club practices points to the fluid ideological nature of therapeutic values and serves as a necessary corrective to the prevailing scholarly view that they are fundamentally conservative" (261).

30. Dana Cloud (in *Control and Consolation*) offers the most cogent version of this critique. See also Ohmann; Wendy Kaminer; Nikolas Rose; Robert Bellah et al.; Philip Rieff; Christopher Lasch; Paul Vitz; Elayne Rapping.

31. Kaminer offers the most forceful version of the latter accusation, claiming that therapeutic rhetoric imagines individuals as devoid of agency.

32. For a historical genealogy of interiority, see Philip Cushman, "Psychotherapy to 1992"; *Constructing the Self*.

33. For a careful description of this shift, see Edward Shorter.

34. For discussions of these movements and the reception of Freud in America, see Cushman, *Constructing the Self*; Steven Starker; Paul Anker; Donald Meyer; Eric Caplan.

35. Eva Moskowitz remarks upon the same historical phenomenon (149).

36. See Jurca; Pfister, "Glamorizing the Psychological," and "On Conceptualizing the Cultural History of Emotional and Psychological Life in America."

37. See Elaine May; Deborah Nelson; Moskowitz.

38. According to Moskowitz, the number of mental disorders listed in the *Diagnostic and Statistical Manual of Mental Disorders* tripled during the first fifteen years of its existence (4).

39. See *New Introductory Lectures*; *Interpretation*.

40. Lears addresses the sense of weightlessness that therapeutic strategies both exacerbated and attempted to mitigate at the turn of the twentieth century. Ehrenreich, Jurca, Pfister (in "Glamorizing the Psychological"), Lionel Trilling (in *Sincerity and Authenticity*), and Whyte, and Cushman (in *Constructing the Self*) comment on the middle-class struggle with banality in the postwar period.

41. Richard Huber, Elizabeth Long (in *The American Dream*), Meyer, Riesman et al., and Whyte all describe the perceived loss of agency that has attended white-collar work in the United States in the twentieth century.

42. For a description of the historical roots of the Protestant ethic, see Max Weber; Huber; Meyer; Elizabeth Long (*The American Dream*). The latter three also discuss the shift in the twentieth century away from the Protestant ethic, as do Riesman, Whyte, Cushman (in *Constructing the Self*), Ehrenreich, and Starker. Ehrenreich notes the persistence of the older worldview even as it becomes increasingly outdated: "The middle class cannot afford to let down its guard; it maintains its position only through continual exertion — through allegiance to the 'traditional values' of hard work and self-denial" (231).

43. See "On Conceptualizing the Cultural History of Emotional and Psychological Life in America"; and "Glamorizing the Psychological."

44. Scholars of the consciousness-raising novel include Lisa Hogeland; Felski; Gayle Greene. For a careful analysis of the New Left's tendency to unify the personal and the political, see Todd Gitlin.

45. Kimberly Chabot Davis argues that scholars have too often mistakenly aligned emotions such as sympathy, empathy, and compassion with conservative ideologies, ignoring contextual variables that help to determine how these emotions function.

46. Hannah Arendt observes: "The *polis*, properly speaking, is not the city-state in its physical location; it is the organization of the people as it arises out of acting and speaking together, and its true space lies between people living together for this purpose, no matter where they happen to be" (198).

47. Moskowitz also notes that the therapeutic "collapses the distinction" between the private and the public (7).

48. Analyzing the message boards associated with Oprah's Book Club, Yung-Hsing Wu notes, "It's not surprising, then, that the message boards should sound a note of fellowship when the topic of the Club's effect comes up. One member pens

a fairly typical comment when she says that 'it is always fun *to read books knowing that others are sharing* in the same experience' (OBCMB, 18 June 2003)" (82).

49. See especially Michael Warner, *Publics and Counterpublics*; Lauren Berlant and Warner, "Sex in Public"; Nick Crossley; Julie Ellison.

50. Obviously radical feminist and black power groups have challenged class as the privileged basis for collective politics. Among scholars, Ernesto Laclau and Chantal Moffe offer the most comprehensive analysis and critique of Marxist class-oriented forms of solidarity, providing a theoretical justification for a variety of alternative modes of identity politics.

51. In formulating the question in this way, I am obviously indebted to Benedict Anderson, who famously posited that the nation is predicated on an imagined solidarity, which print culture works to facilitate. But unlike Benedict, I am especially interested in the role that emotion plays in fostering these communities.

52. Trysh Travis raises a similar question in *The Language of the Heart*, arguing that the difficulty of measuring the political consequences of the affective relationships sponsored in twelve-step recovery groups should not be grounds for dismissing or underestimating these consequences.

53. Elizabeth Long suggests the social meaning of individual-centered discourse as follows: "[Novels] describe how individuals take the world in; how it subtly and unknowingly shapes them; how they, with various levels of accuracy or illusion, perceive the world; and how the world presents them with choices and constraints. They also illuminate, in turn, how individual desires, fears, and dreams impinge on the lives of others and stretch or tear the moral fabric of the social universe. Moreover, novels show an awareness that even these private yearnings and despairs may imply the social in their innermost parts" (*American Dream* 4).

54. See for instance Gillian Bendelow and Simon Williams; William Reddy; and Jeff Goodwin et al.

55. See also Jane Shattuc, *The Talking Cure*; Linda Kerber; Mary Kelley; Berlant, "The Female Complaint."

One. Searching for *Paradise* on *The Oprah Winfrey Show*

1. Channette Romero also notes the earthly connotation of Morrison's "down here," arguing that she is attempting to wrest the idea of paradise away from traditional Christian conceptions (423).

2. Kathleen Rooney (in *Reading with Oprah*), Eva Illouz, Farr and Harker, and Kelley Penfield Lewis all identify these tendencies. After her decision to revive the book club in 2003, Winfrey started placing more emphasis on traditional scholarly approaches to literature, including questions about theme, structure, and narrative, and she invited interpretations from academics on her Web site. For exami-

nations of these new developments, see Sarah Robbins; Rooney, "Everything Old Is New Again."

3. Rooney (in *Reading with Oprah*) notes Winfrey's tendency to treat characters as if they were real people and her lack of emphasis on the fictional status of the novels that she introduces (140). Corinne Squire (in *Empowering Women?*) and Shattuc (in "Oprahfication" and *The Talking Cure*) address the way Winfrey's therapeutic discourse serves to personalize political issues.

4. Sonia Livingstone and Peter Lunt raise the question of whether talk shows can function as the basis for a public sphere. Many scholars have concluded that *Oprah* plays this role, though they tend to position Winfrey as a liminal figure, situated at the border between the public and the private, claiming that her show requires us to rethink our definition of the public sphere. See Shattuc (*The Talking Cure*); Illouz and Nik John; Simon Stow.

5. R. Mark Hall points to the value Winfrey places on the "aha moment" (658).

6. Michael Perry also notes this tension when he observes "the paradoxical nature of book clubs as members read to gain cultural capital, but consciously employ reading strategies that defy consciously elitist readings posed by the academy" (126).

7. See for instance Melanie R. Anderson; Linda Krumholz; Romero; Magali Cornier Michael.

8. Philip Page reaches a similar conclusion, arguing that the text's intepretive difficulties are inseparable from its larger project. He notes that readers will "want to fill in the missing gaps, the apparent holes and spaces in the very surface of the text. But such attempts . . . are bound to fail, focused as they are on narrow pursuits of facts and deductions. Instead, Morrison suggests that readers use their whole selves, pass beyond the merely rational, and truly become co-creators rather than merely passive respondents" (642).

9. For poststructuralist approaches to Morrison's characters, see Deborah McDowell; Madhu Dubey.

10. Farr, Rooney (in *Reading with Oprah*), and Illouz all point to the centrality of identification on Oprah's Book Club.

11. For some accounts of Winfrey's racial politics, which explore her focus on individualism over racial categories, see Janice Peck; Harris and Watson; and Kathleen Dixon.

12. Pattillo-McCoy comments on Americans' contradictory attitudes about race: "Even though America is obsessed with race, some policy makers and even more average citizens act as if race no longer matters. The sweeping assaults on affirmative action programs are prime examples" (1).

13. For some other scholarly accounts of the way black characters function in a culture dominated by white readers, see Penelope Ingram; Richard Dyer; Michael Awkward.

14. For some essays that explore the challenge Morrison poses in *Paradise* to racial essentialism see Richard Schur; Ana Maria Fraile-Marcos; Candice Jenkins.

15. Indeed, several scholars have been tempted to deduce the actual facts of the novel (though the facts seem to involve supernatural occurrences). Sarah Appleton Aguiar, for instance, claims that there is proof that several women at the Convent have already died before they first arrive there. Melanie R. Anderson attempts to discredit this argument by pointing out that Mavis, subsequent to her appearance at the Convent, learns about a warrant for her arrest and that another character, Pallas, actually leaves the Convent at one point (314).

16. Oddly, Perry claims that Morrison and Winfrey "offer a 'class' designed to *overcome* resistance to *Paradise*, rather than to *understand* it" (119), disregarding the sustained attention both figures give to the participants' interpretive difficulties and Morrison's suggestion that these constitute an essential part of the reading experience.

17. Melanie R. Anderson has interpreted the Convent as a model for this state of liminality beyond conventional binaries and identity categories.

18. Romero articulates Morrison's project in similar terms: "[*Paradise*] suggests the importance of holding both of these methods open as a means of creating an earthly paradise, of keeping one eye firmly rooted to the local/material/historical and another looking beyond to the spiritual/mythical/imaginative" (425).

19. In his essay, "Sensations of Loss," Michael Wood notes the difficulty of determining which characters' perspectives we ought to endorse and which we ought to condemn in Morrison's *Paradise*.

20. Several critics have argued that Morrison's attempt to redefine paradise so as to accommodate otherness entails a shift from a narrative of exceptionalism, which ironically shapes Ruby's initial attempt to define itself in opposition to the United States, to a narrative of cosmopolitanism, as embodied in the Convent. See Katrine Dalsgård; Romero; Holly Flint.

21. Fraile-Marcos offers a similar view, claiming that paradise is, according to Morrison, "neither closed nor fixed, but a condition that has to be continuously worked on" (30).

22. Susan Neal Mayberry also notes Morrison's suggestion that conceptualizing and constructing paradise inevitably involves a tension between the familiar and the foreign, between the desire to feel at home and the need to remain open to otherness.

Two. Therapy and Displacement in *Divine Secrets*

1. I am referring to writers such as Sarah Orne Jewett, Mary Wilkins Freeman, and Bret Harte, among others. For some scholarly characterizations of the region-

alist genre, see Tom Lutz; Judith Fetterley and Marjorie Pryse; Kate McCullough; Donna Campbell; Sherrie Inness and Diana Royer; Josephine Donovan.

2. I am referring here to books such as Sheri Reynolds, *The Rapture of Canaan*; Kaye Gibbons, *Ellen Foster*; Billie Letts, *Where the Heart Is*; Brett Lott, *Jewel*; Janet Finch, *White Oleander*; Melinda Haynes, *Mother of Pearl*; and Gwyn Hym Rubio, *Icy Sparks*. Other books not selected for Oprah's Book Club that also exemplify this trend include Barbara Kingsolver, *Animal Dreams*; Sue Monk Kidd, *The Secret Life of Bees*; and Fannie Flagg, *Fried Green Tomatoes at the Whistle Stop Cafe*.

3. For other accounts of this development, see Jack Meltzer; Peter Dreier et al.; Robert Lang.

4. The most famous critiques of the suburbs include works by Lewis Mumford, Whyte, and Riesman. Recent scholars who have sought to revisit and revise these critiques include Kenneth Jackson and Robert Fishman.

5. The attitudes that mobilize their theatrical assumption of blackness are not that different from the motives at work in the production of white minstrel shows in the nineteenth century, which Eric Lott examines in *Love and Theft*.

6. Dyer comments on the perceptions of blackness within white culture as associated with vitality and emotionality rather than reason and rationality (55). Morrison offers a suggestive analysis of the complex affective functions which African American characters are made to perform in white literary culture in *Playing in the Dark*. Pfister also comments on the ways in which therapeutic culture enables these forms of self-valorizing identification in "Glamorizing the Psychological": "The modern bourgeoisie exhibits the tendency to encode some groups it exploits as sexy and primitive (and childish) and then it identifies with these newly encoded groups for therapeutic reasons, as the 'primitive' within itself" (189).

7. Noting, in "The Divine Secrets of the Cultural Studies Sisterhood," that the novel assumes the form of a traditional marriage plot, Travis identifies some of the text's antifeminist impulses. Nevertheless, it is important to acknowledge, as Travis does, the text's demonstrated capacity to inspire the construction of female communities outside the nuclear family — a function not explicitly feminist, but one that poses a challenge to traditional heteronormativity.

8. Moskowitz notes that the therapeutic paradigm has encouraged people to confess their secrets to strangers. She observes that patients during the progressive era were not "accustomed to the idea, readily accepted today, that they should disclose intimate personal facts to perfect strangers. Agnes Moran, a twenty-seven-year-old patient at Boston Psychopathetic Hospital, objected to being asked questions that were, in her words, of a 'very personal character'" (43). Kaminer also notes the recovery movement's tendency to foster the confessional urges of Americans. "The recovery movement combines the testimonial tradition that

serves a greater good, like justice, with the therapeutic tradition in which talking about yourself is its own reward" (30).

9. See the two introductions written, respectively, by Bruce Robbins and Pheng Cheah to the volume they edited, *Cosmopolitics*, 1–44.

10. Robert Putnam writes: "We have not yet faced what is in some respects the deepest and most paradoxical indictment that might be made against advocates of fraternity — that is, the view that fraternity is in some sense at war with itself. Social capital is most easily created *in opposition* to something or someone else" (360–61).

11. In her analysis of Oprah Winfrey, Franny Nudelman notes the strange capacity of therapeutic discourse to facilitate community, relating it to feminist consciousness-raising strategies: "Consciousness-raising and recovery discourse, in particular, regard talk as a means of overcoming isolation and establishing solidarity: in both contexts, testimony creates identifications between the speaker and her audience, thus providing a basis for the development of actual or imagined communities of women" (299).

Three. *Infinite Jest* and the Recovery of Feeling

1. Smith's remarks appear in what Alcoholics Anonymous typically refers to as the Big Book, the text given to all new members: *Alcoholics Anonymous*, 180.

2. As historian of AA, Ernest Kurtz, notes: "What became increasingly clear was that whether primarily because of the titillating view of the underside of human life afforded, or primarily because of the potential for identification, or primarily because a pragmatic people responded to and thrived upon experience, the main marketable commodity that any alcoholic had to offer was his story" (67–68).

3. For some examples of critical responses to the novel, see R. Z. Sheppard; David Gates; Jan McInerney; Michiko Kakutani; Frank Bruni; Dan Cryer; Mark Caro.

4. See John Bradshaw.

5. Mary K. Holland also notes this motif: "Again and again, characters experience adult traumas through the unresolved pain of their childhoods, in the context of the original infant trauma of discovering the parent's disappointing inability or refusal to provide total satisfaction" (231).

6. This is obviously a broad and hyperbolic claim; as Catherine Toal rightly argues, *Infinite Jest* understates the tendency of popular culture to allure its viewers by dramatizing and provoking intense sentiment (319).

7. His descriptions of contemporary culture echo, in an unhappy register, some of the basic characterizations of postmodern culture made by Jameson in *Postmodernism*.

8. As Jeff Gonzales notes, much of the criticism on Wallace focuses on his ef-

forts to escape postmodernist irony. In his essay, Gonzales focuses on what he sees as Wallace's purpose in his later fiction — to imagine forms of community that do not threaten participants' sense of their own authenticity — which Gonzales reads as distinct from the project of *Infinite Jest*. While Gonzales offers a persuasive interpretation, I would argue that there is somewhat more continuity between the earlier and later work than he acknowledges.

9. Kurtz provides a historical and theoretical analysis of the organization in *Not-God*. Nan Robertson's *Getting Better* is an interesting historical/personal account of AA. Travis offers a very smart examination of the organization's publication history in *Language of the Heart*. See also Gregory Bateson; Paul Antze.

10. In an insightful reading, David Morris treats *Infinite Jest* as an illustration of reason's limitations and of the need to recognize ways of experiencing time dependent upon the habits and rituals that function outside the agency of reason.

11. Iannis Goerlandt argues that readers can escape the atmosphere of irony that Wallace produces only by breaking away from the addictive narrative of the text altogether; they must, as one disgruntled reader quoted by Goerlandt insists, "put the book down and slowly walk away" (324).

12. See for instance Brian James Oak; A Customer; E. A. Glaser; B. Johnson; Derk Koldewyn; Fred J. Solinger; Tkurie; Abby Ridge.

13. Katherine Hayles notes the recursive quality of the novel: "*Infinite Jest* creates cycles within cycles within cycles. Imagine a huge novel that has been run through the recursive feedback loops of an intelligent agent program and then strung out along the page" (5).

14. Catherine Nichols cogently describes *Infinite Jest*'s carnivalesque tactics, which function, in her view, ironically, to counter the "carnivalesque qualities of postmodern culture" (3).

15. Timothy Jacobs (in "The Brothers Incandenza") also notes this tendency of the narrator's voice to haunt the consciousness of his characters. He claims that Wallace's purpose is to underscore the fictional status of his work in the service of supporting its allegorical function. In another essay ("American Touchstone"), he contends that Wallace "effaces himself in the production of his art" (226). As will become clear shortly, I interpret *Infinite Jest* rather differently; to me the text and its metafictional interventions read as a somewhat equivocal attempt at self-expression.

16. According to Wallace, the clearest and most influential formulations of the death of the author appear in Roland Barthes, "The Death of the Author"; Jacques Derrida, *Margins of Philosophy*; and Martin Heidegger, *Poetry, Language, Thought* ("Greatly Exaggerated" 138–41).

17. Brian McHale describes this phenomenon as follows: "Frame-breaking is risky business. Intended to establish an absolute level of reality, it paradoxically *relativizes* reality; intended to provide an ontologically stable foothold, it only

destabilizes ontology further. For the metafictional gesture of sacrificing an illusory reality to a higher, 'realer' reality, that of the author, sets a precedent: why should this gesture not be *repeatable*? What prevents the author's reality from being treated in its turn as an illusion to be shattered? Nothing whatsoever, and so the supposedly absolute reality of the author becomes just another level of fiction, and the *real* world retreats to a further remove" (197).

18. Several reviewers on Amazon remark that the self-consciousness of the novel thwarted their emotional responses. J. Rosenbaum for instance writes: "It is generally quite difficult to empathize with the characters in the book when most of them are used as vehicles for Wallace's observations. This book is extraordinarily self indulgent."

19. After Wallace's suicide, A. O. Scott in fact acknowledged his intense identification with the author: "When, as an undergraduate with a head full of literary theory and a heartsick longing for authenticity, I first encountered David Foster Wallace, I experienced what is commonly called the shock of recognition. Actually, shock is too clean, too safe a word for my uncomfortable sense that not only did I know this guy, but he knew me" ("The Best Mind").

20. Wallace articulates this explicitly in his essay on Kafka: "No wonder [my students] cannot appreciate the really central Kafka joke — that the horrific struggle to establish a human self results in a self whose humanity is inseparable from that horrific struggle" (27).

21. In calling attention to the ontological status of the fictional world, postmodernist fiction, according to McHale, does not, as the standard narrative often suggests, turn away from attempts to represent the so-called real world. On the contrary, McHale argues, postmodernist fiction is constantly dramatizing the moments of exchange, contact, interpenetration, resemblance, and dissimilarity between the fictional and the real world in order to produce a better understanding of both — of how the real world shapes the act of fiction production and how the act of fiction production shapes the real world. In his book on David Foster Wallace, Marshall Boswell seems to uphold the anti-mimetic thesis in order to throw into relief Wallace's own revolt against the self-referential, hermetic quality of postmodernist fiction. But as his comments in "E Unibus Pluram" acknowledge, Wallace himself recognizes the inadequacy of any theory that radically severs his postmodernist forefathers from the realist project.

22. Calling Wallace a post-postmodernist author, Robert McLaughlin also identifies what he sees as a shift of "emphasis": "The emphasis among the younger writers I've talked about here, the post-postmodernists, is less on self-conscious wordplay and the violation of narrative conventions and more on representing the world we all more or less share. Yet in presenting that world, this new fiction nevertheless has to show that it's a world that we know through language and lay-

ers of representation; language, narrative, and the processes of representation are the only means we have to experience and know the world, ourselves, and our possibilities for being human. The better we understand them and how they operate, the better we can disengage them from the institutions that encourage the cynical despair that perpetuates the status quo and claim them for our own purposes."

Four. The Pain of Reading *A Million Little Pieces*

1. The overall tone of the journalistic coverage of the scandal was accusatory and judgmental. Certain writers, including Brian Bethune, Matthew Flamm, and Laura Vanderkam were especially outraged, treating James Frey's actions as irresponsible and unforgivable. Others, including Roy Clark, Marco della Cava, Samuel Freedman, Erica Jong, and Susan Salter Reynolds acknowledged mitigating factors, including the ambiguity of the memoir genre and the difficulty of upholding a rigid distinction between fact and fiction. Still others, such as Rob Long and Heather King, took the opportunity to point out that Frey's book was a disaster even by artistic standards. See also Jonathan Darman; Carol Memmott; Mark Peyser et al.; Lev Grossman et al.; Scott Martelle and Scott Collins; Collins and Matea Gold; Wyatt, "Treatment Description," "Frey Says Falsehoods Improved His Tale," "Live on 'Oprah,'" "Pieces' Editor," "Questions for Others"; Virginia Heffernan; David Carr; Richard Siklos; Frank Rich.

2. He makes this observation on *Oprah* 26 January 2006, and in "Truthiness 101: From Frey to Alito."

3. Laura Quinney writes, "Whatever historical moment evolved the grimness of the truth, it is not, as one might expect, strictly a Romantic or post-Romantic phenomenon. Twentieth-century preoccupations and tastes have made the phenomenon palpable" (xviii–xix).

4. Leigh Gilmore notes the importance of the confessional form in autobiography: "Autobiography cannot in this context be seen to draw its social authority simply from a privileged relation to real life. Rather, authority is derived through autobiography's proximity to the rhetoric of truth telling: the confession" ("Policing" 57).

5. According to Quinney, Samuel Johnson's *Rasselas* equates this "fierce impersonality" with wisdom (75).

6. Travis reads Frey's truth criteria as predicated upon an effort to embrace an antisentimental modernist aesthetic, which she terms "terrible honesty." See her afterword in *The Language of the Heart.*

7. This, at least, is how Theador Adorno understands the meaning of the term —though he finds it nonsensical.

8. See *Sincerity and Authenticity*, 95; 145–47; 152–53.

9. For a persuasive analysis of the complex rhetorical strategies members of the

American middle class employ in order to appropriate authentic forms of struggle and suffering, see Jurca.

10. For an intelligent analysis of the media coverage of the drug war in the United States, see Jimmie Reeves and Richard Campbell.

11. The connection between the middle class and illegal drugs has been well documented. See, for instance, Gordon Witkin; Reeves and Campbell.

12. As Eve Kosofsky Sedgwick observes: "The simplest answer, I think, to the question, 'Why now?' — why the twentieth century, and most of all its final quarter, should turn out to be the site of this epidemic of addiction and addiction attribution — must lie in the peculiarly resonant relations that seem to obtain between the problematics of addiction and those of the consumer phase of international capitalism" (135).

13. Mumford provides an early and influential view of suburbia's alienation from reality: "This [suburbia] was not merely a child-centered environment; it was based on a childish view of the world in which reality was sacrificed to the pleasure principle" (494).

14. For some explorations of the relationship between addiction and gender, see Mariana Valverde; John William Crowley.

15. Frey's resistance both to emasculation and to his middle-class identity announces itself most markedly in his spare nonironic writing style, which he characterized in a *New York Observer* interview as a reaction against the "effete" works promoted by master's programs in the United States (Joe Hagan 1).

16. For critical analyses of Winfrey's therapeutic strategies see Dixon; Illouz; D. T. Max; Rooney, *Reading with Oprah*; Shattuc; Corinne Squire; and Sherryl Wilson. Shattuc in particular addresses the ways in which Winfrey tends to personalize problems that have political or social origins.

17. Jaime Harker and Travis (in her afterword to *The Language of the Heart*) both read Frey as opposing a masculinist notion of serious literature to the therapeutic, feminine protocols at work on *Oprah*.

18. See for instance Shirley Neuman; Mary Mason.

19. In their analysis of her book club, Farr, Rooney (in *Reading with Oprah*), Illouz, and Max all observe Winfrey's emphasis on resemblance-based identification.

20. For a history of consciousness-raising groups, see Alice Echols; Flora Davis. Nudelman notes the resemblance between Winfrey's therapeutic strategies and consciousness-raising (CR) practices in the 1970s (300). Rapping traces the historical and logical connections between CR and the recovery movement.

21. In previous decades, Winfrey's strategies were even more in keeping with Frey's. Prior to her decision to raise the tone of her show in 1994, she frequently presented her viewers with extreme, transgressive, scandalous scenarios similar to the ones offered on her competitors' talk shows, such as *The Jerry Springer Show*,

The Geraldo Rivera Show, and *The Sally Jesse Raphael Show*. For some examinations of this shift, see Hall; Maria McGrath.

22. In *Columbia Journalism Review*, Freedman asserts, "Fiction and nonfiction make fundamentally different compacts with a reader and are held to fundamentally different standards" (53). In *USA Today*, Clark remarks, "The next time you pick up a memoir, you should expect that the price of the book seals an implied contract between you and the author" (13A). Also writing for *USA Today*, Laura Vanderkam describes the Frey scandal as "shattering the compact between writers and readers into a million little pieces" (11A).

23. For a discussion of effective alternatives to the disease model of alcohol and AA, see Fingarette.

24. An example of an important conservative figure invested in recuperating the discourse of individual responsibility is David Brooks. See for instance "The Columbine Killers" and "Virtues and Victims."

25. For a good ethnographic examination of American individualism, see Bellah et al.

26. Numerous scholars have pointed out Winfrey's commitment to a bootstraps ideology and her tendency to hold individuals responsible for their problems and their successes, rather than historical, political, or structural causes. See Peck; Tarshia Stanley; Sherryl Wilson; Illouz; Cloud, "Hegemony or Concordance?"; Debbie Epstein and Deborah Steinberg; Jeffrey Decker. Malin Pereira corroborates this general assessment, while arguing that a critique of this bootstraps ideology constitutes the repressed political unconscious of *Oprah*.

27. In their essay, "Oprah Winfrey and Women's Autobiography," Illouz and John expand upon this observation: "In other words, Winfrey always defines her hurdles as psychological rather than material ones, despite the fact of difficult material conditions as well. Furthermore, Winfrey's career has been punctuated by the construction of what can be called 'psychic events'" (93).

Five. The Politics of Interiority in *The Pilot's Wife*

1. A highly successful writer, Anita Shreve has published thirteen novels in the past two decades, including *The Weight of Water* and *Body Surfing*. Like *The Pilot's Wife*, most of these texts focus on middle-class female protagonists and their personal, psychological dilemmas.

2. In his reading of Jane Austen, D. A. Miller suggests that free indirect discourse might be conceptualized as a form of identification between the narrator and the character (57–60).

3. Famously describing the modernist focus on the subjective, Erich Auerbach observed, "At the time of the first World War and after — in a Europe unsure of itself, overflowing with unsettled ideologies and ways of life, pregnant with disaster

—certain writers distinguished by instinct and insight find a method which dissolves reality into multiple and multivalent reflections of consciousness" (551). Lears and Michael Levenson also explore the turn to the subjective provoked by the bewildering changes that characterized modernity. For treatments of this trend later in the century, see Elaine Tyler May; Radway, "Research Universities" and *Feeling*.

4. The most obvious modernist text that exemplifies this anguished tone is Ford Madox Ford, *The Good Soldier*. But of course one can find many instances of acute epistemological distress in Beckett, Conrad, T. S. Eliot, Faulkner, James, and Wharton among others.

5. See my discussion of this under "The Therapeutic Turn" in the introduction.

6. This fact about novelistic form is symptomatic of the more general political reality observed by Berlant and Warner that an individual's claim on privacy depends upon his or her adherence to various sexual, cultural, and economic conventions. See Berlant and Warner, "Sex in Public"; Berlant, *The Queen*, 220; Warner, "Zones." Deborah Nelson also considers the paradox that intrusive norms serve to police and protect individual privacy in the postwar United States.

7. See for instance flyover; soybaby; M. Asali; Marmalinde "marmalinde."

8. Describing Kathryn's bland fashion choices, reviewer Laura Jamison makes a similar observation: "Kathryn is not someone who dresses in couture; she is Everywoman. Like so much else in this book, the fashion choices seem designed to invite the identification of a mass readership" (37).

9. Derrida's analysis in *Politics of Friendship* of the unsettling consequences of Carl Schmitt's teleological definition of the political suggests this as an irrepressible possibility.

10. In fact Shreve has written a history of feminist consciousness-raising practices. See *Women Together, Women Alone*.

11. For other critics who suggest that Shreve is difficult to classify, see Charlie Hill; Rebecca Ascher-Walsh; Tom Shone; Ron Charles; Susan Isaacs; David Willis McCullough.

12. Several readers on Amazon do remark that Jack is more interesting than Kathryn. See for instance Susan E. Neill; Marmalinde "marmalinde."

13. May comments upon the central role that the domestic sphere plays in cold war ideology.

14. Recently, numerous scholars have addressed the social and political character of psychological states, especially various modes of affect. See for instance Ellison; Bendelow and Williams. Warner has also written very eloquently in *Publics and Counterpublics* on the need to rethink the notion of the public sphere in order to embrace styles of affect ordinarily excluded by an emphasis on dispassionate, disembodied debate.

15. In "Poor Eliza," Berlant describes the danger as follows: "As when a refrigerator is opened by a person hungry for something other than food, the turn to sentimental rhetoric at moments of social anxiety constitutes a generic wish for an unconflicted world, one where structural inequities, not emotions and intimacies, are epiphenomenal" (646).

Six. Reading *The Kite Runner* in America

1. See for instance: K. Solomon; Olga Comas Bacardi; Lori D Widmer "Reader"; K. M. Sowka; Michael Werner; Logan Creek; SB Reader; Nathan Crabtree; I Luv Books; Annie "bookwishes4"; Lee A. Rubinstein; nodice; Jeff T. Blevins; Shana Punim.

2. For descriptions of these responses to the book, see Patricia Kay; C. Marken; Birgit A. Jensen; Christine K. Sartory; Timothy Kearney; Marsha Marks. *The Kite Runner* made it onto best-seller lists in September 2004. By April 2005 it had gone through seventeen printings, and over 1.4 million copies had been sold. It remained on best-seller lists as late as August 11, 2008, and in 2007 DreamWorks released a feature film version of the book. See Craig Wilson; Wyatt, "Wrenching Tale."

3. For some positive reviews that also describe the reading experience as painful, see Michaela Jones; Beausoir; Julie A. Boyd; Donna K. Jenner; Amira A. Clow; Patrick Carlin; Chloe L. Moushey; Peggy G. Lambdin; 1KAT; doc peterson; M. Schijvens; Gerber Daisy; The Stinker; Lover of books; Justin Snow; M. Colleen Talley; Hector Guerra; C. A. Begum; Yasaman Mostajeran; L. Jean-Louis; K. Kuehl; L.K.B.H.; K. Folmar; Mark L. Harris; S. E. Duke; Rebecca of A Better Cause; NC; enthusiastic reader.

4. Edward Said, of course, was one of the first scholars to explore the dangers of exoticization, in *Orientalism*.

5. For especially emphatic testimonies to this effect, see Brian K. Tarumoto; Judith R. Wright; James E. O'Leary; Girl Chronicles; Phoebe Snow; Brace Gfeen; Cassandra L. Warren; Click Chick; L. A. Atkins; D. Smith; "margymc"; S. Masula; Janet M. Cortez.

6. Readers who appreciate the absence of a distinct political position include Wave Tossed; William R. Siggelkow; P. E. Lee; Click Chick; Annie "Annie"; Robin Friedman; mdscifi_lover; prcarolyn.

7. Readers who identified themselves as members of book clubs include: C. J. Procko; E. Haroldsen; Connie V.; Nancy J. Coughlin; Shelly Belden; C. Davis; M. Nichols; D. Maynard; H. Boehning; Avid Reader; Debbie; Linda; "doves wing"; W. Jamison; Laura K; Gentle Reader; Susan B.; Virginia Nuckols; Nathan Crabtree; sb-lynn; BethDeHart; nekko1; L. Roth; snowblaze; Melissa Niksic; Learning

All The Time; Acme Reader; R. Boadway; trish's Dish; A Mom at Home; Douglas M. Dixon; Happy Reader; Eileen Davidoff; Shana Punim.

8. See Jon T; Cheryl Tran; K. Rominger ; Sherry Johnson; Judith Anne; C. Kim; Judith R. Wright; Paul Fellows; B. Vander Eyk; S. Masand; M. D. Copeland; B. Flanagan; LZ-1; Carolyn Rowe Hill; Denise; Jessica K.; Scorpion1664; SB Reader; John K. Addis; Bibliophile; kattepus; ThomsEBynum; J. Fiorani; Wendy Somerlot Bittel; Maryam Habib Khan; Michele Cozzens; Jack L. Langdon; Tea Molino; Louise D. Somes; J. M. McCormick; S. Langner; D. Smith; Carol A. Sym; A reader 7/16/04; Daffy Du; Professor Joseph L. McCauley; A reader 12/16/04; "blissengine"; M. T. Guzman; M. J Leonard; Cathy O'Connor; Kim keenan; Ayesha Riaz; Andy P.

9. See Squidhunter; Stacy Eichhorn; Roni; Aaron Black; Gene Koo; applepiebooks; Sabad One; Amer Dahmash.

10. See M. McDonald; mtspace; Roy Munson; Deborah Palladino; Michael A. Lacombe; edith lawrence; Paul Fellows; Josh J. Riley; The Stinker; Vijay B. Kumar; Cindy C.; Josh Daniels; Dr Cathy Goodwin; Jennifer McCormick; Luther; Robin Friedman; Stephanie Henry; J. Olcott; Anne Lebrecht; Linda K. Faigaohall; The Inspired One; C. Leibbrand; Eileen Rieback; debonairbear; A reader 8/20/03; Francis J. Mcinerney.

11. Said comments on this in *Orientalism*, but he focuses more directly on media coverage of the Islamic world in *Covering Islam*.

12. Here I am referring to Paul Gilroy's notion of "strategic universalism," which can be read as a response to Gayatri Spivak's "strategic essentialism." Two influential works of scholarship that reinforce a binaristic understanding of Islam and the West are Samuel Huntington's *The Clash of Civilizations* and Bernard Lewis's *The Crisis of Islam*. See also Said, "Clash."

13. Of course, paradoxically, this pain is also pleasurable; in her work on tragedy, Laura Quinney points to a number of thinkers, including Burke, Hume, Kant, and Deleuze, who have explored this double effect (xv).

14. See for instance Hector Guerra; enthusiastic reader; Patrick Carlin; SDSonn.

15. See PW; R. Bakker; sb-lynn; D. C. Smith; Dean Blobaum; applepiebooks.

16. For some reviews that suggest this response, see UNC; Lori D Widmer; Yuni; S. Schultz; George R. Odell; Kent Holland; Cheryl Morris; Josh J. Riley; Shelley C. Raker; Cassandra L. Warren; Luther; Anne Lebrecht; K. L. Cotugno; Jerry Caveglia; laleh hamadani; Reader "tisha69."

17. For detailed historical accounts of this period, see Raja Anwar; M. Hassan Kakar; Ralph Magnus and Eden Naby; David Edwards, *Before Taliban*.

18. For examples of reviews that juxtapose these two characterizations, see Kar-

rah Trainer; M. McDonald; Stephanie L. Warfel; mtspace; A. Rutherford; Yasmin Mansoor; Cenk Sumbas; Enchanted-reader; j old school; Yuni; Dolly A. Berthelot; Ashley Blackwell; Kent Holland; Wave Tossed; D. K. Miles; George R. Odell; Cynthia K. Robertson; Michael Werner; Ellen VandeWater; Suzanne Somers; M. J. Smith; Dayle; Frederick A. Babb; ReadBks1182; Susan B.; dougrhon; Timothy Kearney; Sunsara Taylor; Catherine J. Thomson; Patricia Kay; Maclen; Ed Foltz; sb-lynn; Tom Arnold; Mary Reinert; Robin Friedman; J. Olcott; K. Folmar; B. Mellon; nekko1; Missie Dowey; Michael S. Rudman MD; A reader 7/8/04; "themage7"; Mary Whipple; M. L. Nieves; Robbie; William E. Adams; PR Kgregus; C. L. Tobin.

19. See Amira A. Clow; Patrick Carlin; Sonya D. Stutts; E. Alavi; M. Patel; Molly J. Mathias; Mooch; Christine K. Sartory; Justin Snow; Hector Guerra; Yasaman Mostajeran; Cathleen A. Dennison; Richard Nelson; Mary Parker; Tracy Oshima; S. E. Duke; Megan Brizzolara; Anne Fitten Glenn (author); "osudebbie"; Analis M.; kehroll; hi; Traci Watson.

20. See, for instance Sancho Mahle; Dolly A. Berthelot; Sylvanna M. Vargas; Kent Holland; Chloe L. Moushey; M. J. Smith; Grace; Lover of books; Charlene Sanderson; Tom Arnold; Greg Henderson; L.K.B.H.; Michele Cozzens; J. Olcott; Anne Lebrecht; Grady Harp; C. G. Johnson; Patricia Kramer; L. Poor; A reader 7/8/04; Gul A. Zikria M.D.; "bernardetreves"; B. Capossere; A. Rajamani; trish's Dish; Traci Watson.

21. See for instance E. Dillon; C. B. Collins Jr.; A New York Reader; Harold R. Zeckel; anduarto; Steve Koss; kattepus; Jennifer M-R; D. C. Smith; Naz; More Over; Manola Sommerfeld; E. Abrams.

22. For an illuminating exploration of Pashtun culture, see Edwards, *Heroes*.

23. Edwards, in *Before Taliban*, Ahmed Rashid, and Hosseini, in his second novel, *A Thousand Splendid Suns*, describe the set of extreme and anomalous conditions that enabled the Taliban to assume power. The Soviet occupation and the ensuing civil war killed 1.5 million Afghans and rendered millions more destitute. The Taliban, comprising refugees educated in ascetic conditions in madrasas on the border between Afghanistan and Pakistan, had not participated in the ethnic and political feuds that divided the country after the occupation, and they promised to bring peace and unity to a desperate population that no longer trusted its leaders. Moreover, according to Rashid, the United States may well have provided covert aid to the Taliban in the hopes that the group would produce sufficient stability to enable the production of a natural gas pipeline.

24. In *The Next Attack*, published in 2005, Daniel Benjamin and Steven Simon point out that a quarter of Americans have negative stereotypes of Muslims; a quarter believe that Muslims value life less than other people; and more than half

believe that it would be justifiable to curb the civil rights of Muslims in the United States in order to defend the country against terrorist attacks.

25. See for instance Karisa; A. Krafft; Cassandra L. Warren; LBR; "mom3xover"; Gary Griffiths.

26. See for instance Megan Brizzolara; Violet Bandong.

27. According to Berlant, Americans frequently view sentiment, especially "painful feeling," as a unifying experience, both predicated on and, at the same time, capable of overcoming cultural and class differences ("Poor Eliza" 641).

Conclusion

1. Pfister has pointed out that psychological concepts have largely served the needs of the middle class. See "On Conceptualizing the Cultural History of Emotional and Psychological Life in America."

2. For a discussion of how the victim has become a paradoxically empowering status, see Jurca; Moskowitz; Kaminer.

3. See for instance Cloud, *Control and Consolation*; Jameson; Bellah et al.; Vitz.

4. Cheah observes a similar phenomenon: "Politics must be forced to include the variable power of sympathetic imagination to define collectivities of belonging and responsibility in the absence of that long history of face-to-face interaction that Dewey thought was necessary to community" (8–9). See "Introduction Part II," in *Cosmopolitics*.

5. This dichotomy between the apparently individual scope of reference and the larger social resonances of psychological discourse is one that Shattuc also discusses. See "Oprahfiction" and *Talking Cure*.

6. Quirk also notes the ways in which the therapeutic paradigm has allied itself with multiculturalism in order to produce feelings of cross-cultural identification. He argues that such feelings tend to efface perceptions of difference in favor of perceptions of commonality. I would argue that the two need not be treated as mutually exclusive.

7. See for instance Rey Chow; Doris Sommer.

8. See for instance Stacey Margolis; Berlant, "Poor Eliza."

9. Elizabeth Barnes, for instance, reads the effort to elicit sympathy as a form of coercion.

BIBLIOGRAPHY

Books and Articles

Adams, Timothy Dow. *Telling Lies in Modern American Autobiography*. Chapel Hill: UNC P, 1990.

Adorno, Theodor W. *The Jargon of Authenticity*. Trans. Knut Tarnowski and Frederic Will. Evanston: Northwestern UP, 1973.

Aguiar, Sarah Appleton. "'Passing On' Death: Stealing Life in Toni Morrison's *Paradise*." *African American Review* 38 (2004): 513–19.

Alcoholics Anonymous: The Story of How Many Thousands of Men and Women Have Recovered from Alcoholism. 3rd ed. New York: Alcoholics Anonymous World Services, 1976.

Anderson, Benedict. *Imagined Communities: Reflections on the Origin and Spread of Nationalism*. London: Verso, 1983.

Anderson, Melanie R. "'What would be on the other side?': Spectrality and Spirit Work in Toni Morrison's *Paradise*." *African American Review* 42 (2008): 307–21.

Anker, Paul. *Self-Help and Popular Religion in Modern American Culture: An Interpretive Guide*. Westport: Greenwood Press, 1999.

Antze, Paul. "Symbolic Action in Alcoholics Anonymous." *Constructive Drinking: Perspectives on Drink from Anthropology*. Ed. Mary Douglas. Cambridge: Cambridge UP, 1987. 149–81.

Anwar, Raja. *The Tragedy of Afghanistan: A First-Hand Account*. Trans. Khalid Hassan. New York: Verso, 1988.

Arendt, Hannah. *The Human Condition*. Chicago: U of Chicago P, 1958.

Armstrong, Nancy. *Desire and Domestic Fiction: A Political History of the Novel*. New York: Oxford UP, 1987.

Ascher-Walsh, Rebecca. "Past Imperfect." *Entertainment Weekly* 27 April 2001: 110–11.

Auerbach, Erich. *Mimesis: The Representation of Reality in Western Literature*. Trans. Willard Trask. Garden City: Doubleday, 1957.

Awkward, Michael. *Negotiating Difference: Race, Gender, and the Politics of Positionality*. Chicago: U of Chicago P, 1995.

Barnes, Elizabeth. *States of Sympathy: Seduction and Democracy in the American Novel*. New York: Columbia UP, 1997.

Barthes, Roland. "The Death of the Author." *Image, Music, Text*. Ed. and trans. Stephen Heath. New York: Hill, 1977. 142–48.

Bateson, Gregory. "The Cybernetics of the Self: A Theory of Alcoholism." *Psychiatry* 34 (1971): 1–18.

Bellah, Robert, et al. *Habits of the Heart: Individualism and Commitment in American Life*. Berkeley: U of California P, 1985.

Bendelow, Gillian, and Simon J. Williams, eds. *Emotions in Social Life: Critical Themes and Contemporary Issues*. New York: Routledge, 1998.

Benjamin, Daniel, and Steven Simon. *The Next Attack: The Failure of the War on Terror and a Strategy for Getting It Right*. New York: Times, 2005.

Berlant, Lauren. "Compassion (and Withholding)." *Compassion: The Culture and Politics of an Emotion*. Ed. Lauren Berlant. New York: Routledge, 2004. 1–13.

——. "The Female Complaint." *Social Text* 19/20 (1988): 237–59.

——. "Poor Eliza." *American Literature* 70 (1998): 635–68.

——. *The Queen of America Goes to Washington City*. Durham, NC: Duke UP, 1997.

——, and Michael Warner. "Sex in Public." *Critical Inquiry* 24 (1998): 547–66.

Berúbé, Michael. *The Left at War*. New York: NYU P, 2009.

Bethune, Brian. "Truth or Consequences." *MacLean's* 10 April 2006: 68.

Bhabha, Homi K. "The Other Question: Difference, Discrimination, and the Discourse of Colonialism." *Black British Cultural Studies: A Reader*. Ed. Houston A. Baker, Jr., et al. Chicago: U of Chicago P, 1996. 87–106.

Boorstin, Daniel. *The Americans: The Democratic Experience*. New York: Random House, 1973.

Booth, Wayne. *The Company We Keep: An Ethics of Fiction*. Berkeley: U of California P, 1988.

Bordo, Susan. *Unbearable Weight: Feminism, Western Culture, and the Body*. Berkeley: U of California P, 1993.

Boswell, Marshall. *Understanding David Foster Wallace*. Columbia: U of South Carolina P, 2003.

Botton, Alain de. *How Proust Can Change Your Life: Not a Novel*. New York: Pantheon, 1997.

Bourdieu, Pierre. *Distinction: A Social Critique of the Judgement of Taste*. Trans. Richard Nice. Cambridge: Harvard UP, 1984.

Bradshaw, John. *Homecoming: Reclaiming and Championing Your Inner Child*. New York: Bantam, 1990.

Brooks, David. "The Columbine Killers." *New York Times* 15 May 2004: A17.

————. "Virtues and Victims." *New York Times* 9 April 2006, sec. 4: 12.

Brooks, Peter. *Reading for Plot: Design and Intention in Narrative*. New York: Knopf, 1984.

Bruni, Frank. "The Grunge American Novel." *New York Times Magazine* 24 March 1996: 38.

Burke, Kenneth. "Literature as Equipment for Living." *The Philosophy of Literary Form: Studies in Symbolic Action*. Baton Rouge: Louisiana State UP, 1941. 293–304.

Campbell, Donna M. *Resisting Regionalism: Gender and Naturalism in American Fiction, 1885–1915*. Athens: Ohio UP, 1997.

Caplan, Eric. *Mind Games: American Culture and the Birth of Psychotherapy*. Berkeley: U of California P, 1998.

Caro, Mark. "The Next Big Thing: Can a Downstate Author Withstand the Sensation over His 1,079-Page Novel?" *Chicago Tribune* 23 February 1996: 1.

Carr, David. "Oprah Trumps Truthiness." *New York Times* 30 January 2006: C1.

Casanova, Pascale. *The World Republic of Letters*. Trans. M. B. DeBevoise. Cambridge: Harvard UP, 2004.

Chapman, Mary, and Glenn Hendler, eds. *Sentimental Men: Masculinity and the Politics of Affect in American Culture*. Berkeley: U of California P, 1999.

Charles, Ron. "Remembrance of Things Past — and Stale." *Christian Science Monitor* 5 April 2001: 21.

Cheah, Pheng. "Introduction Part II: The Cosmopolitical — Today." Cheah and Robbins 20–44.

————, and Bruce Robbins, eds. *Cosmopolitics: Thinking and Feeling Beyond the Nation*. Minneapolis: U of Minnesota P, 1998.

Cheever, John. "The Worm in the Apple." *The Housebreaker of Shady Hill and Other Stories*. New York: Harper, 1958. 106–12.

Chow, Rey. *Writing Diaspora: Tactics of Intervention in Contemporary Cultural Studies*. Bloomington: Indiana UP, 1993.

Cioffi, Frank. "'An Anguish Become Thing': Narrative as Performance in David Foster Wallace's *Infinite Jest*." *Narrative* 8 (2000): 161–81.

Clark, Roy Peter. "How to Fix the Memoir Genre." *USA Today* 11 April 2006: 13A.

Cloud, Dana. *Control and Consolation in American Culture and Politics: Rhetoric of Therapy*. Thousand Oaks CA: Sage, 1998.

————. "Hegemony or Concordance? The Rhetoric of Tokenism in 'Oprah': Winfrey's Rags-to-Riches Biography." *Critical Studies in Mass Communication* 13 (1996): 115–37.

Collins, Scott, and Matea Gold. "Winfrey Throws Book at Frey." *Los Angeles Times* 27 January 2006: A22.

Crain, Caleb. *American Sympathy: Men, Friendship, and Literature in the New Nation.* New Haven: Yale UP, 2001.

Crossley, Nick. "Emotion and Communicative Action: Habermas, Linguistic Philosophy and Existentialism." Bendelow and Williams 16–38.

Crowley, John William. *The White Logic: Alcoholism and Gender in American Modernist Fiction.* Amherst: U of Massachusetts P, 1994.

Cryer, Dan. "A Triumphant Volley of Obsessions." *Newsday* 12 February 1996: 13.2.

Cushman, Philip. *Constructing the Self, Constructing America: A Cultural History of Psychotherapy.* Reading, MA: Addison, Wesley, 1995.

———. "Psychotherapy to 1992: A Historically Situated Interpretation." *A History of Psychotherapy: A Century of Change.* Ed. Donald K. Freedheim. Washington, D.C.: American Psychological Association, 1992. 21–64.

Dalsgård, Katrine. "The One All-Black Town Worth the Pain: (African) American Exceptionalism, Historical Narration, and the Critique of Nationhood in Toni Morrison's *Paradise.*" *African American Review* 35 (2001): 233–48.

Damrosch, David. *What Is World Literature?* Princeton: Princeton UP, 2003.

Darman, Jonathan. "The Wrath of Oprah." *Newsweek* 2 February 2006: 42–43.

Davis, Flora. *Moving the Mountain: The Women's Movement in America Since 1960.* New York: Simon & Schuster, 1991.

Davis, Kenneth C. *Two-Bit Culture: The Paperbacking of America.* Boston: Houghton Mifflin, 1984.

Davis, Kimberly Chabot. "Oprah's Book Club and the Politics of Cross-Racial Empathy." Farr and Harker 141–62.

Decker, Jeffrey Louis. *Made in America: Self-Styled Success from Horatio Alger to Oprah Winfrey.* Minneapolis: U of Minnesota P, 1997.

della Cava, Marco R. "Truth Falls to 'Pieces' After Suspect Memoir." *USA Today* 16 January 2006: 1D.

Derrida, Jacques. *Margins of Philosophy.* Trans. Alan Bass. Chicago: U of Chicago P, 1982.

———. *Politics of Friendship.* Trans. George Collins. New York: Verso, 1997.

Dixon, Kathleen. "The Dialogic Genres of Oprah Winfrey's 'Crying Shame.'" *Journal of Popular Culture* 35 (2001): 171–91.

Domina, Lynn. "From Autobiography to Infinity: Mary McCarthy's *Memories of a Catholic Girlhood* and *How I Grew.*" *a/b: Auto/Biography Studies* 10 (1995): 68–86.

Donaldson, Scott. *The Suburban Myth.* New York: Columbia UP, 1969.

Donovan, Josephine. *New England Local Color Literature: A Women's Tradition.* New York: F. Ungar, 1983.

Douglas, Ann. *The Feminization of American Culture.* New York: Knopf, 1977.

Dreier, Peter, John Mollenkopf, and Todd Swanstrom. *Place Matters: Metropolitics for the Twenty-First Century*. Lawrence: UP of Kansas, 2001.

Dubey, Madhu. *Black Women Novelists and the Nationalist Aesthetic*. Bloomington: Indiana UP, 1994.

Dyer, Richard. *White*. London: Routledge, 1997.

Echols, Alice. *Daring to Be Bad: Radical Feminism in America, 1967–1975*. Minneapolis: U of Minnesota P, 1989.

Edwards, David B. *Before Taliban: Genealogies of the Afghan Jihad*. Berkeley: U of California P, 2002.

———. *Heroes of the Age: Moral Fault Lines on the Afghan Frontier*. Berkeley: U of California P, 1996.

Ehrenreich, Barbara. *Fear of Falling: The Inner Life of the Middle Class*. New York: Pantheon, 1989.

Eliot, T. S. "Tradition and the Individual Talent." *The Sacred Wood*. London: Methune, 1920. 42–53.

Ellison, Julie. *Cato's Tears and the Making of Anglo-American Emotion*. Chicago: U of Chicago P, 1999.

Epstein, Debbie, and Deborah Lynn Steinberg. "American Dreamin': Discoursing Liberally on *The Oprah Winfrey Show*." *Women's Studies International Forum* 21 (1998): 77–94.

Epstein, Jason. *Book Business: Publishing Past, Present, and Future*. New York: Norton, 2001.

Farr, Cecilia Konchar. *Reading Oprah: How Oprah's Book Club Changed the Way America Reads*. New York: SUNY P, 2005.

———, and Jaime Harker. Introduction. Farr and Harker 1–12.

———, and Jaime Harker, eds. *The Oprah Affect: Critical Essays on Oprah's Book Club*. Albany: SUNY UP, 2008.

Felski, Rita. "After Suspicion." *Profession* (2009): 28–35.

———. *Beyond Feminist Aesthetics: Feminist Literature and Social Change*. Cambridge: Harvard UP, 1989.

Fetterley, Judith, and Marjorie Pryse. *Writing out of Place: Regionalism, Women, and American Literary Culture*. Urbana: U of Illinois P, 2003.

Fiedler, Leslie A. *Love and Death in the American Novel*. New York: Criterion, 1960.

———. "The Middle against Both Ends." *Mass Culture: The Popular Arts in America*. Ed. Bernard Rosenberg and David Manning White. New York: Free Press, 1964. 537–47.

Finch, Janet. *White Oleander*. Boston: Little, Brown, 1999.

Fingarette, Herbert. *Heavy Drinking: The Myth of Alcoholism as a Disease*. Berkeley: U of California P, 1988.

Fish, Stanley. *Is There a Text in This Class? The Authority of Interpretive Communities*. Cambridge: Harvard UP, 1980.

Fisher, Philip. *Hard Facts: Setting and Form in the American Novel*. New York: Oxford UP, 1987.

Fishman, Robert. *Bourgeois Utopia: The Rise and Fall of Suburbia*. New York: Basic, 1987.

Flagg, Fannie. *Fried Green Tomatoes at the Whistlestop Cafe*. New York: Random House, 1987.

Flamm, Matthew. "Truth, Fiction and Frey." *The Nation* 13 February 2006: 5–6.

Flint, Holly. "Toni Morrison's *Paradise*: Black Cultural Citizenship in the American Empire." *American Literature* 78 (2006): 585–612.

Foucault, Michel. "What Is an Author?" *Foucault Reader*. Ed. Paul Rabinow. New York: Pantheon, 1984. 101–20.

Fraile-Marcos, Ana María. "Hybridizing the 'City upon a Hill' in Toni Morrison's *Paradise*. *Melus* 28 (2003): 3–33.

Freedman, Mary E. Wilkins. *New England Nun, and Other Stories*. New York: Harper, 1891.

Freedman, Samuel. "The Predictable Scandal: The Book World's Devotion to Truth Runs Much Deeper than James Frey and the Memoir." *Columbia Journalism Review* March/April 2006: 50–53.

Freud, Sigmund. *Interpretation of Dreams*. Trans. A. A. Brill. 3rd ed. London: MacMillan, 1915.

———. *New Introductory Lectures on Psychoanalysis*. Trans. James Strachey. New York: Norton, 1965.

Frey, James. *A Million Little Pieces*. New York: Anchor, 2003.

Friedan, Betty. *The Feminine Mystique*. New York: Norton, 1963.

Frye, Northrop. "Literature as Therapy." *The Eternal Act of Creation: Essays, 1979–1990*. Bloomington: Indiana UP, 1993. 21–34.

Gal, Susan. "A Semiotics of the Public/Private Distinction." *Differences* 13 (2002): 77–95.

Galbraith, John Kenneth. *The Affluent Society*. Boston: Houghton Mifflin, 1958.

Garnham, Nicholas. "Political Economy and Cultural Studies: Reconciliation or Divorce?" *Critical Studies in Mass Communication* 12 (1995): 62–71.

Garreau, Joel. *Edge City: Life on the New Frontier*. New York: Anchor, 1992.

Gates, David. "Levity's Rainbow." *Newsweek* 19 February 1996: 80.

Gibbons, Kaye. *Ellen Foster*. New York: Vintage, 1990.

Giddens, Anthony. *Modernity and Self-Identity: Self and Society in the Late Modern Age*. Cambridge: Polity Press, 1991.

Gilmore, Leigh. *The Limits of Autobiography: Trauma and Testimony*. Ithaca: Cornell UP, 2001.

———. "Policing Truth: Confession, Gender, and Autobiographical Authority." *Autobiography & Postmodernism*. Eds. Kathleen Ashley, Leigh Gilmore, and Gerald Peters. Amherst: U of Massachusetts P, 1994. 54–78.

Gilroy, Paul. *Against Race: Imagining Political Culture beyond the Color Line*. Cambridge: Harvard UP, 2000.

Gitlin, Todd. *The Sixties: Years of Hope, Days of Rage*. New York: Bantam, 1987.

Goerlandt, Iannis. "'Put the Book Down and Slowly Walk Away': Irony and David Foster Wallace's *Infinite Jest*." *Critique* 47 (2006): 310–28.

Gonzales, Jeff. "'That Our Endless Journey Home Is in Fact Our Home': Reconsidering David Foster Wallace." Unpublished Essay.

Goodwin, Jeff, et al. *Passionate Politics: Emotions and Social Movements*. Chicago: U of Chicago P, 2001.

Greco, Albert N. "Shaping the Future: Mergers, Acquisitions, and the U.S. Publishing, Communications, and Mass Media Industries, 1990–1995." *Publishing Review Quarterly* 12 (1996): 5–15.

———, et al. *The Culture and Commerce of Publishing in the 21st Century*. Stanford: Stanford UP, 2007.

Greene, Gayle. *Changing the Story: Feminist Fiction and the Tradition*. Bloomington: Indiana UP, 1991.

Grossberg, Lawrence. "Cultural Studies vs. Political Economy: Is Anybody Else Bored with This Debate?" *Critical Studies in Media Communication* 12 (1995): 72–81.

Grossman, Lev, et al. "The Trouble with Memoirs." *Time* 23 January 2006: 58–62.

Guillory, John. *Cultural Capital: The Problem of Literary Canon Formation*. Chicago: U of Chicago P, 1993.

———. "The Ordeal of Middlebrow Culture." *Transition* 67 (1995): 82–92.

Habermas, Jürgen. *The Structural Transformation of the Public Sphere: An Inquiry into a Category of Bourgeois Society*. Trans. Thomas Burger. Cambridge: MIT P, 1989.

Hagan, Joe. "Meet the Staggering Genius." *The New York Observer* 3 February 2003: 1.

Hall, R. Mark. "The 'Oprahfication' of Literacy: Reading Oprah's Book Club." *College English* 65 (2003): 646–67.

Harker, Jaime. "Afterword: Oprah, James Frey, and the Problem of the Literary." Farr and Harker 321–33.

Harris, Jennifer, and Elwood Watson. "Introduction: Oprah Winfrey as Subject and Spectacle." Harris and Watson 1–31.

———, eds. *The Oprah Phenomenon*. Lexington: UP of Kentucky, 2007.

Harte, Francis Brett. *The Luck of Roaring Camp, and Other Sketches*. Boston: Fields, Osgood, & Co., 1870.

Hayles, N. Katherine. "The Illusion of Autonomy and the Fact of Recursivity: Virtual Ecologies, Entertainment, and *Infinite Jest*." *New Literary History* 30 (1999): 675–97.

Haynes, Melinda. *Mother of Pearl*. New York: Hyperion, 1999.

Heffernan, Virginia. "Ms. Winfrey Takes a Guest to the Televised Woodshed." *New York Times* 27 January 2006: A16.

Heidegger, Martin. *Poetry, Language, Thought*. Trans. Albert Hofstadter. New York: Harper, 1971.

Herman, Ellen. *The Romance of American Psychology: Political Culture in the Age of Experts*. Berkeley: U of California P, 1995.

Hill, Charlie. "Small-Town Scandal." *New Statesman* 1 December 2008: 53.

Hogeland, Lisa Marie. *Feminism and Its Fictions: The Consciousness-Raising Novel and the Women's Liberation Movement*. Philadelphia: U of Pennsylvania P, 1998.

Holland, Mary K. "'The Art's Heart's Purpose': Braving the Narcissistic Loop of David Foster Wallace's *Infinite Jest*." *Critique* 47 (2006): 218–42.

Holland, Norman N. *The Dynamics of Literary Response*. New York: Oxford UP, 1968.

Hosseini, Khaled. *The Kite Runner*. New York: Riverhead, 2003.

———. *A Thousand Splendid Suns*. New York: Riverhead, 2008.

Howe, Irving. "Realities and Fictions." *Partisan Review* 26 (1959): 131.

Huber, Richard. *The American Idea of Success*. New York: McGraw, 1971.

Hughes, Rhalee A. "A Means to Measure." *Publishing Research Quarterly* 21 (2005): 12–28.

Huntington, Samuel P. *The Clash of Civilizations and the Remaking of the World Order*. New York: Simon, 1997.

Hutton, Tatiana. "Bookscan: A Marketing Tool or Literary Homogenizer?" *Publishing Research Quarterly* 18 (2002): 46–51.

Illouz, Eva. *Oprah Winfrey and the Glamour of Misery: An Essay on Popular Culture*. New York: Columbia UP, 2003.

———, and Nik John. "Oprah Winfrey and Women's Autobiography." Harris and Watson 87–99.

Ingram, Penelope. "Racializing Babylon: Settler Whiteness and the 'New Racism.'" *New Literary History* 32 (2001): 159–76.

Inness, Sherrie A., and Diana Royer, eds. *Breaking Boundaries: New Perspectives on Women's Regional Writing*. Iowa City: U of Iowa P, 1997.

Isaacs, Susan. "Summer Camp for Lovers." *New York Times Book Review* 6 June 1993: 50.

Iser, Wolfgang. *The Act of Reading: A Theory of Aesthetic Response*. Baltimore: Johns Hopkins UP, 1978.

Jackson, Kenneth T. *Crabgrass Frontier: The Suburbanization of the United States*. New York: Oxford UP, 1985.

Jacobs, Timothy. "American Touchstone: The Idea of Order in Gerald Manley Hopkins and David Foster Wallace." *Comparative Literature Studies* 38 (2001): 215–31.

———. "The Brothers Incandeza: Translating Ideology in Fyodor Dostoevsky's *The Brothers Karamazov* and David Foster Wallace's *Infinite Jest*." *Texas Studies in Language and Literature* 49 (2007): 265–92.

Jameson, Fredric. *The Political Unconscious: Narrative as a Socially Symbolic Act*. New York: Routledge, 1983.

———. *Postmodernism, or, The Cultural Logic of Late Capitalism*. Durham: Duke UP, 1991.

Jamison, Laura. "Carry on Baggage." *New York Times Book Review* 7 June 1998: 37.

Jenkins, Candice M. "Pure Black: Class, Color, and Intraracial Politics in Toni Morrison's *Paradise*." *Modern Fiction Studies* 52 (2006): 270–96.

Jewett, Sarah Orne. *The Country of Painted Firs*. Boston: Houghton Mifflin, 1897.

Jong, Erica. "The Truth about Books (and Us)." *USA Today* 7 February 2006: 11A.

Joyce, James. "The Dead." *Dubliners*. New York: Penguin, 1992. 175–225.

———. *Portrait of the Artist as a Young Man*. New York: Penguin, 1992.

Jurca, Catherine. *White Diaspora: The Suburb and the Twentieth-Century American Novel*. Princeton: Princeton UP, 2001.

Kakar, M. Hassan. *Afghanistan: The Soviet Invasion and the Afghan Response, 1979–1982*. Berkeley: U of California P, 1995.

Kakutani, Michiko. "Books of the Times: A Country Dying of Laughter." *New York Times* 13 February 1996: 17.

Kaminer, Wendy. *I'm Dysfunctional, You're Dysfunctional: The Recovery Movement and Other Self-Help Fashions*. New York: Vintage, 1993.

Kelley, Mary. *Private Woman, Public Stage: Literary Domesticity in Nineteenth-Century America*. New York: Oxford UP, 1984.

Kenner, Hugh. "The Uncle Charles Principle." *Joyce's Voices*. Berkeley: U of California P, 1978. 15–38.

Kerber, Linda K. "Separate Spheres, Female Worlds, Woman's Place: The Rhetoric of Women's History." *Meanings for Manhood: Constructions of Masculinity in Victorian America*. Ed. Mark C. Carnes and Clyde Griffen. Chicago: U of Chicago P, 1990.

Kidd, Sue Monk. *The Secret Life of Bees*. New York: Viking, 2002.

King, Heather. "Why James Frey Doesn't Get It." *Publishers Weekly* 23 January 2006: 216.

Kingsolver, Barbara. *Animal Dreams*. New York: HarperCollins, 1990.

Krumholz, Linda. "Reading and Insight in Toni Morrison's *Paradise*." *African American Review* 36 (2002): 21–34.

Kurtz, Ernest. *Not-God: A History of Alcoholics Anonymous*. Center City, MN: Hazelden Educational Services, 1979.

Laclau, Ernesto, and Chantal Mouffe. *Hegemony and Socialist Strategy: Towards a Radical Democratic Politics*. Trans. Winston Moore and Paul Cammack. London: Verso, 1985.

Lang, Robert. *Edgeless Cities: Exploring the Elusive Metropolis*. Washington, D.C.: Brookings Institute Press, 2003.

Larry King Live, CNN, 11 January 2005.

Larson, Magali Sarfatti. *The Rise of Professionalism: A Sociological Analysis*. Berkeley: U of California P, 1977.

Lasch, Christopher. *The Culture of Narcissism: American Life in the Age of Diminishing Expectations*. New York: Norton, 1978.

Leach, Laurie F. "Lying, Writing, and Confrontation: Mary McCarthy and Lillian Hellman." *LIT: Literature Interpretation Theory* 15 (2004): 5–27.

Lears, T. J. Jackson. *No Place of Grace: Antimodernism and the Transformation of American Culture 1880–1920*. New York: Pantheon, 1981.

Letts, Billie. *Where the Heart Is*. New York: Warner, 1995.

Levenson, Michael. *A Genealogy of Modernism: A Study of English Literary Doctrine, 1908–1922*. New York: Cambridge UP, 1984.

Levinson, Marjorie. "What Is New Formalism?" *PMLA* 122 (2007): 558–69.

Lewis, Bernard. *The Crisis of Islam: Holy War and Unholy Terror*. New York: Modern, 2003.

Lewis, Kelley Penfield. "The Trouble with Happy Endings: Conflicting Narratives in Oprah's Book Club." Farr and Harker 211–34.

Lewis-Kraus, Gideon. "The Last Book Party: Publishing Drinks to a Life after Death." *Harper's Magazine*. March 2009: 41–51.

Livingstone, Sonia, and Peter K. Lunt. *Talk on Television: Audience Participation and Public Debate*. London: Routledge, 1994.

Long, Elizabeth. *The American Dream and the Popular Novel*. Boston: Routledge, 1985.

———. *Book Clubs: Women and the Uses of Reading in Everyday Life*. Chicago: Chicago UP, 2003.

———. "Textual Interpretation as Collective Action." *Discourse* 14 (1992): 104–30.

———, and Janice Radway. "The Book as Mass Commodity: The Audience Perspective." *Book Research Quarterly* 3 (1987): 9–30.

Long, Rob. "Reality Bites." *The National Review* 13 February 2006: 30–31.

Lott, Brett. *Jewel*. New York: Pocket, 1999.

Lott, Eric. *Love and Theft: Black Minstrelsy and the American Working Class*. New York: Oxford UP, 1993.

Lukács, Georg. *The Theory of the Novel: A Historico-Philosophical Essay on the Forms of Great Epic Literature*. Trans. Anna Bostock. Cambridge, MA: MIT P, 1987.

Lutz, Tom. *Cosmopolitan Vistas: American Regionalism and Literary Value*. Ithaca: Cornell UP, 2004.

Macdonald, Dwight. *Against the American Grain*. New York: Random House, 1962.

Magnus, Ralph, and Eden Naby. *Afghanistan: Mullah, Marx, and Mujahid*. Boulder: Westview Press, 1998.

Marcuse, Herbert. "The Affirmative Character of Culture." *Negations: Essays in Critical Theory*. Trans. Jeremy J. Shapiro. Boston: Beacon, 1968. 88–133.

Margolis, Stacey. "Huck Finn; Or, Consequences." *PMLA* 116 (2001): 329–43.

Martelle, Scott, and Scott Collins. "Oprah Winfrey Defends Memoir's Author in On-Air Call." *Los Angeles Times* 12 January 2006: A17.

Mason, Mary. "The Other Voice: Autobiographies of Women Writers." *Autobiography: Essays Theoretical and Critical*. Ed. James Olney. Princeton: Princeton UP, 1980. 207–35.

Max, D. T. "The Oprah Effect." *New York Times Magazine* 26 December 1999: 36–41.

May, Elaine Tyler. *Homeward Bound: American Families in the Cold War Era*. New York: Basic, 1988.

Mayberry, Susan Neal. "'Everything about Her Had Two Sides to It': The Foreigner's Home in Toni Morrison's *Paradise*." *African American Review* 42 (2008): 565–78.

McCaffery, Larry. "An Interview with David Foster Wallace." *The Review of Contemporary Fiction* 13 (1993): 127–50.

McChesney, Robert. "Is There Any Hope for Cultural Studies?" *Monthly Review: An Independent Socialist Magazine* 47 (March 1996): 1–18.

McClurg, Jocelyn. "On the Syllabus: Professors' Painful Lessons." *USA Today* 14 April 2003: 4d.

McCullough, David Willis. "Sea of Glass." *New York Times Book Review* 14 April 2002: 14.

McCullough, Kate. *Regions of Identity: The Construction of America in Women's Fiction*. Stanford: Stanford UP, 1999.

McDowell, Deborah. "'The Self and the Other': Reading Toni Morrison's *Sula* and the Black Female Text." *Critical Essays on Toni Morrison*. Ed. Nellie Y. McKay. Boston: G. K. Hall, 1988. 77–90.

McGee, Micki. *Self-Help, Inc.: Makeover Culture in American Life*. New York: Oxford UP, 2005.

McGrath, Maria. "Spiritual Talk: *The Oprah Winfrey Show* and the Popularization of the New Age." Harris and Watson 125–45.

McHale, Brian. *Postmodernist Fiction*. London: Routledge, 1987.

McInerney, Jay. "The Year of the Whopper." *New York Times Book Review* 3 March 1996: 8.

McLaughlin, Robert L. "Post-Postmodern Discontent: Contemporary Fiction and the Social World." *Symploke* 12 (2004): 53–69.

Meltzer, Jack. *Metropolis to Metroplex: The Social and Spatial Planning of Cities*. Baltimore: Johns Hopkins UP, 1984.

Memmott, Carol. "'Million Little' Problems Follow Writer." *USA Today* 30 January 2006: 1D.

———. "Winfrey Grills 'Pieces' Author, Apologizes for Backing Book." *USA Today* 27 January 2006: 1E.

Meyer, Donald B. *The Positive Thinkers: Religion as Pop Psychology from Mary Baker Eddy to Oral Roberts*. New York: Pantheon, 1980.

Michael, Magali Cornier. "Re-Imagining Agency: Toni Morrison's *Paradise*." *African American Review* 36 (2002): 643–61.

Miller, D. A. *Jane Austen, or, The Secret of Style*. Princeton: Princeton UP, 2003.

Miller, Laura. "David Foster Wallace: Interview." *Salon* 9 March 1996. http://www.salon.com/books/feature/1996/03/09/wallace

Miller, Nancy K. "The Entangled Self: Genre Bondage in the Age of Memoir." *PMLA* 122 (2007): 537–48.

"A Million Little Lies." The Smoking Gun. Ed. William Bastone. 8 January 2006. Court TV. http://www.thesmokinggun.com/archive/0104061jamesfrey1.html

Milliot, Jim. "Chains, Internet Ruled Bookselling in 2007." *Publishers Weekly* 7 April 2008: 8.

Mills, C. Wright. *White Collar: The American Middle Classes*. New York: Oxford UP, 1951.

Mobilio, Albert. "Olympia Faces Desire." *New York Times Book Review* 26 December 1999: 10.

Moretti, Franco. "Serious Century: From Vermeer to Austen." *The Novel Volume I: History, Geography, and Culture*. Ed. Franco Moretti. Princeton: Princeton UP, 2006. 369–400.

Morris, David. "Lived Time and Absolute Knowing: Habit and Addiction from *Infinite Jest* to the *Phenomenology of Spirit*." *Clio* 30 (2001): 375–415.

Morrison, Toni. *Paradise*. New York: Penguin, 1997.

———. *Playing in the Dark: Whiteness and the Literary Imagination*. New York: Vintage, 1993.

Moskowitz, Eva. *In Therapy We Trust: America's Obsession with Self-Fulfillment.* Baltimore: Johns Hopkins UP, 2001.

Mumford, Lewis. *The City in History: Its Origins, Its Transformations, and Its Prospects.* New York: Harcourt, 1961.

Nelson, Deborah. *Pursuing Privacy in Cold War America.* New York: Columbia UP, 2002.

Nelson, Sara. "Talk Show Blues." *Publishers Weekly* 30 January 2006: 5.

Neuman, Shirley. Introduction. *Autobiography and Questions of Gender.* Ed. Shirley Neuman. London: Frank Cass, 1991. 1–11.

Nichols, Catherine. "Dialogizing Postmodern Carnival: David Foster Wallace's *Infinite Jest.*" *Critique* 43 (2001): 3–14.

Nudelman, Franny. "Beyond the Talking Cure: Listening to Female Testimony on the *Oprah Winfrey Show.*" Pfister and Schnog 297–315.

Ohmann, Richard. "The Shaping of a Canon: U.S. Fiction, 1960–1975." *Politics of Letters.* Middletown, CT: Wesleyan UP, 1987.

Oprah Winfrey Show. Harpo Productions Inc., 6 March 1998.

———. Harpo Productions Inc., 26 October 2005.

———. Harpo Productions Inc., 26 January 2006.

"Our Country and Our Culture: A Symposium." Ed. William Phillips and Philip Rahv. *Partisan Review* 19 (1952): 282–326.

"Our Country and Our Culture: II." Ed. William Phillips and Philip Rahv. *Partisan Review* 19 (1952): 420–50.

"Our Country and Our Culture: III." Ed. William Phillips and Philip Rahv. *Partisan Review* 19 (1952): 562–97.

"Over One-Third of Americans Read More Than Ten Books in Typical Year." *Harris Poll* 37.7 April 2008. http://www.harrisinteractive.com/harris_poll/index.asp?PID=891

Page, Philip. "Furrowing All Brows: Interpretation and the Transcendent in Toni Morrison's *Paradise.*" *African American Review* 35 (2001): 637–49.

Papinchak, Robert Allen. "Testing the Water." *Writer* November 2001: 26–29.

Pattillo-McCoy, Mary. *Black Picket Fences: Privilege and Peril among the Black Middle Class.* Chicago: U of Chicago P, 1999.

Peck, Janice. "Talk about Racism: Framing a Popular Discourse of Race on *Oprah Winfrey.*" *Cultural Critique* 27 (1994): 89–126.

Pereira, Malin. "Oprah's Book Club and the American Dream." Harris and Watson 191–205.

Perloff, Marjorie. "Presidential Address 2006: It Must Change." *PMLA* 122 (2007): 652–62.

Perry, Michael. "Resisting Paradise: Toni Morrison, Oprah Winfrey, and the Middlebrow Audience." Farr and Harker 119–39.

Peyser, Mark, et al. "The Ugly Truth: When James Frey Embellished His Rap Sheet in His Best-Selling Memoir, Did He Cross the Line into Fiction?" *Newsweek* 23 January 2006: 62–64.

Pfister, Joel. "Glamorizing the Psychological: The Politics of Performances of Modern Psychological Identities." Pfister and Schnog 167–213.

———. "On Conceptualizing the Cultural History of Emotional and Psychological Life in America." Pfister and Schnog 17–62.

———, and Nancy Schnog, eds. *Inventing the Psychological: Toward a Cultural History of Emotional Life in America.* New Haven: Yale UP, 1997.

Pietsch, Michael, et al. "Always Another Word." *Harper's Magazine* January 2009: 26–30.

"President Bush's Address on Terrorism before a Joint Meeting of Congress." *New York Times* 21 September 2001: B4.

Putnam, Robert. *Bowling Alone: The Collapse and Revival of American Community.* New York: Simon & Schuster, 2000.

Quinney, Laura. *Literary Power and the Criteria of Truth.* Gainesville: U of Florida P, 1995.

Quirk, Kevin. "Correcting Oprah: Jonathan Franzen and the Uses of Literature in the Therapeutic Age." Farr and Harker 253–76.

Radway, Janice. "The Book-of-the-Month Club and the General Reader: On Uses of 'Serious' Fiction." *Critical Inquiry* 14 (1988): 516–38.

———. *A Feeling for Books: The Book-of-the-Month Club, Literary Taste, and Middle-Class Desire.* Chapel Hill: UNC P, 1997.

———. *Reading the Romance: Women, Patriarchy, and Popular Culture.* Chapel Hill: UNC P, 1984.

———. "Research Universities, Periodical Publication, and the Circulation of Professional Expertise: On the Significance of Middlebrow Authority." *Critical Inquiry* 31 (2004): 203–28.

Rapping, Elayne. *The Culture of Recovery: Making Sense of the Self-Help Movement in Women's Lives.* Boston: Beacon, 1996.

Rashid, Ahmed. *Taliban: Militant Islam, Oil, and Fundamentalism in Central Asia.* New Haven: Yale UP, 2001.

Reddy, William. *The Navigation of Feeling: A Framework for the History of Emotions.* New York: Cambridge UP, 2001.

Reeves, Jimmie Lynn, and Richard Campbell. *Cracked Coverage: Television News, the Anti-Cocaine Crusade, and the Reagan Legacy.* Durham: Duke UP, 1994.

Reynold, Sheri. *The Rapture of Canaan.* New York: Berkley Books, 1995.

Reynolds, Susan Salter. "The Truth about Memoirs: Uproar over James Frey's Bestseller 'A Million Little Pieces' Unearths a Literary Minefield." *Los Angeles Times* 13 January 2006: E1.

Rich, Frank. "Truthiness 101: From Frey to Alito." *New York Times* 22 January 2006, sec. 4: 16.

Rieff, Philip. *The Triumph of the Therapeutic: Uses of Faith after Freud.* New York: Harper, 1966.

Riesman, David, et al. *Lonely Crowd: A Study of the Changing American Character.* New Haven: Yale UP, 1950.

Robbins, Bruce. "Introduction Part I: Actually Existing Cosmopolitanism." Cheah and Robbins 1–19.

Robbins, Sarah. "Making Corrections to Oprah's Book Club: Reclaiming Literary Power for Gendered Literacy Management." Harris and Watson 227–57.

Robertson, Nan. *Getting Better: Inside Alcoholics Anonymous.* New York: Morrow, 1988.

Romero, Channette. "Creating the Beloved Community: Religion, Race, and Nation in Toni Morrison's *Paradise*." *African American Review* 39 (2005): 415–30.

Rooney, Kathleen. "Everything Old Is New Again: Oprah's Book Club Returns with the Classics." Farr and Harker 295–320.

———. *Reading with Oprah: The Book Club That Changed America.* Fayetteville: U of Arkansas P, 2005.

Rose, Nikolas. *Inventing Our Selves: Psychology, Power, and Personhood.* Cambridge: Cambridge UP, 1996.

Ross, Andrew. *No Respect: Intellectuals and Popular Culture.* New York: Routledge, 1989.

Rubin, Gwyn Hym. *Icy Sparks.* New York: Viking, 1998.

Rubin, Joan Shelley. *The Making of Middlebrow Culture.* Chapel Hill: UNC P, 1992.

Ryan, Mary P. *Women in Public: Between Banners and Ballots, 1825–1880.* Baltimore: Johns Hopkins UP, 1992.

Said, Edward. "The Clash of Ignorance." *Nation* 22 October 2001: 11–13.

———. *Covering Islam: How the Media and the Experts Determine How We See the Rest of the World.* New York: Pantheon, 1981.

———. *Orientalism.* New York: Pantheon, 1978.

Schaub, Thomas. *American Fiction in the Cold War.* Madison: U of Wisconsin P, 1991.

Schmitt, Carl. *The Concept of the Political.* Trans. J. Harvey Lomax. Chicago: U of Chicago P, 1996.

Schriffin, Andre. *The Business of Books: How International Conglomerates Took Over Publishing and Changed the Way We Read.* London: Verso, 2000.

Schur, Richard L. "Locating Paradise in the Post-Civil Rights Era: Toni Morrison and Critical Race Theory." *Contemporary Literature* 45 (2004): 276–99.

Scott, A. O. "The Best Mind of His Generation." *New York Times* 20 September 2008: Wk 1.

———. "The Panic of Influence." *The New York Review of Books* 10 February 2000: 39–43.

Sedgwick, Eve Kosofsky. "Epidemics of the Will." *Tendencies.* Durham: Duke UP, 1993. 130–43.

Sennett, Richard. *The Fall of Public Man.* New York: Knopf, 1977.

Shamir, Milette, and Jennifer Travis. *Boys Don't Cry? Rethinking Narratives of Masculinity and Emotion in the U.S.* New York: Columbia UP, 2002.

Shattuc, Jane M. "The Oprahfication of America." *Television, History, and American Culture: Feminist Critical Essays.* Ed. Mary Beth Haralovich and Lauren Rabinovitz. Durham: Duke UP, 1999.

———. *The Talking Cure: TV Talk Shows and Women.* New York: Routledge, 1997.

Sheppard, R. Z. "Mad Maximalism." *Time* 19 February 1996: 70.

Shone, Tom. "Poets in Love." *New York Times Book Review* 22 April 2001: 34.

Shorter, Edward. *A History of Psychiatry: From the Era of the Asylum to the Age of Prozac.* New York: Wiley, 1997.

Shreve, Anita. *The Pilot's Wife.* Boston: Little, Brown, 1998.

———. *Women Together, Women Alone: The Legacy of the Consciousness-Raising Movement.* New York: Viking, 1989.

Siklos, Richard. "I Cannot Tell a Lie (from an Amplification)." *New York Times* 5 February 2006, sec. 3: 3.

Sommer, Doris. "Resistant Texts and Incompetent Readers." *Poetics Today* 15 (1994): 523–51.

Spectorsky, A. C. *The Exurbanites.* Philadelphia: Lippincott, 1955.

Spivak, Gayatri Chakravorty. *In Other Worlds: Essays in Cultural Politics.* New York: Methuen, 1987.

Squire, Corinne. "Empowering Women? *The Oprah Winfrey Show.*" *Feminist Television Criticism: A Reader.* Ed. Charlotte Brunsdon, Julie D'Acci, and Lynn Spigel. Oxford: Clarendon, 1997. 99–110.

Stanley, Tarshia L. "The Specter of Oprah Winfrey: Critical Black Female Spectatorship." Harris and Watson 35–50.

Starker, Steven. *Oracle at the Supermarket: The American Preoccupation with Self-Help Books.* New Brunswick: Transaction, 1989.

Stow, Simon. "The Way We Read Now: Oprah Winfrey, Intellectuals, and Democracy." Farr and Harker 277–93.

Tebbel, John William. *Between Covers: The Rise and Transformation of Book Publishing in America.* New York: Oxford UP, 1987.

Toal, Catherine. "Corrections: Contemporary American Melancholy." *Journal of European Studies* 33 (2003): 305–22.

Tompkins, Jane, ed. *Reader-Response Criticism: From Formalism to Post-Structuralism*. Baltimore: Johns Hopkins UP, 1980.

——. *Sensational Designs: The Cultural Work of American Fiction, 1790–1860*. New York: Oxford UP, 1985.

——. "Sentimental Power: *Uncle Tom's Cabin* and the Politics of Literary History." *Sensational Designs* 122–46.

Travis, Trysh. "The Divine Secrets of the Cultural Studies Sisterhood: Women Reading Rebecca Wells." *American Literary History* 15 (2003): 134–61.

——. *The Language of the Heart: A Cultural History of the Recovery Movement from Alcoholics Anonymous to Oprah Winfrey*. Chapel Hill: UNC P, 2009.

Trilling, Lionel. *The Liberal Imagination: Essays on Literature and Society*. New York: Charles Scribner's Sons, 1950.

——. *Sincerity and Authenticity*. New York: Harcourt, 1972.

Valverde, Mariana. *Diseases of the Will: Alcohol and the Dilemmas of Freedom*. Cambridge: Cambridge UP, 1998.

Vanderkam, Laura. "When Fiction Masquerades as Truth." *USA Today* 17 January 2006: 11A.

Venuti, Lawrence. *The Scandals of Translation: Toward an Ethics of Difference*. London: Routledge, 1998.

Veroff, Joseph, Richard Kulka, and Elizabeth Douvan. *Mental Health in America: 1957 to 1976*. New York: Basic, 1981.

Vitz, Paul C. *Psychology as Religion: The Cult of Self-Worship*. Grand Rapids: W. B. Eerdmans, 1977.

Wallace, David Foster. "E Unibus Pluram: Television and U.S. Fiction." Wallace, *A Supposedly Fun Thing*, 21–82.

——. "Greatly Exaggerated." Wallace, *A Supposedly Fun Thing* 138–45.

——. *Infinite Jest*. Boston: Little, Brown, 1996.

——. "Laughing with Kafka." *Harper's* July 1998: 23–27.

——. "Octet." *Brief Interviews with Hideous Men: Stories*. Boston: Little, Brown, 1999.

——. *A Supposedly Fun Thing I'll Never Do Again: Essays and Arguments*. Boston: Little, Brown, 1997

Warner, Michael. *Publics and Counterpublics*. Cambridge, MA: Zone Books, 2002.

——. "Zones of Privacy." *What's Left of Theory*. Ed. Judith Butler, John Guillory, and Thomas Kendall. New York: Routledge, 2000. 75–113.

Weber, Max. *The Protestant Ethic and the Spirit of Capitalism*. Trans. Stephen Kalberg. Chicago: Fitzroy Dearborn, 2001.

Weinstein, Cindy. *Family, Kinship, and Sympathy in Nineteenth-Century American Literature*. New York: Cambridge UP, 2004.

Wells, Rebecca. *Divine Secrets of the Ya-Ya Sisterhood.* New York: Harper-Perennial, 1997.

———. *Little Altars Everywhere.* New York: HarperPerennial, 1996.

Whyte, William H. *The Organization Man.* New York: Simon & Schuster, 1956.

Wilson, Craig. "*Kite Runner* Catches the Wind: Tale of Afghan Boys Becomes a Hit — and Basis of a Film — through Word of Mouth." *USA Today* 19 April 2005: 1D.

Wilson, Sherryl. *Oprah, Celebrity, and Formations of Self.* New York: Palgrave, 2003.

Wilson, Sloan. *The Man in the Gray Flannel Suit.* New York: Simon & Schuster, 1955.

Witkin, Gordon. "The Men Who Created Crack." *U.S. News and World Report* 19 August 1991: 44–53.

Wood, Michael. "Sensations of Loss." *The Aesthetics of Toni Morrison: Speaking the Unspeakable.* Ed. Marc C. Conner. Jackson: U of Mississippi P, 2000. 114–23.

Wu, Yung-Hsing. "The Romance of Reading Like Oprah." Farr and Harker 73–87.

Wyatt, Edward. "Frey Says Falsehoods Improved His Tale." *New York Times* 2 February 2006: E1.

———. "Live on 'Oprah,' a Memoirist Is Kicked Out of the Book Club." *New York Times* 27 January 2006: A1.

———. "'Pieces' Editor Now Says He Was Fooled by Frey." *New York Times* 4 February 2006: B7.

———. "Questions for Others in the Frey Scandal." *New York Times* 28 January 2006: B7.

———. "Treatment Description in Memoir Is Disputed." *New York Times* 24 January 2006: E1.

———. "Wrenching Tale by an Afghan Immigrant Strikes a Chord." *New York Times* 15 December 2004, late ed.: E1+.

Yates, Richard. *Revolutionary Road.* Boston: Little, Brown, 1961.

Young, John. "Toni Morrison, Oprah Winfrey, and Postmodern Popular Audiences." *African American Review* 35 (2001): 181.

Reviews

Infinite Jest Amazon Customer Reviews
    Abby Ridge 12/29/99
    B. Johnson 3/1/02
    Brian James Oak 6/3/04
    A Customer 6/28/03

Derk Koldewyn 2/16/01
E. A. Glaser 4/15/02
Fred J. Solinger 12/5/00
J. Rosenbaum 5/10/04
Tkurie 3/15/00

The Kite Runner Amazon Customer Reviews
1KAT 6/22/05
A. Krafft "Alexis" 3/28/05
A. Rajamani 11/7/05
A reader 8/20/03
A reader 12/16/04
A reader 7/8/04
A reader 7/16/04
A. Rutherford 9/21/05
Aaron Black "Skeptic" 3/11/05
Acme Reader 11/22/05
Amer Dahmash 10/9/05
Amira A. Clow 9/12/05
Analis M. 12/30/05
Andrew W. Johns "ResQgeek" 5/31/05
anduarto "anduarto" 7/19/05
Andy P "AP" 10/27/05
Anne Fitten Glenn (author) 9/28/04
Anne Lebrecht "www.annelebrecht.com" 1/2/05
Annie "Annie" 2/14/05
Annie "bookwishes4" 2/14/05
applepiebooks 12/1/05
Ashley Blackwell 8/20/05
Avid Reader 8/2/05
Ayesha Riaz "ashriaz" 12/1/05
B. Capossere 8/23/03
B. Flanagan "barbara@flanagans.com" 7/19/05
B. Mellon 12/10/04
B. Udy "Bookaholic" 8/10/05
B. Vander Eyk 5/13/05
beachlvr 8/7/04
Beausoir 9/26/05
"bernardetreves" 9/2/03
BethDeHart 3/9/05

Bibliophile "Rachel" 3/7/05

Birgit A. Jensen "Book lover" 8/23/05

"blissengine" 10/10/03

Book Maven "Ma Maven" 8/4/2005

Brace Gfeen 3/14/05

Brian K. Tarumoto 8/31/05

Bruce Stern 6/17/05

C. A. Begun "Book Nut" 4/29/05

C. B. Collins Jr. 8/27/05

C. Davis 8/20/05

C. G. Johnson "C. J. The Soul Man" 11/14/04

C. Kim "Fitness buff and Buffy buff" 9/8/05

C. J. Procko "Booker T." 9/29/05

C. L. Tobin 10/13/05

C. Leibbrand 11/29/04

C. Marken 6/6/05

Carol A. Sym 8/31/04

Carolyn Rowe Hill "author of The Dead Angel" 5/7/05

Cassandra L. Warren 3/7/05

Catherine J. Thomson 4/15/05

Cathleen A. Dennison 3/29/05

Cathy O'Connor 12/29/05

Cenk Sumbas 9/13/05

Chai Trek "roosting chicken" 3/17/05

Charlene Sanderson 4/9/05

Cheryl Morris 7/23/05

Cheryl Tran 9/18/05

Chloe L. Moushey 7/17/05

Christine K. Sartory "Kite Lover!" 5/23/05

Christopher G. Kenber "chris kenber" 12/20/04

Cindy C. "TLC Book club girl" 4/19/05

Click Chick 2/16/05

Connie V. 9/27/05

Cynthia K. Robertson 8/8/05

D. C. Smith "rabid bookfiend" 11/14/04

D. K. Miles "dkmiles1" 8/10/05

D. Maynard 8/4/05

D. Smith 9/22/04

Daffy Du 4/25/04

Dayle 6/9/05

Dean Blobaum 11/4/04

Debbie "Debbie" 3/31/05

debonairbear 8/31/03

Deborah Palladino 9/1/05

Denise "Denise" 6/1/05

doc peterson 6/19/2005

Dolly A. Berthelot "Dr. Dolly, Communication Consultant, Writer, Editor"
    8/23/05

Donna K. Jenner 9/19/05

Douglas M. Dixon 10/16/05

dougrhon "dougrhon" 5/2/05

doves wing 6/7/05

Dr Cathy Goodwin 3/3/05

E. Abrams 10/10/05

E. Alavi 8/22/05

E. Dillon "Erica Kostro" 9/26/05

E. Haroldsen "Readaholic" 9/28/05

Ed Foltz 3/30/05

edith lawrence "reader obsessed" 8/17/05

Eileen Davidoff "one avid reader" 10/12/05

Eileen Rieback 7/18/04

Ellen VandeWater 7/21/05

Elspeth 8/14/05

Enchanted-reader 9/4/05

enthusiastic reader 6/19/04

Francis J. Mcinerney 6/25/03

Frederick A. Babb "An Author" 6/6/05

Gary Griffiths 12/11/05

Gene Koo 2/3/05

Gentle Reader 5/25/05

George R. Odell "IDEO" 8/9/05

Gerber Daisy 5/24/05

Girl Chronicles "Girl Chronicles" 7/1/05

Grace 5/3/05

Grady Harp 12/16/04

Greg Henderson 2/3/05

Gul A. Zikria M.D. 9/15/03

H. Boehning "helenB" 8/2/05

Happy Reader 10/14/05

Harold R. Zeckel 6/5/05

Hector Guerra 5/1/05
hi 11/1/05
I Luv Books 2/16/05
Iles Fan "Gary" 9/4/2005
The Inspired One 12/13/04
J. Fiorani 2/11/05
J. M. McCormick "crazyforgems" 11/6/04
J. Olcott "Love2Read" 1/3/05
j old school "Jerry" 8/30/05
Jack L. Langdon 1/8/05
James E. O'Leary 7/26/05
Janet M. Cortez "The Omnivorous Reader" 10/17/05
Jeff T. Blevins 12/14/05
Jennifer McCormick 2/10/05
Jennifer M-R 1/8/05
Jerry Caveglia 9/20/03
Jessica K. 5/26/05
John K. Addis 3/14/05
Jon T 9/20/05
Josh Daniels "jd83" 3/30/05
Josh J. Riley 7/14/05
Judith Anne 9/8/05
Judith R. Wright 8/8/05
Julie A. Boyd "book lover" 9/21/05
Justin Snow 5/2/05
K. Folmar "Texas Mom" 12/30/04
K. Kuehl "Phi Beta" 2/10/05
K. L. Cotugno 8/31/04
K. M. Sowka "William Sowka" 7/28/05
K. Rominger "Dream with your eyes open . . ." 9/12/05
K. Solomon 9/26/05
Karisa 6/19/05
Karrah Trainer 9/28/05
kattepus "Karin" 2/28/05
kehroll 12/6/05
Kent Holland 8/14/05
Kim keenan 12/19/05
L. A. Atkins "Lesley" 11/9/04
L. Jean-Louis "justLauren" 3/2/05
L.K.B.H. "alfie henry" 1/17/05

L. Poor "L.Poor" 7/20/04

L. Roth 11/21/04

laleh hamadani 9/8/03

Laura K 5/30/05

LBR Wease 11/30/04

Learning All the Time "Its Never Too Late to . . ." 12/2/05

Lee A. Rubinstein "rubindue" 7/1/04

Linda 7/19/05

Linda K. Faigaohall 12/31/04

Logan Creek 7/1/05

Lori D Widmer "Reader" 9/9/05

Louise D. Somes "Lucy in Dallas" 11/21/05

Lover of books 5/3/05

Luther 2/2/05

LZ-1 6/27/05

M. Colleen Talley "Colleen" 5/1/05

M. D. Copeland "avid opinionist" 7/26/05

M. J. Smith 6/30/05

M. L. Leonard "MikeonAlpha" 8/7/03

M. L. Nieves 12/22/05

M. McDonald 9/23/05

M. Nichols 8/11/05

M. Patel 7/16/05

M. Schijvens 6/8/2005

M. T. Guzman "squeakychu" 9/29/03

Maclen 3/31/05

Manola Sommerfeld 12/7/05

margymc 8/8/03

Mark L. Harris 12/4/04

Marsha Marks "wwwflyingbytheseatofmypants.net" 4/30/05

Mary Parker "Mary P" 1/9/05

Mary Reinert 1/16/05

Mary Whipple 6/11/03

Maryam Habib Khan 1/24/05

mdscifi lover 12/1/04

Megan Brizzolara 10/19/04

Melissa Niksic 12/12/05

Michael A. Lacombe 8/23/05

Michael S. Rudman MD 9/6/04

Michael Werner "MindTrekker" 7/23/05

Michael Cozzens 1/12/05
Michaela Jones 9/28/05
Michele Cozzens 1/12/05
Michelle E. 9/5/05
Missie Dowey 11/18/04
Molly J. Mathias "luv2teach" 7/13/05
A Mom at Home 11/2/05
"mom3xover" 12/31/03
Mooch 6/16/05
More Over "Paul Moreno" 12/8/05
mtspace "Reader, Cook, Gardener, Critic" 9/21/05
Nancy J. Couglin "momcat" 9/1/05
Nathan Crabtree "singer" 3/25/05
Naz 9/15/04
NC 9/6/04
nekkol "nekkol" 12/2/04
A New York Reader 8/12/05
nodice 12/30/05
Olga Comas Bacardi 9/24/05
"osudebbie" 1/18/04
P. E. Lee "Lizzard" 5/25/05
P. Newton "AZ Minis" 8/29/05
Patricia Kay "writer and reader" 4/9/05
Patricia Kramer 11/9/04
Patrick Carlin 9/2/05
Paul Fellows 8/4/05
Peggy G. Lambdin 7/7/05
Phoebe Snow "Knack" 6/29/05
PR Kgregus 10/18/05
prcarolyn 10/12/05
Professor Joseph L. McCauley "Joseph L. McCauley" 2/4/04
PW 7/25/05
R. Bakker 6/29/05
R. Boadway "HF Buff" 11/6/05
ReadBks1182 "lizzybennet" 6/2/05
Reader "tisha69: 7/20/03
Rebecca of A Better Cause 10/14/04
Richard Nelson 3/23/05
Robbie 11/29/05
Robin Friedman 1/5/05

Rone Prinz "artist/traveler" 10/27/05
Roni 5/3/05
Roy Munson 9/15/05
S. E. Duke 11/24/04
S. Langner 10/17/04
S. Masand 7/27/05
S. Masula "LovelyBooks" 12/17/05
S. Schultz 8/22/05
Sabad One 11/7/05
Sancho Mahle 9/2/05
sb-lynn 3/19/05
SB Reader 4/24/05
Scorpion1664 "Scorpion1664" 5/15/05
SDSonn 5/4/05
Shana Punim 10/8/05
Shelley C. Raker 5/2/05
Shelly Belden 8/25/05
Sherry Johnson 9/11/05
snoblaze 7/1/04
Sonya D. Stutts "LuvnRed" 8/22/05
Squidhunter 7/3/05
Stacy Eichhorn "StacyAnn" 6/17/05
Stephanie Henry "Book Addict" 1/4/05
Stephanie L. Warfel 9/22/05
Steve Koss 4/6/05
The Stinker 5/21/05
Sunsara Taylor "Sunsara Taylor" 4/19/05
Susan B. "Greedyreaders" 5/25/05
Suzanne Somers "Suzieknits2" 7/21/05
Sylvanna M. Vargas "Sylvanna" 8/19/05
Tea Molino 12/20/04
Teacher "Book Lover" 1/27/05
"themage7" 7/23/03
ThomsEBynum 2/16/05
Tim A. 11/19/04
Timothy Kearney 4/30/05
Tom Arnold "A beach bum" 3/8/05
Traci Watson "a bit of a book snob" 10/7/05
Tracy Oshima 11/24/04
trish's Dish 11/3/05

UNC "Baird" 9/23/05
Vijay B. Kumar 5/13/05
Violet Bandong "Candyband" 10/15/04
Virginia Nuckols 3/31/05
W. Jamison 6/3/05
Wave Tossed 8/12/05
Wendy Somerlot Bittel 1/28/05
William E. Adams 11/16/05
William R. Siggelkow 8/8/05
Yasaman Mostajeran "www.inspiremecoach.com" 3/31/05
Yasmin Mansoor "all for superb products" 9/18/05
Yuni "nut stud" 8/25/05

The Pilot's Wife Amazon Customer Reviews
flyover 1/16/00
M. Asali 9/28/00
Marmalinde "marmalinde" 12/27/99
soybaby 1/20/00
Susan E. Neill 2/1/03

INDEX

Freud, Sigmund, 18–19, 21, 28
Frey, James: *A Million Little Pieces*,
2–3, 40, 126, 127–49, 200; attitude
toward drug addiction, 137–39, 144–
45; bodily pain, 131–32; controversy,
127–29, 142–43; individual agency,
145–47; masculinity, 139–40; mini-
malist style, 133–34; notion of truth,
134–35, 141–42
Friedan, Betty, 27
Frye, Northrop: "Literature as Therapy," 29

Gal, Susan, 33
Garreau, Joel, 73
gender roles, 77, 139, 141, 165
Gilmore, Leigh, 129, 141
Guillory, John, 15, 48

Habermas, Jürgen, 32–36
HarperCollins, 87–88
Harpo Productions, 45, 148
Heffernan, Virginia, 149
Herman, Ellen, 19
highbrow culture, 3, 4, 7, 30, 39, 48, 65,
112, 126, 166
Holland, Norman: *The Dynamics of
Literary Response*, 29–30
Hosseini, Khaled: cultural specificity
of fiction, 179, 182, 185–87; depiction
of the Taliban, 190–91; humanism,
188–89, 192; *The Kite Runner*, 40–41,
172, 175–98, 201, 203, 206, 207; orientalism, 182; politics, 191–96; sado-
masochism, 184–85; treatment of
universal themes, 179–81
Howe, Irving, 7

identification, 1, 14, 31, 36, 52–54, 68,
72, 89, 98, 107–8, 113–14, 119–20, 122–

23, 128, 132, 141, 143, 147, 151, 155, 161,
169–70, 178–79, 182–83, 184–88, 197
Illouz, Eva, 148–49
inner child, 21–23, 29, 101–2, 123
interiority, 18, 25, 37, 123, 152, 159–60,
199
irony: and addiction, 108; in popular
culture, 40, 103, 105

Jameson, Fredric, 41, 158
Joyce, James, 152–54
Jurca, Catherine, 31

Kenner, Hugh, 153
King, Gayle, 47–48, 51, 65

Larry King Live, 128, 143–44
Larson, Magali Sarfatti, 77
Lasch, Christopher, 41, 81, 199–200
Lears, T. J. Jackson, 19
left, 1–2, 12, 17, 27, 32, 34, 161, 206
literary fiction, 2, 9–10, 11, 12, 14–16,
28–30, 45, 46–48, 66, 68, 151, 166–
67, 179
Little, Brown, 120–21
Long, Elizabeth, 14–15
lowbrow culture, 2, 4, 166
Lukács, Georg, 31
Lutz, Tom, 83

Macdonald, Dwight, 3–8, 10, 11, 13, 15
Max, D. T., 44, 52
McGee, Micki, 200
McHale, Brian, 124–25
memoir genre, 128–29, 131, 142–43,
147–48
Mencken, H. L., 92
middle class, 12–13, 20, 22, 136–37, 166,
199; apathy, 100–3; authenticity,
136–37, 139, 142, 146–47; norms, 160

170–71; focus on the middle class, 158–60, 161; literary status, 166–67; *The Pilot's Wife*, 40, 152–73, 200, 203, 204–5; treatment of subjective knowledge, 156–58; use of free indirect discourse, 154–55, 159–60, 168
Smith, Robert, 97–98
Smoking Gun concept, 128
suburbia, 31, 73, 75, 81, 84, 136–39, 159, 162, 170–71, 203; postwar, 4–8, 15
sympathy, 2, 36, 54–55, 181, 188–90, 194–95, 203–7

technoburbs, 73–75, 202
therapeutic paradigm, 17–20, 23–26, 35–38, 52, 72, 78, 80–81, 85, 90, 91–94, 99, 127–28, 131, 158, 160, 168, 171–72, 199–202
Toal, Catherine, 123
Tompkins, Jane, 13, 195
Travis, Trysh, 81, 88, 90
Trilling, Lionel, 28, 136
truthiness, 129–32

Uncle Charles Principle, 153–55
Updike, John, 73

Veterans Administration, 19

Wallace, David Foster: attitude toward irony, 105–6, 108, 113–14; "E Unibus Pluram," 105; "Greatly Exaggerated," 116–17; *Infinite Jest*, 39–40, 95, 99–126, 204, 206, 207; interview with Larry McCaffery, 101, 123; interview with Laura Miller, 106, 117, 120; narrative experimentation, 110–12, 122–26; "Octet," 117–19; publicity campaign, 120–21; relationship to

his audience, 100; role as author-protagonist, 115–22; suicide, 121; use of endnotes, 110–11, 116
War on Terror, 152, 170–71, 178, 191–96, 202
Warner, Michael, 36, 87
Wells, Rebecca: attitude toward African Americans, 75–76; cosmopolitanism, 83–84; critique of therapy, 79–82, 85–87, 93–94; *Divine Secrets of the Ya-Ya Sisterhood*, 39, 72–95, 202, 204, 207; *Little Altars Everywhere*, 87–88; narrative strategies, 88–89; regionalist perspective, 74–75, 77, 80–84, 86, 91; relation to feminism, 77; Ya-Ya clubs inspired by, 90–91
Wharton, Edith, 166
whiteness, 14, 76
Whyte, William, 6, 136
Wilson, Bill, 97–98
Wilson, Sherryl, 64
Wilson, Sloan, 6
Winfrey, Oprah, 144, 146; book club, 43–70, 176, 204; January 26 episode on *A Million Little Pieces*, 127, 129, 141–43, 147–49; March 6 episode on *Paradise*, 44–61, 64–70, 71, 106; October 26 episode on *A Million Little Pieces*, 128, 132, 136–39, 140; position on civil rights, 56; relation to feminism, 141
women readers, 13–14, 160–61
women's fiction, 149, 151, 158
world literature, 177–78

Yates, Richard, 6, 73
Young, John, 44